W9-AET-524

T·H·E
C·O·U·N·T·R·Y
K·I·T·C·H·E·N

BOOKS Family Circle

❦

EDITORIAL

Editor, Family Circle Books — Carol A. Guasti
Assistant Editor — Kim E. Gayton
Project Editor — Leslie Gilbert Elman
Copy Editor — Laura Crocker
Book Design — Bessen, Tully & Lee
Cover Photo — Maris/Semel
Illustrations — Lauren Jarrett
Editorial Assistant — Kate Jackson
Editorial Production Coordinator — Celeste Bantz
Editorial Freelancer — Kristen Keller
Typesetting — Alison Chandler, Caroline Cole, Maureen Harrington
Indexer — Candace Gylgayton

MARKETING

Director, Family Circle Books & Licensing — Margaret Chan-Yip
Direct Marketing Manager — Jill E. Schiffman
Fulfillment/Planning Coordinator — Carrie Meyerhoff
Administrative Assistant — Dianne Snively

❦

Published by The Family Circle, Inc.
110 Fifth Avenue, New York, NY 10011

Copyright® 1990 by The Family Circle, Inc.

All rights reserved. No part of this book may be reproduced in any form or by any electronic means, including information storage and retrieval systems, without permission in writing from the publisher, except by a reviewer who may quote brief passages in a review.

Manufactured in the United States of America

10 9 8 7 6 5 4 3 2 1

Library of Congress Cataloging in Publication Data
Main entry under title:

Family circle the country kitchen.
Includes index.
1.Country decorating.   2.Country crafts and cooking.
I.Family Circle, Inc.   II.Title: The Country Kitchen.

1990   90-80373

ISBN 0-933585-18-7

Other Books By Family Circle

BEST-EVER RECIPES

THE BEST OF FAMILY CIRCLE COOKBOOK SERIES
(Pub. Dates: 1985 – 1989)

BUSY COOK'S BOOK

GOOD HEALTH COOKBOOK

MAKE IT COUNTRY

THE FAMILY CIRCLE CHRISTMAS TREASURY SERIES
(Pub. Dates: 1986 – 1990)

FAVORITE NEEDLECRAFTS

HINTS, TIPS & SMART ADVICE

To order **FamilyCircle** books, write to Family Circle Books, 110 Fifth Avenue, New York, NY 10011.

To order **FamilyCircle** magazine, write to Family Circle Subscriptions, 110 Fifth Avenue, New York, NY 10011.

T·A·B·L·E O·F
C·O·N·T·E·N·T·S

W·E·L·C·O·M·E T·O T·H·E
C·O·U·N·T·R·Y K·I·T·C·H·E·N

If home is where the heart is, then the heart of the country home is the kitchen. Always welcoming, yet guided by respect for common sense and practicality, the kitchen is the natural gathering place in any country home.

Part wish book, part work book, *The Country Kitchen* shows you how to make your work space beautiful. There are inspiring overviews, from vintage Victorian to relaxed Southwestern country. First we explain the remodeling done and identify the country elements, then we move in for a closer look at sensible and beautiful uses of existing space.

You'll also find a chapter of kitchen crafts, and one devoted to vegetables, herbs and flowers. Plus, there's a chapter with delicious homestyle recipes!

The best country kitchens are practical and beautiful, comfortable and homey. This book can help you meld these elements in your own home.

THE
H·E·A·R·T
OF THE HOME

Work is not the curse, but drudgery is.
—Henry Ward Beecher

Each kitchen in this chapter is a "country" kitchen, comfortable and inviting. But each is also a "working" kitchen, complete with state-of-the-art appliances and easy-care fixtures that save time and energy. This chapter shows you how to mix your favorite elements of country decor with modern technology to create a kitchen that's both beautiful and functional.

All of the kitchens shown expand or improve upon existing spaces. The room in the photo at left started as a standard kitchen. By adding open shelves, a hanging pot rack and a greenhouse window over the sink, the space was used to maximum effect, while retaining the room's country flavor.

Some of these kitchens have a very dramatic country look. Others show a simple, clean country style. But all adhere to the creed of country living: they are places to work in comfort and beauty.

C·O·U·N·T·R·Y K·I·T·C·H·E·N S·T·Y·L·E·S

What is work? and what is not work?
are questions that perplex
the wisest of men.
—Bhagavadgita

KITCHEN · IMPROVEMENT CHECKLIST · ONE

Determining Your Needs

The first step in your kitchen improvement plan should be a thorough assessment of your present kitchen, and your family's needs. Careful planning will cut down on problems, and save you money. Use the following guidelines to determine your kitchen needs.

1. Which tasks do you perform in your kitchen?
- [ ] Food preparation and cooking
- [ ] Food storage
- [ ] Family dining
- [ ] Entertaining
- [ ] Professional cooking
- [ ] Bar service
- [ ] Sewing or household business
- [ ] Laundry

2. Which of the above tasks does your kitchen already accommodate adequately?

3. Which of the above tasks do you want to accommodate in your kitchen improvement?

4. Provide for the basics first. The kitchen's primary functions are food preparation, cooking and food storage. Think about the types of foods you buy, and the way you cook. Then ask yourself if you have:
- [ ] Enough counterspace and work surfaces?
- [ ] Proper lighting for work areas?
- [ ] Adequate storage for fresh foods?
- [ ] Adequate storage for shelf-stable foods?
- [ ] Space for countertop appliances?

5. Do you plan to buy new major appliances? If so, which of the following will you replace or add:
- [ ] Stove
- [ ] Wall oven
- [ ] Free-standing cooktop
- [ ] Microwave oven
- [ ] Refrigerator
- [ ] Freezer
- [ ] Dishwasher
- [ ] Trash compactor
- [ ] Washing machine/dryer

6. Consider the eating area of your kitchen.
- [ ] How many people must it accommodate?
- [ ] Do you need more space?
- [ ] Can you get by with less space?
- [ ] Do you prefer a table, or a countertop eating surface?
- [ ] Is the eating area positioned so it doesn't interfere with the work area?

7. Think about the extras. Make a wish list of special features you'd want for your "dream" kitchen.
- [ ] Butcherblock countertop cutting area
- [ ] Pastry marble
- [ ] Island cooktop
- [ ] Small food prep sink
- [ ] Wet bar
- [ ] Built-in wine rack
- [ ] Laundry area
- [ ] Desk area
- [ ] Sewing area
- [ ] Walk-in pantry

8. Prioritize. Use the list below to rank your needs (with 1 being the most important).
- [ ] Countertop work areas
- [ ] Additional cabinets
- [ ] Fresh food storage (refrigerator/freezer)
- [ ] Pantry storage
- [ ] Electricity (additional outlets/power capability)
- [ ] Island (with or without a secondary sink and/or a cooktop)
- [ ] Appliances (make a complete list in order of importance)
- [ ] Eating area
- [ ] Primary sink
- [ ] Ventilation
- [ ] Lighting
- [ ] Appliance storage/organization
- [ ] Additional task areas (desk, sewing area, laundry, and so on)

9. Aesthetic improvements. Which of the following need replacing or refurbishing?
- [ ] Cabinets
- [ ] Floors
- [ ] Countertops
- [ ] Walls/ceiling

10. Go comparison shopping. Using your "wish list," try to get an idea of what your dream kitchen will cost. Window shop for appliances, and bring home brochures and sales information. Be sure to write down the dimensions of the items that interest you. Do the same for floors, cabinets, counters, and so on.

11. Compare your "dream" kitchen to your budget and available space. This is the most difficult stage, because it involves both compromise and ingenuity.
- [ ] Approach the problem with a flexible attitude, and keep your priorities firmly in mind. For example, are you willing to live with the floor you have in order to afford the countertops you want? Can your cabinets be repainted rather than replaced?
- [ ] Call on a design pro. Now that you're organized, you're ready to talk to a professional about making your kitchen dreams come true. For more about choosing a kitchen designer, see page 33.

All In The Family

This kitchen blends the best of Colonial country with modern conveniences to serve a large, busy family.

▼ This is a room built for activity, allowing many tasks to be performed at once— the entire family can work together to get dinner on the table.

▼ Two entrances to the kitchen—one on each side of the island—let traffic flow freely so nothing gets in the way of meal preparation.

▼ The Colonial-inspired decor uses warm cherrywood cabinetry, naturally finished on the island, and comb-painted along the wall. The refrigerator and dishwasher were camouflaged with matching panels.

▼ To bridge the 18th and 20th centuries, the existing ceiling beams were left intact, but the ceiling itself was dropped to house recessed lighting.

▼ A polished granite countertop calls attention to the island—the kitchen's showpiece. In addition to a sink and cooktop, the island features plenty of below eye-level storage. The counter at the end of the island is great for breakfast, homework-with-a-snack, or just keeping the cook company.

▼ In the main sink area, the countertop is standard laminate—less costly than the granite. By keeping the sink counter simple, the island is further spotlighted as the center of the kitchen.

▼ Little touches—an open spice rack, pineapple trivet wallhanging, dried flowers hung from ceiling beams— all contribute to a homey feeling.

▼ Underneath it all, the floors are covered with brick-look ceramic tiles.

ELEMENTS OF DESIGN

The Craft of Cabinetry

Cabinets typically account for one third to one half of the total cost of a kitchen remodeling job. When you choose yours, choose them carefully. Remember that cabinets are a long-term investment. You may redecorate in a few years' time, but chances are you won't replace your cabinetry. Select something you can live and work with for many years to come.

Cabinet Types

▼ Stock cabinets are available in a variety of styles and materials, but only in certain standard sizes that grow in 3-inch increments. They offer quick delivery and moderate prices, but little artistic license. Stock cabinets may force you to compromise the dimensions of your kitchen redesign.

▼ Factory-custom units cost more, but offer flexibility. They are built to individual order, so their sizes can be altered to suit your design. You can customize materials, finish and hardware. You also may be able to select interior options, such as pull-out shelves, spice racks and drawer dividers.

▼ True custom cabinetry, made by local cabinetmakers or shops, provides the ultimate creative freedom. It also is more costly than factory-built cabinetry. (For more tips on custom cabinetry, see page 14.)

Cabinet Styles

▼ Traditional frame-style cabinets feature doors that are hinged to a front frame and project from the cabinet box. The hinges and hardware are visible, and may be quite decorative. Most often made of wood, frame-style cabinets are the standard choice for a country kitchen.

▼ Euro-style cabinets (now made in the U. S.) feature doors that are hinged directly to the side of the cabinet box. The hinges are concealed inside the cabinets, and knobs or pulls often are replaced by notches hidden under the doors and drawers. These cabinets usually are made of plastic laminate, and are favored in contemporary kitchen design.

▼ While the dilineation between the tradition frame-style cabinets and the sleek Euro-style cabinets generally holds true, some manufacturers will offer traditional-style cabinets in plastic laminate, or frameless styles in wood.

Cabinet Hardware

▼ Select cabinet hardware that will not catch on clothing. Also remember that an intricate or fancifully-designed knob may look alluring by itself in the store, but when 10 or 20 knobs are on display in a kitchen, those ornate knobs can be overwhelming. If you are striving for an authentic period style, consult a book on period furniture design. Iron hinges and wooden knobs were most common in Colonial designs.

Evolution, Not Revolution

Generations have cooked in this room, each adding something special from their own era. Rather than stripping away the existing eclectic decor and starting again from scratch, this kitchen is a study in how beautifully the vintage old can blend with the necessary new to create a room that's practical, comfortable and country cozy.

▼ The many types and shades of wood used in this kitchen are product of different "improvements" over time. The cabinetry in a deep red-brown, the lighter hues of the ceiling planks and the blond pine of the modern butcherblock work table all work together to create a rich, warm atmosphere. Brightness is added by the many touches of white used throughout the kitchen in the white walls, laminate countertops, new sink and appliances, and ruffled café curtains.

▼ A vintage 1920's stove provides extra storage space. The free-standing stove in the center of the room is an authentic wood burning stove very much in use for heating the kitchen area during the winter.

▼ "In plain sight" is the motto of this hard-working kitchen. Glass doored pantry cabinets display a collection of pretty — and practical — pottery and stoneware. Spices are lined up on the windowsill behind the sink for easy access. Often used pots and pans are hung on a rack above the butcherblock table, with mixing bowls and casserole dishes tucked away within reach on the shelf below the table.

> **Cookery has become an art,**
> **a noble science.**
> — Robert Burton

From the Heartland
(photo, page 4)

Careful restoration uncovered the turn-of-the-century charm of this Midwestern Victorian kitchen. Much of the period housing in the middle of America is from the Victorian era; prior to that, the Midwest basically was a frontier.

▼ To retain the authentic atmosphere of this vintage room, many of the original fixtures were left intact, including the porcelain sink with its brass fittings and the wood-burning stove.

▼ The molding and wainscotting were painted a soft moss green, and are set off by the walls done in a complimentary pale shade of green.

▼ The seemingly random arrangement of paintings and prints adds to the Victorian style, as do the collection of period kitchen implements. The antique pedestal table and matching chairs complete the look.

ELEMENTS OF DESIGN
The Work Triangle

A kitchen's efficiency is measured by the "work triangle," a concept developed at the University of Illinois in the 1950's. To determine your own work triangle, make a quick sketch of your present kitchen that notes the location of the refrigerator, sink, and stove or cooktop. Draw a triangle connecting these three work centers — this is your work triangle.

▼ The principle of the work triangle is to minimize the number of steps you take to go back and forth between the three work centers. The greater the number of steps, the less efficient the layout. However, too few steps between the work areas can be just as inefficient and inconvenient.

▼ To measure the efficiency of your work triangle, add the lengths of the legs of the triangle. The sum should be greater than 12 feet, and less than 23 feet.

The Heat is On!
Stoves and Ovens

Gas or electric? The precise control of gas now is matched by electric induction burners without the potential danger of open flames. You can choose a stove that combines a cooktop and oven, or one with separate components. Each option has its advantages.

▼ A full stove takes up less space and provides a larger oven than a wall unit. If you opt for a full stove, get one with edges that protrude over the countertop to eliminate dirt-trapping between the stove and cabinets. A stove without a back panel leaves the backsplash visually unbroken, and has easy-to-reach controls in the front.

▼ A separate cooktop and wall oven offers greater design flexibility than a full stove. Some electric cooktops come with interchangeable induction burners and solid-disc burners, offering a more even heat than gas. Griddles, grills, and other accessories also are available. Cooktops made in Europe are known for their superb performance and good looks, but are smaller than American models.

▼ Built-in wall ovens are small enough to consider having two ovens, and can be installed at eye level. Units are available with both microwave and conventional radiant heat.

▼ A microwave oven is safe and efficient, serving a busy family well. If you are considering getting a microwave, plan for it now; you might lose working space to accommodate it after your kitchen is completed.

▼ A commercial stove is large and requires a 6-inch airspace in the back, making it project 36 inches into the room. It needs powerful ventilating fans, is difficult to clean, and throws off a lot of heat. However, the oven capacity is much larger than a conventional oven.

Bright White, Warm Wood

By removing the wall between the kitchen and the family room, this space was transformed into an airy, open-plan cooking/eating/living area.

▼ The brightness of cabinets, walls and ceilings painted white is tempered by the soft warm gold of pine wood in the cabinets, countertops, stools and exposed ceiling beams.

▼ Wooden cabinets with clearly visible slats were painted a glossy white to provide an airy backdrop for cabinet doors and drawers made of 100-year-old heart pine. Although the pantry cabinets are covered by solid doors with white hardware, there are glass panels on the china and glassware cabinet.

▼ Hardwood countertops are shined to a soft glow. They require more care than synthetic countertops, but the look is incomparable.

▼ The cooktop island is a veritable treasure trove of storage, with cabinets under the cooktop, open shelves opposite, and a built-in wine rack on one side.

▼ The breakfast counter opens onto the family room, permitting unrestricted flow of conversation during meal preparation. And under the counter is another roomy storage area.

▼ To maintain the simple lines of the room, the appliances have been recessed so they don't obstruct the walkways or compete with the decor.

ELEMENTS OF DESIGN
Finishing Touches for Cabinets

Cabinet Looks

▼ Wood is by far the most popular cabinet material, accounting for 75 percent of all cabinet sales. The interiors of wooden cabinets usually are made of plywood or particleboard, while the exposed elements — doors, drawer fronts and front frames — are made of solid wood or veneers.

▼ Almost any wood can be crafted into kitchen cabinets: oak, cherry, maple, mahogany, walnut, ash, birch, and soft woods such as various pine species. Solid wood construction uses solid boards that usually are ¾ inch thick. Less-costly laminated units have thin wood veneers over particleboard.

▼ Wood can be stained, painted, pickled, or finished naturally. For a natural look that allows you to see and feel the wood grain, use a penetrating oil (this often is called a Swedish finish). For added protection against stains, apply a coat of paste wax.

▼ Matte or glossy lacquer finishes, usually sprayed on at the factory, provide more protection. The most durable finish is multiple coats of polyurethane, available in satin or gloss.

▼ Wooden cabinets can easily be refinished to change their look, and scratches are simple to repair. When choosing a natural wood finish, ask for samples and compare them with your existing trim and molding.

▼ If you're planning to paint your cabinets *(see page 21)*, have them made from birch veneer plywood, which absorbs paint better than other wood veneers. If you're going to stain your cabinets, experiment on a piece of scrap wood until you achieve the shade you want. Then stain the cabinets.

▼ Plastic-laminate, available in matte and high-gloss finishes in many colors, is durable and easy to care for, but difficult to refinish or repair. The laminate usually is applied to particleboard, and should be on the inside and outside surfaces of the cabinet.

▼ Steel cabinets are uncommon these days. Those that are available are quite costly.

Cabinet Quality Checks

▼ Be sure doors and drawer fronts are mounted solidly, and joints are clean and tight. Run your hand over the surfaces; they should be smooth and even.

▼ Stained finishes should be consistent in color; streaks or trapped dust particles are an indication of sloppy workmanship.

▼ Open and close the samples. Doors should open and close quietly and easily. Drawers should glide smoothly on runners without wobbling.

▼ Another sure sign of quality is how well the cabinet interiors are finished. They should be clean and neat, with no obvious seams, dried glue, or loose joints.

COUNTRY WAYS
Wish on an Eyelash

Many people still believe in making a wish on a dropped eyelash. Here's the proper way to be sure your wish comes true: When you lose an eyelash (it doesn't count if you pull one out), place it on the back of your left hand. Close your eyes, and make a wish. Then hit the palm of your left hand, from underneath, with the back of your right hand to make the eyelash fly away. If, after three tries, the eyelash still sticks to your left hand, the wish will not come true.

If this is the case, pick up the eyelash and burn it. It's said that someone who wants to cause you harm needs only one of your eyelashes to work the spell. Burning the eyelash ensures that it will not fall into the hands of evil doers.

S·M·A·L·L
S·P·A·C·E D·E·S·I·G·N·S

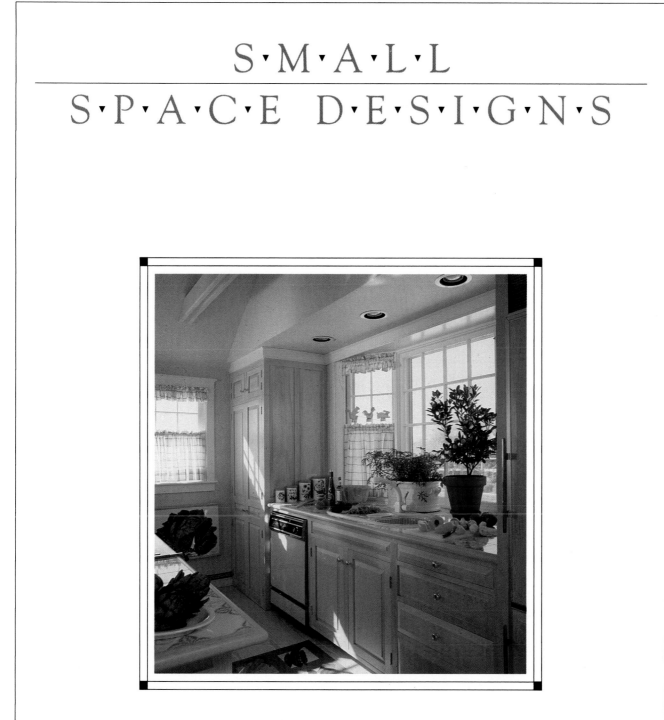

Cozy Country Cottage

This tiny kitchen, made pretty with French country accents, is both space smart and appealing.

▼ Storage is a priority, so the sink area is bracketed by a roomy closet and extra-large paneled refrigerator.

▼ Blond pine cabinetry and flooring visually enlarge a small area; white trim furthers the airy feeling.

▼ Large French country floral tiles top the counters and introduce a dash of color, echoed in the café curtains.

▼ The bay window is perfect for plants; the three bowl sink features a detachable sprayer for easy watering. Whimsical silhouette ornaments in the window actually are targets from a shooting gallery.

ELEMENTS OF DESIGN

Custom Kitchen Cabinets

Commissioning a local cabinetmaker or cabinet shop to build kitchen cabinets offers the ultimate in creative freedom. Design, materials, finishes and specialized interior features are limited only by your imagination and budget. Awkward dimensions, strange angles, uneven floors and walls, and other design problems all can be solved. You even can have the cabinets built as separate, freestanding units, so that you can take them with you if you move.

▼ Depending on design complexity and materials, custom cabinets usually are more expensive than built-to-order factory units, and are much more expensive if you want them to resemble fine furniture. (Some shops do offer a few basic styles at reasonable prices.) Scheduling also can be a problem; the best cabinet shop in your area may be backlogged for a year. Still, if you have very specific needs, appreciate quality craftsmanship, and have the budget, custom cabinets can pay handsome rewards.

▼ If you're working with a designer or architect, he or she probably can recommend a good cabinet shop. If not, check the Yellow Pages under "Cabinets" or "Cabinetmakers." Most shops offer both design and fabrication services, but they also can work from detailed plans.

▼ You should have the cabinetmaker visit the room before building the cabinets; it will give him or her a chance to check dimensions, and spot any potential problems you or a designer may have missed. The cabinetmaker also might offer valuable suggestions for a better or more economical design.

▼ As you would with any contractor, work out the details in advance: design, materials, hardware, finishes, construction and payment schedules, who will install the finished cabinets, and so on. Check the shop's references, and inspect some of their past work before you commit any money.

Enamel Cookware

Enamel-on-metal cookware has been used for centuries, and remains a favorite of chefs today. Prized for their stain and scratch resistance, porcelain enamel-coated pots and pans are available in a variety of styles and colors.

▼ You're likely to find a great difference in both weight and price between enamel-on-cast-iron cookware and enamel-on-steel cookware. However, both types of cookware should be cared for in the same manner. The porcelain enamel that coats the cookware essentially is a form of glass, so it can crack. Avoid banging the cookware against hard surfaces, and do not the use cookware if the enamel is cracked or chipped. In some cases, the enamel may melt if it is exposed to an extremely high temperature for a prolonged time.

▼ Wash porcelain enamel-coated pots in warm, sudsy water using a sponge or cloth. To remove stubborn stains, soak the pot, or use a non-abrasive cleanser and non-abrasive scrubber. If the enamel becomes discolored, scrub it with a mixture of lemon juice and salt, or with chlorine bleach, and then wash and rinse the pot thoroughly.

Painting Techniques

There are any number of painting techniques you can use to add texture to your cabinets or walls, or to achieve a desired effect.

▼ Antiquing: Paint, varnish, or glaze is applied to a surface, then wiped or blotted off to create a weathered or aged look.

▼ Bleaching or Pickling: White or light-colored paint is applied to wood, then wiped off while the paint is still damp to let the grain of the wood show through.

▼ Combing: A comb (often of heavy cardboard) is pulled across a freshly painted surface to make a pattern of wavy stripes.

▼ Dragging: A dry paintbrush is dragged across a freshly glazed surface to add texture and a pattern of fine lines.

▼ Glazing: A thin layer of an oil-base paint is applied over a previously painted surface for an almost-transparent effect.

▼ Graining: The technique of dragging some type of object, such as a feather or a stick, through fresh glaze to produce a wood-grain effect.

▼ Marbling: To create the look of marble, several colors are blended and streaked using a brush or sponge. Often veins are added.

▼ Spattering: Paint is first thinned, then splashed lightly across a surface, usually with a paintbrush.

▼ Sponging: To achieve a softly textured effect, a sponge is used to dab paint over a surface, or to blot excess paint off a surface.

▼ Stippling: The tip of a dry brush is dabbed firmly over a freshly glazed or painted surface to create a matte finish.

▼ Trompe l'oeil painting: "Fool-the-eye" technique in which a picture is painted to look three dimensional.

We put our love where we have put our labor.
— Ralph Waldo Emerson

Lighting

Lighting your kitchen may be more complicated than you realize. Lighting essentials for a kitchen should include good general, or ambient, lighting, plus "task" lighting at work areas such as the sink, stove and countertops.

▼ A centrally located ceiling fixture generally will provide enough ambient lighting for an average-size kitchen. Larger kitchens may require several ceiling lights to provide enough illumination.

▼ All work surfaces need task lighting, which is brighter and more concentrated than ambient lighting. Under-cabinet fluorescent fixtures often are used to light countertops, but recessed lights in the ceiling have the added benefit of lighting the inside of cabinets. Position recessed lights slightly back from the front edge of the counter or cooktop so that your body doesn't cast a shadow onto the work surface.

▼ To light an island or dining area, consider using a hanging pendant or chandelier. Set these lights at least 30 inches higher than the surface they are to illuminate.

▼ Build flexibility into your kitchen lighting scheme. Put lighting fixtures on individual switches so that your lighting can be varied to suit the task or time of day. A fixture over the sink, for example, may be necessary only for after-dinner clean-up. A hanging lamp over the table may be more effective on a dimmer switch.

▼ Before remodeling, consult your contractor, designer, or a lighting consultant for kitchen lighting schemes to suit your personal needs.

*L*a Cuisine Française

A kitchen equipped for a master chef is absolutely charming in French country style.

▼ Beautiful hand-painted ceramic tiles set the scene in this small but highly workable kitchen. Tinted ever-so-slightly, they provide color and a cheerful pattern without making the walls too busy. The smooth, glossy tiles also reflect available light into dark spaces.

▼ A commercial stove is the pièce de résistance for this "cook's kitchen." The overhead ventilation system is a must for safe operation of such a powerful stove. It features two recessed lights to make working easier.

▼ In addition to ceiling lights, there's fluorescent task lighting mounted under the cabinets over the sink.

▼ The tile countertops are lovely to look at, but for serious chopping and food preparation, there's a butcherblock counter next to the stove. The wooden edging around the tiled countertops complements the butcherblock and adds a homey touch.

▼ Instead of doored upper cabinets, the owner opted for open pantry shelving throughout the kitchen, with one glass-doored cabinet over the sink. Down below, the custom-made tongue and groove cabinets hold cleaning items.

▼ This kitchen shows a real love of surface texture, from the wall tiles to the paneled cabinets. The floors are covered with terra cotta tiles in warm shades of red-gold. The kitchen table is a French marble-topped baker's table that is ideal for dining, and doubles as a surface for rolling pie crusts.

He that eateth well, drinketh well;
he that drinketh well, sleepeth well;
he that sleepeth well, sinneth not;
he that sinneth not goeth straight
through Purgatory to Paradise.
—William Lithgow

ELEMENTS OF DESIGN
Countertops

All the countertops in your kitchen do not have to be the same. For the main work area, select a smooth, water-resistant, durable material. Granite is extra durable. Corian also is quite sturdy. Laminate does not wear as well. However, the most popular choices for country kitchen countertops are wood and tile. Here are a few things you should know about these materials.

Wood

▼ Dense hardwoods, such as maple and mahogany, are the best choices for countertops. Wood countertops (except those used for chopping) should have a tough surface finish, such as multiple coats of polyurethane, to make them smooth, waterproof and wipeable.

▼ Butcherblock, which is made from strips of oak or maple laminated together, is another popular choice. All the joints of butcherblock counters should be absolutely square and tight.

▼ Wood countertops that will be used for chopping should be finished with natural mineral oil. Renew the finish periodically. Remember that the surface will show the marks of your cutting and chopping.

Tile

▼ Ceramic tile, while not a good choice for the primary food preparation area, works well for the counter area around the stove because it can take hot pots without cracking or scorching.

▼ Grouting is the major drawback to tile countertops. Although glazed tiles are impervious to stains, grout is not. The grout, slightly lower than the tile surfaces, also make counters bumpy. If you choose tile for your countertops, consider including at least one smooth work area made from granite, Corian, or wood. Larger tiles (12 inches square) maximize the flat tile area of the countertop, cutting down on grout lines as well. Two 12-inch tiles with a bullnose edging will fit the standard counter depth without cutting.

▼ When choosing tile, select a product designed for countertop use; some tiles are made for walls only. Glazed tiles are the easiest to clean. Or try an unglazed tile with a low absorption rate (called "impervious" or "vitreous"). Avoid using heavily textured tiles on counters.

▼ Treat the grout with a silicone sealer after it has fully cured, about 30 days after installation.

In Ship Shape

Embark on a voyage of culinary pleasure in this kitchen inspired by a ship's galley.

▼ A U-shaped kitchen doesn't have to be cramped; good design can make it a pleasure to work in. This design uses every inch of available space to best advantage. The look is deliberately angular and clean to make the limited space seem larger than it is.

▼ Unadorned square windows around all three walls at counter height give the space breadth and let in air and light. Two of the windows on each wall open out; the center window panels are stationary.

▼ Below the counter, oak cabinets and drawers hold kitchen necessities. Ventilation holes for the cooktop and dishwasher (next to the sink) were drilled into the cabinet baseboards.

▼ Overhead cabinets would have cramped this small space. Open cabinet shelving, which holds dishes, glasses and often-used ingredients, performs the same function with an airy feeling. The top of the cabinet shelving is used to display a collection of baskets.

▼ Because windows occupy most of the wall space, switches for the overhead lights were installed waist-high on the cabinets. Another set of lights is mounted under the cabinets above the sink.

▼ A newly installed paneled ceiling gives a nod to old-fashioned country in this modern country kitchen. The ceiling beams camouflage track lighting. A forged steel pot rack is a practical choice for storing extra-large pots and pans.

G o West!

Warm, simple and built for maximum efficiency, this suburban kitchen is a perfect blend of southwestern and early American country.

▼ The primary function of this Texas kitchen is fast and efficient food preparation for a modern family. From the built-in microwave oven to the trash compactor to the high-powered hot water spigot at the sink, all the modern appliances are here. There's even (dare we say it?) a portable TV to entertain the cook. Any upgrading or remodeling had to be done without sacrificing ease and convenience.

▼ The major addition here was an island with a cooktop (the ventilation system is concealed below). Shelves built into the side of the island hold cookbooks, food stuffs and what nots, so everything is right at hand.

▼ Decorative painting, in a unique mix of early American and southwestern styles, makes the kitchen "country." The spacious cabinets were upgraded with a coat of custom-mixed paint in a sunwashed shade of Williamsburg blue. The stenciled oakleaf and acorn border adds Colonial charm.

▼ Laminate countertops were replaced with rugged butcherblock, and a ceramic tile backsplash was added. The same southwestern gold ceramic tiles were used on the island countertop.

▼ Completing the look, there are decorative accents in both southwestern and early American styles. The unique handcrafted wrought iron pot rack takes center stage. Over the sink, showcase shelving holds pottery in desert colors. The breakfast counter stools are an updated version of early American Windsor chairs.

ELEMENTS OF DESIGN
Prepare to Paint
The success of any painting job depends on proper surface preparation.

▼ Previously painted surfaces, if in good condition, should be cleaned and rinsed thoroughly to remove dirt and grease. Glossy finishes must be roughened with fine sandpaper or commercial deglossing liquid in order to give the cabinets "tooth" to hold the new paint.

▼ Scrape off any loose or chipping paint. Then feather the edges with sandpaper so that the chipped spots will not show once they're painted. Spot-prime any areas of exposed bare wood or metal. To paint stained or varnished objects, clean and sand or degloss the surfaces, then remove any wax on the finish.

▼ Raw or stripped wood should be sanded, sealed, and primed prior to painting.

▼ If painting cabinets, remove the doors and drawers, which will be painted separately, and the hardware.

COUNTRY WAYS
The Round-Up Cook
Every cattle round-up outfit in the Old West traveled with a cook who prepared the cowboys' meals. Very often, the cook was the highest paid man in the group; cowboys always were available, but a good cook was hard to come by.

▼ With an outfit of twenty men on a round-up that lasted several months, a lot depended on the cook's happiness in his job. Riders often quarreled among themselves, but a rider who harassed the cook would soon find himself out of a job. Wise cowboys were always ready to pitch in to keep the cook happy.

▼ To insure cooperation, the cook often posted signs such as these around his wagon:
If you can't wash dishes, don't eat.
A busy cook loves a full wood box.
A full water bucket makes a happy cook.
Stray men are not exempt from helping wash dishes, bringing wood or water.
The well is just 110 steps from the kitchen, mostly downhill both ways.

ELEMENTS OF DESIGN

Bleaching and Whitewashing

Bleaching, sometimes called pickling, and whitewashing give a lovely translucent look to wood flooring of any type—strip, plank or parquet. The easiest way to achieve this look is to buy it. Many leading wood floor manufacturers offer a bleached or whitewashed finish on prefinished floors.

▼ To bleach or whitewash an existing floor, you first must remove the existing finish. Usually, this means sanding. It a good idea to hire a professional for this messy, laborious job. If you prefer to do it yourself, you'll need to rent a commercial floor sander.

Bleaching

▼ Like linen or cotton, wood is composed of fibers that can be bleached to a lighter color, or even to white. Wood floors can be bleached with laundry bleach, concentrated sodium hypochlorite, oxalic acid, or a special two-part bleach for wood (one chemical is brushed or wiped on immediately after the other). The first two bleaches can be used to remove small stains. To bleach an entire floor, one of the latter two chemicals is recommended.

▼ After you have applied oxalic acid or a two-part bleach to the floor and allowed it to dry, you can bleach the floor again to achieve a lighter color. Bleaches react differently to different woods, so it is best to experiment first on an unobtrusive part of the floor.

▼ Once you have achieved the desired shade, the bleach must be neutralized with a solution of 1 part vinegar to 1 part water. Let the floor dry thoroughly, then sand it with fine, 240-grit sandpaper. This smooths the grain raised by the bleaching process. Vacuum the floor, rinse it again, and let the floor dry.

▼ Top the bleached floor with a protective surface coat of varnish, or a penetrating sealer.

Whitewashing

▼ Whitewashing creates a softer effect than bleaching. Thinned white or light-colored paint is applied to the wood and wiped off, so a thin layer of the color remains but the grain of the wood shows through. The process can be repeated until the desired shade is reached. Once the whitewash dries, lightly sand the floor, and apply a protective surface coating or a penetrating finish.

White Open Spaces

Sunshine floods this farmhouse-style kitchen. The bright, white walls are warmed by the soft, bleached wood floor, and wood tables and chairs.

▼ Knocking down the wall between the kitchen and the spare room doubled the size of this kitchen. To the left of the kitchen, a small porch/laundry room was enclosed, adding more space and welcome sunlight. The back porch doorway was retained, and the porch door replaced with reinforced glass French doors. A whitewashed ceiling beam covers the spot where the wall once stood.

▼ Pulling up the linoleum tile revealed a fir wood floor that was then stripped and bleached. The kitchen is at the back of the house, so the owner by-passed window curtains, preferring to let the sun shine in.

▼ The bright white of the cabinets, walls and ceiling is offset by light olive tiles on the countertops and stove backsplash. The green, almost a neutral, echoes the colors of the garden outside.

▼ To achieve an old-fashioned feeling in keeping with the home's 1917 vintage, wired glass was used in the upper cabinet doors. Down below, and in the dining area, painted wooden cabinets and drawers are reminiscent of a butler's pantry. Clean chrome fixtures—the stove hood, wired glass, faucet, drawer pulls, and towel bar—blend well with the simple white and pale green treatment.

▼ A butcherblock table placed in the center of the kitchen provides a handy work space. The kitchen table, used mostly for family meals, is antique pine.

ELEMENTS OF DESIGN
Appliance Camouflage

Appliances present a major dilemma in a country kitchen design: how to reconcile their sleek, high-tech looks with the rustic or period styles of country decorating. We recommend two solutions: hiding them, or making them blend in with their surroundings. You'll find examples of both solutions throughout this book.

▼ Small appliances—from microwave ovens to cordless hand mixers—can be hidden fairly easily behind hinged or sliding cabinet doors. For instance, try concealing a microwave above the counter behind a cabinet door that lifts up and slides back. If you decide to hide your microwave, remember that you must provide for proper ventilation.

▼ A tall corner cabinet that's flush with the countertop can be an excellent hiding place for a blender, food processor, mixer, coffee maker, and so on. Consider when and how you use these appliances, and use your imagination to devise a workable arrangement—retractable shelves, turntables—anything's possible! Build the cabinet around a power source so you don't have to move the appliances to use them.

▼ For large appliances such as refrigerators, dishwashers and trash compactors, the camouflage method is best; it would be impractical to put them behind closed doors. Select appliances that can be installed flush with cabinets, and can accept custom trim panels. Most cabinet manufacturers offer matching appliance panels, but you'll have to know your appliances' dimensions. It is best to select your appliances before ordering your cabinets. *(For more clever ideas for appliance camouflage, see Chapter III, Kitchen Close-Ups, page 78.)*

> **Our God is great
> and the cook is his prophet.**
> —Jerome K. Jerome

A Turn-of-the-Century Twist

A cheery kitchen combining the ornate decor of turn-of-the-century America with the ambience of an old-fashioned saloon.

▼ This kitchen invites everyone to come in and cook. The work island is built for action, with a double sink, cooktop and built-in motor for small appliances.

▼ A "private garden" is created by using botanical tile throughout the kitchen. The tile runs all around the countertops and right up the walls, filling the kitchen with trails of hand-painted ivy and potted plants. A few real plants scattered about add dimension and texture to their painted counterparts.

▼ Stock cabinets were given the look of a turn-of-the-century saloon by being "gussied-up" with ornate metal hardware. To further the saloon theme, some of the cabinet doors have had their center panel removed and etched glass panels put in their place.

▼ The showpiece of the room takes you back 100 years—a hanging brass lamp fixture with green glass shades. This beautiful chandelier helps pull all the decorating elements in the room together, while also providing plenty of light for the island.

▼ Because this room has such an opulent feeling, details are kept to a minimum: a single ruffled curtain and hand-painted canister set are all that's needed.

DO·IT·YOURSELF·DECOR

K·I·T·C·H·E·N
F·A·C·E·L·I·F·T·S

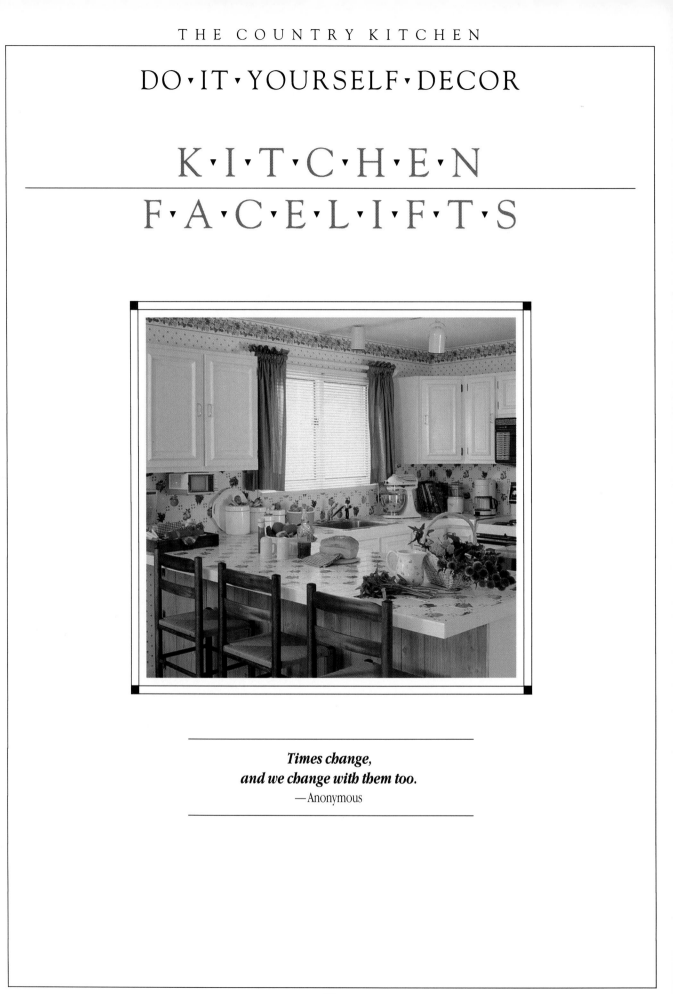

Times change,
and we change with them too.
—Anonymous

Country Facelift

This standard suburban kitchen didn't need a major overhaul. The appliances and cabinets were fine, and so was the basic layout. What were needed were a few cosmetic changes to give it a new country look.

▼ Gone are the plain white walls and tired Formica countertops. In their stead: marvelous hand-painted tiles that evoke the garden-fresh look of the French countryside. If you wish, you can install tiles yourself. Sand the surfaces you're planning to tile, lay the tiles with thin set mortar, and fill in with grout.

▼ Glossy white paint and new brass hardware revive ordinary dark wooden cabinets. The change from dark to light gave the room a new personality immediately. Along the top, a floral wallpaper border complements the tile below.

▼ Narrow white wooden blinds are a practical choice that also add charm to a less-than-lovely window. Gathered on a decorative wooden rod, pretty curtains that pick up the blue in the tile and wallpaper border give the window a finished look.

▼ The pre-renovation track lighting remains, focused on the primary work areas. It provides good light, and costs far less than adding new recessed lighting.

▼ Old blends with new easily, from the quaint canister set to the TV tucked under a cabinet.

▼ The rustic ladderback bar stools were purchased unfinished, and stained with dye *(directions, page 32)*.

ELEMENTS OF DESIGN
Ventilation

Proper ventilation not only will rid your kitchen of smoke and odors, but will remove the moisture generated by cooking. Excessive moisture damages wall and ceiling finishes, and can lead to rot and mildew inside the walls.

▼ The most effective way to remove moisture and odors is with a ventilating hood above the cooktop or stove. Two types commonly are available. One vents directly to the outside by means of a duct. The other, a ductless model, passes odor- and moisture-laden air through a filtering system and returns it to the kitchen. Models with ducts are preferable because they also remove excess heat generated by cooking.

▼ Make sure your stove hood has enough fan capacity to move 100 cubic feet of air per minute (CFM) for each linear foot of hood length. If you are installing a restaurant-style stove with burners that produce almost twice the heat of those on a normal stove, install an exhaust fan with greater capacity. Stove manufacturers can provide the recommended CFM capacity needed to handle your model. Check with your local building department for guidelines about the correct installation of restaurant stoves.

▼ Some consumer cooktops include a built-in exhaust fan, designed to duct to the outside. With some models, however, the fan's effectiveness decreases as the duct length increases, because the blower motor lacks the power to push the air beyond a given distance. Be sure to check the strength of the fan motor and the length of the exhaust duct before installing a new cooktop.

▼ Windows are good, simple ventilation devices. Your kitchen should have windows that can be opened. When you're remodeling, consider adding more windows to aid cross-ventilation.

▼ Ventilators of gas appliances must be maintained properly to ensure your family's good health. Filters should be cleaned or replaced three or four times a year. Ducts should be checked periodically for cracks and blockage. If you smell gas, open a window and telephone the gas company.

STAINED FURNITURE

Materials: Unfinished furniture; extra-fine sandpaper; tack cloth; No. 29 Royal Blue Rit® Liquid Dye; wide mouth container; 2-inch-wide paintbrush; sponge; satin polyurethane.

Directions:

1. Sand the unfinished furniture smooth, and wipe off all the sawdust with the tack cloth.

2. Pour the liquid dye into the wide mouth container. Apply the dye to the furniture with the paintbrush, blending the brush strokes into the grain of the wood. Allow the dye to dry. Repeat the process until you achieve the tone desired. Allow the dye to dry.

3. Rinse the sponge several times to make sure it is clean. Dampen the sponge, and wipe the entire dyed surface of the furniture, rinsing the sponge often. Let the furniture dry completely.

4. Using a clean paintbrush, seal the stained furniture with one or two coats of the polyurethane; sand lightly between coats.

ELEMENTS OF DESIGN
Creative Cabinet Changes

It's possible to improve your cabinets without replacing them. When you're on a strict budget, or your kitchen simply needs "freshening," this is the way to go.

▼ Replace worn solid cabinet doors with glass doors. Throughout this book, you'll see many variations of glass cabinet doors: solid panes, leaded glass, sand-blasted designs, and more.

▼ Glass doors, once only a European preference, now are being offered by some American manufacturers. We recommend stile-and-rail doors — glass bordered by wooden frames — for their easy installation. You'll find them ready-made in standard sizes at stores that sell modular cabinets and wall units. Bring your cabinet measurements with you when you shop.

▼ Painting and stenciling also give cabinets new life. Just covering dark wooden cabinets with a few coats of glossy white paint will change the look of the entire kitchen. Or change your kitchen's color scheme by changing the color of the cabinets — try Williamsburg blue, hunter green, or pastel yellow. Use our stenciling techniques *(directions, pages 154-155)* to add motifs or borders on the cabinet doors.

COUNTRY WAYS
From Little Acorns . . .

▼ In bygone days, many people carried an acorn with them to ward off disease and insure long life. Acorns were considered especially lucky for men.

▼ In many homes, acorns were used as pulls for window shades. Women crocheted or knit covers for the acorns, and chains to attach them to the shades.

K I T C H E N · I M P R O V E M E N T
C H E C K L I S T · T W O

Choosing A Design Professional

If you want to remodel rather than just redecorate your kitchen, it's best to call on a professional. Unlike redoing a living room or bedroom, where you can get by with an eye for color and the skill to mix wallpaper paste, kitchen remodeling requires expertise in plumbing, electrical wiring, cabinetry and space planning. Mistakes can be demoralizing, as well as very expensive.

An architect, interior designer, or builder is not necessarily the right person for a kitchen remodeling job. Your first choice should be a Certified Kitchen Designer (CKD). A CKD has received formal training in kitchen design from the National Kitchen & Bath Association, has met the Association's requirements, and has passed tests for certification. Most CKDs have at least seven years of experience in the field. For a listing of CKDs in your region, write to the

National Kitchen & Bath Association
124 Main Street
Hackettstown, NJ 07840.

Here are some additional tips to help you choose a design professional wisely.

1. Ask friends and co-workers for recommendations. Visit their kitchens to inspect the work. Ask about costs and work habits.

☐ How close was each designer's final fee to his or her original cost estimate?

☐ Was the work done on schedule?

☐ Were the workers overly disruptive?

☐ What did your friend like and dislike about the designer's work?

2. Check the name of each designer with the Better Business Bureau.

☐ Are there any outstanding complaints against the designer?

3. Examine each designer's portfolio.

☐ Ask to see before-and-after photos of the work.

☐ Ask to visit a kitchen that the designer has remodeled; some satisfied customers will be gracious enough to allow this.

4. Check details.

☐ What types of cabinets and appliances does the designer use most often?

☐ How well are storage units integrated in the overall design?

☐ Which of the designer's special techniques (window treatments, "signature" cabinet designs, appliance camouflage, and so on) can be used in your remodel?

5. Assess the personal chemistry between you and each designer you interview.

☐ Is the designer someone you can spend a great deal of time with? Remember, a kitchen remodel is not done overnight!

☐ Will the designer listen to suggestions? It's true that kitchen design is an art, but a good designer is an artist who is willing to bend to his or her client's needs. After all, it's your kitchen.

☐ Do you and the designer communicate well? If the designer always is too busy to talk, choose another designer.

☐ Does the designer have good taste? Everyone has a personal idea of "fabulous." Be sure yours agrees with your designer's.

A PLACE TO
D·I·N·E

If any man hunger, let him eat at home.
—I Corinthians

S ome of the most vivid memories of childhood center around the dining table: family conferences, homework sessions, late-night heart-to-hearts, and of course, daily meals.

Whether you have a separate room for dining, or set aside a corner of your country kitchen, this chapter will show you how to create your own unique dining area. Explore the variety of styles available in both round and square tables— from French country to Southwest, Victorian to Colonial. There are tables that easily make room for one more, and space-saving tables for smaller rooms.

Fresh flowers, a watermelon basket of cut fruit, a selection of just-baked muffins—these are just a few of the country-style centerpieces we suggest to add the finishing touch to your dining table. By creating the perfect place to dine, you can make every meal a memorable one.

A F·A·M·I·L·Y A·F·F·A·I·R

An' all us other children,
when the supper things is done,
We set around the kitchen fire
an' has the mostest fun.
—James Whitcomb Riley

Touches of Country

This 450-foot kitchen/dining room was designed to be high-tech, but the owner wanted to bring a country flavor to the room, especially the dining area. The charmingly eclectic result was achieved by adding just the right country accents.

▼ Since the window in the corner is quite small, the light, bright quality of the room is achieved by the use of track lighting, floor-to-ceiling white laminate shelving and a mirror in the wine alcove — all adding or reflecting light into the room.

▼ The open pantry-style shelving is filled with collections of Meissen and Royal Copenhagen china, giving the dining area true country charm. In the alcove, stainless steel commercial shelving holds a collection of fine wines.

▼ The simplicity of the white-on-white overall design is warmed by the red-brown floor of Mexican quarry tile. The beautiful oak table and chairs actually are junk shop treasures that the owner refinished. On the table, instead of place mats, oversize linen napkins were spread on the diagonal at each setting. The framed maps of French wine country are from the 1930's.

Away From It All
(photo, page 34)

A cozy corner, filled with natural light and the warmth of wood, is the perfect setting for a country meal.

▼ The big corner window makes this dining area work. By using only a valance and white tie-back curtains, the window itself is unobstructed. The view of the garden and the natural sunlight set off the richness of the wood table, chairs and cupboard.

▼ The showpiece in this dining nook is the hand-carved wooden cupboard. In true country style, it's not only beautiful to look at, it also provides good storage.

▼ The red tile flooring is reminiscent of colonial brick, and the petit-patterned wallpaper looks like old-fashioned calico. Ruffled chair pads make the well-worn Windsor-style chairs more comfortable.

▼ The turn-of-the-century green glass chandelier is wired to a dimmer switch. The ceiling beams hold a decorative collection of baskets and copper cookware. A spatterware pitcher and bowl were filled with fresh flowers for the perfect country centerpiece.

COUNTRY WAYS
Wine: A Bottle of Red, A Bottle of White . . .

▼ *Storing.* Ideally, a wine bottle should be stored on its side at a temperature of 55°, but most wines will keep perfectly well at up to 70° (a cellar or cool closet work well). A wine's worst enemies are heat and fluctuations in temperature. Heat will cause wine to age prematurely and deteriorate. Fluctuating temperatures contract and expand the cork, which allows air to seep in and oxidize the wine.

▼ *Serving.* White wine should be chilled for one hour in the refrigerator, or for 20 minutes in an ice bucket before serving. Red wines should be served at around 65° for the optimum bouquet and taste.

▼ *Breathing.* Before you serve red wines such as cabernet sauvignon, they need to breathe — be exposed to the air — to improve their flavor. The amount of time varies. Most cabernets need at least 15 minutes, while a 20-year-old wine needs less

than one minute. The process can be accelerated by pouring the wine into a decanter.

▼ *Pouring.* A wineglass never should be filled more than half full. This is so the wine can be gently swirled to release its aroma. The best all-purpose wineglass is the 10-ounce tulip shape.

▼ *Appearance.* Any wine should appear clear, not cloudy. A red wine should be clear ruby red or garnet, with the slightest hint of brown if it is more than six years old. A white wine should be clear, with greenish or golden aspects.

▼ *Bouquet.* To fully appreciate a wine's aroma (also called "nose"), gently swirl the wine in the glass a few times to release its aroma upward. A wine's bouquet always should be pleasant and slightly fruity. An odor of bad eggs or sulphur are signs of a wine that has gone bad.

Meals by the Fireside

A wonderful fireplace was discovered behind a plaster wall during the renovation of this 18th century home. The homeowners found the old mantel at a flea market, and refurbished the home's original wainscoting and hardwood floors themselves.

▼ To fit the modern necessities into this kitchen without destroying its charm, the owners opted for an L-shape arrangement along two walls, making the fireside dining area the focal point of the room.

▼ The room was decorated and furnished as a "room with many purposes," just as a true Colonial kitchen would have been. The drop-leaf table and Windsor chairs are ideal companions for one another. There's even a cozy rocker tucked by the fireplace.

▼ The oak cabinets are standard-size stock models, selected for their simple styling. The brown-tiled countertops are edged in wood.

▼ Pewterware and tin candle sconces are the perfect accents for this early American eating area. Underfoot is a braided rag rug in harmonious shades of blue.

COUNTRY WAYS
Pewter

Pewter, sometimes called the poor man's silver, was widely used in Colonial America; Paul Revere was a pewtersmith by trade.

▼ Pewter is an alloy, a combination of two or more metals. Its primary ingredient, tin, is mixed with copper, antimony, bismuth, zinc, or lead. It is the tin that gives pewter its luster. Pewter color ranges from mousy grey to bright silver, depending on the combination of metals used and the amount of polishing done during manufacturing. Since pewter is rather soft, most pieces are left plain or are simply engraved. The shape of the piece dictates its decorative quality.

▼ Pewter is highly collectible. Pieces from 18th century America are extremely rare, because it is thought many were melted down to make ammunition in the Revolutionary War.

▼ Reproductions of Colonial pewter pieces now are available. Choose from pewter pitchers, bowls, candlesticks, plates and more to decorate your home and your table.

Here Comes The Sun

If you like a dining nook that's crisp and airy, come to Scandinavian country!

▼ Several shades of fresh ivy green mixed with pristine white make this eating area cool and inviting. The simplicity of the color scheme unites the furnishings.

▼ Note how the petite table provides just the right focal point for a cozy seating arrangement. The garden furniture is roomy, sturdy, and is made even more comfortable with awning-striped seat cushions and lacy handkerchief pillows. The arrangement is what you might have under a shady elm in the garden — ideal for a relaxing respite while enjoying fresh fruit and cookies.

▼ The bare wooden floor actually is outdoor decking. On the side, a small scatter rug in bright greens adds a splash of color.

▼ In keeping with the al fresco theme, the striped wallpaper is decorated with hand-stenciled ivy leaves. And there's real Swedish ivy too!

▼ True to Scandinavian country, this room is as light-filled as possible. The table, which features the darkest wood tones, is topped with white linen. The hutch is painted white, and displays a collection of white porcelain. The only touch of frills are found in lace accents: on pillows, the tablecloth, windows, even as a shelf trim.

**At a round table
there is no dispute of place.**
—Anonymous

ELEMENTS OF DESIGN
The Kitchen Table

The table is the choice spot for family conferences, study sessions and, of course, marvelous meals. In this book, you'll see tables in all shapes and sizes. Some came from retailers, others from antique dealers, some were custom-made, and others have been in the family for generations.

▼ The "perfect" dining table truly is a matter of personal taste. Wood is the most common material used for tables — and a virtual must for a country kitchen — yet a marble-topped wrought-iron table would be lovely in a French country or Americana soda-fountain setting.

▼ Most kitchen tables seat at least four people, and usually six to eight. However, a breakfast nook or tiny apartment kitchen might best be served by a table for two, with a larger dining table in the living/dining area.

▼ There is one rule to keep in mind: Before you buy, sit at the table. Be sure it feels comfortable to you, that everyone has leg room and elbow room, and that everyone can reach the surface. If possible, choose your chairs at the same time you choose your table. If you already own the chairs, bring one with you when you shop for a table. It is crucial that the table and chairs look and feel right together.

A Room with Room

When the owners of this house moved in, they realized their dining area had suddenly grown—and they only had smaller furnishings to fill the space! Here's how they gave this space the warm and inviting feeling of an old farmhouse.

▼ In center stage: a pretty round oak table, slightly smaller in size than a standard table. Surrounding it are armchairs tied with plump seat cushions. Underneath is an area rag rug—note how this rug visually reduces the floor space around the table.

▼ Around the perimeter of the room, there's plenty of space for an accent table, dry sink and hutch. The corner hutch is an eye-catching variation on the standard hutch. The hutch doors are left open, to "cozy up" the room.

▼ By the way, the owners didn't track down the perfect table, chairs or side pieces at an antique shop or auction. All the furnishings in this room are antique reproductions—the same look at a much lower cost.

▼ Also contributing to the farmhouse motif are the wonderful "treasures" in this room: floral paintings, Shaker boxes, old-time crockery, beautiful china pieces. They help make this dining room a place that's welcoming to all.

ELEMENTS OF DESIGN

Colonial Tables

Gateleg tables and trestle tables are two Colonial styles still popular today. If you're looking for a country-style dining table with a little visual interest, consider purchasing one of these classic styles.

▼ The gateleg table features unique hinged legs that support drop leaves on either side of the table that fold flat when not in use. A gateleg table may have as many as eight legs — four stationary legs that support the center of the table, and four fold-out legs. The butterfly table is similar to the gateleg table but, instead of folding legs, has supporting "wings" that fold out from the table frame without actually touching the ground.

▼ Trestle tables were the most commonly used table in America from the mid-1600's through the mid-1800's. They consist of a plank top supported on upside down T-shaped trestles, or uprights, stabilized with a stretcher bar. The sawbuck table is a variation on the trestle table. Instead of trestles, it has crossed legs that resemble those of a sawhorse.

▼ Colonial-style tables usually have turned legs and knob or pear-shaped feet. They are decorated simply, and are very sturdy. Most Colonial furniture was made from American woods such as pine, maple, oak, ash, birch, cherry, or walnut.

Breakfast by the Bay

If your kitchen/dining area is fortunate enough to have a special feature like a bay window, place your dining table there to take advantage of the natural light.

▼ The window treatment offers sunlight as well as privacy. Imagine how different this area would look with streamlined shades instead of full curtains. The curtains "soften" the predominantly wood furnishings and are made of light fabric that diffuses sunlight. Note how the curtain fabric also complements the fabric of the seat cushions.

▼ Overhead, a tin chandelier makes this area accessible for night time dining as well.

▼ Simple Early American furnishings lend a homey look to this eating nook. The more modern banquette is covered in traditional red and white plaid fabric that is used again for the place mats.

▼ Three different patterned fabrics — a floral and two plaids — work together beautifully because they are united by the color scheme and their traditional motifs. Splashy polka dots, awning stripes, or art deco prints would be out of place here.

▼ The center of the table is brightened with red tulips. They are hearty, inexpensive, colorful and lush — you only need a few to fill a vase or pitcher. Choose flowers to match your decor, or your mood.

One cannot think well,
love well, sleep well,
if one has not dined well.
—Virginia Woolf

Vintage Victorian

If you long for a dining room with a formal air, consider recreating the elegance of the Victorian era.

▼ The highly polished dark wood of the dining table and matching carved ladder-back chairs forms the focal point of this pretty room. The tie-on chair seats are made from the same fabric as the heavy, tie-back curtains, which are hung on decorative rods.

▼ Rather than cover the table with a cloth, the setting of scalloped lace-edged place mats with crisp white linen napkins reveals the rich tones of the wood. The crystal water and wine glasses and the heavily carved silver utensils further add to the elegance of the setting.

▼ An antique tablecloth is dramatically draped over an inexpensive bamboo screen. The plate rack is a reproduction piece that is the perfect setting for a collection of antique plates. The fancy lighting fixture also is a reproduction.

▼ Other touches of Victoriana include the brass bird cage, the polished wood molding, the miniature lamps on the table instead of candles and the large potted fern. The centerpiece is typical of a period country bouquet: A seemingly random collection of posies in a white porcelain container.

A child should always say what's true
And speak when he is spoken to,
And behave mannerly at the table:
At least as far as he is able.
— Robert Louis Stevenson

ELEMENTS OF DESIGN

Variations on a Country Theme

Even if you love country decor, you can tire of seeing the same elements in room after room. By substituting new items for standard country fare, your own country style will emerge.

▼ Country decor is a mix of many different periods and influences. The "perfect" country home is one in which you feel most comfortable, whether your home is filled with pieces handed down through the generations, or newly crafted objects that you love.

▼ The following are suggested substitutions for standard country items. Try to select pieces that are crafted from natural materials, such as wood, iron, tile, or natural fibers.

Standard Fare	Variations
Windsor or ladderback chairs	Wicker chairs
	Breuer chairs
	Wrought iron chairs
	Upholstered chairs
Round oak or trestle table	Glass top/metal base
	Marble top/wood base
	Painted wood
Knotty pine woodwork	High-gloss white painted woodwork
	Dry-brushed woodwork
	Marbling or other decorative finish
Wide-board floors	Prefinished planks
	Ceramic tile or look-alike vinyl
	Brick or look-alike vinyl
	Black-and-white checkerboard in tile, vinyl, or painted wood
	Slate or stone
Hooked rug	Dhurrie
	Rag rug
	Oriental
18th century folk art	Vintage utilitarian objects hung as art
	Contemporary native paintings (from Haiti, Mexico, the U.S.)
	Contemporary crafted objects

ELEMENTS OF DESIGN
Light Effects

If you're adding or moving windows in your kitchen, you should be aware of the different kinds of light that come from different directions and orientations.

▼ Northern light is soft and diffuse, which is why many artists prefer it, but north-facing windows are the least energy efficient in cold climates. Southern light is best for solar gain in winter, but south-facing roof glazing requires summer shading. Eastern morning light is soft and pleasing with little glare. Western light is harsh, causes heat gain in summer and, left unchecked, will fade furnishings.

▼ A window's placement, as much as its size, affects natural light entry. Skylights and windows high on a wall admit more light deeper into rooms than the same size units placed lower on the wall. Work areas, such as kitchen counters, are better lit by reflected natural light than by harsher direct light.

COUNTRY WAYS
Weather Vanes

The earliest American weather vanes were not the decorative tin fixtures we know. In fact, topping one's home with something as ornate as a crowing rooster or trotting horse would have been considered vulgar and unseemly.

▼ Early American weather vanes were made of lightweight wood, such as pine or cedar. Some were as simple as a slab of wood, or even a cloth streamer, attached to a stick; the word "vane" comes from the Anglo-Saxon word for flag.

▼ The farmers who used weather vanes to predict the weather already knew the directions of east, west, north and south, so the vanes were not marked for this purpose.

Early American Influence

Old-fashioned pine blended with Williamsburg blue and parchment white gives this dining room real Colonial flavor. It's a color scheme that's been in fashion since the days of our founding fathers — and it still looks great!

▼ Parchment white wallpaper imprinted with a soft blue leaf design was used to brighten the upper walls. Coordinating wallpaper in a reverse white-on-blue pattern defines the wainscoting. The drapes and tie-on seat cushions were made from fabric that matches the wallpaper.

▼ Six ladderback chairs with woven rush seats were painted Williamsburg blue to match the chair rail on the wall. They blend perfectly with the pine sawbuck table *(see Colonial Tables, page 44)*.

▼ An oval braided rug in blue and white is a Colonial country "must." Here the rug covers the table area, but still allows the wide plank flooring to show in the lower-traffic areas.

▼ Instead of a standard hutch, the owner hung a plate rack on the wall over a narrow side table. The rack holds new ironstone and pewter plates.

▼ Would you believe there are real candles in this colonial chandelier? It's made from a section of a balustrade spindle or newel post turning, with bent sections of heavy-duty fencing wire for arms, and ball finials as candleholders.

▼ The decorative accents in this dining room look like antiques, but actually are beautiful modern replicas. The American primitive portrait between the windows is a museum reproduction. The tin wall sconces and duck decoys also are new versions of classic objects.

The city has a face,
the country a soul.
—Jacques De Lacretelle

ELEMENTS OF DESIGN

Window Wonderland

Buying windows involves making choices about size, shape, materials, finish, and optional equipment. The more you know, the better prepared you are to select the best windows for your needs.

Stock Windows vs. Custom-Made Windows

▼ In the past, if you wanted a window other than a few standard sizes and shapes (mostly rectangles), you had to have the window custom-made by a local millwork shop. Today, though custom millwork shops still exist, the distinction between stock windows and custom windows has virtually disappeared.

▼ Most leading window manufacturers not only offer a staggering array of stock shapes and sizes — including half-rounds, octagons and trapezoids, traditional casement, double-hung, awning, hopper, bay and bow units, skylights, and patio doors of every description — but they also provide custom services at factory prices. What's more, most units can be built to specification with precisely the frame, glazing, hardware and finish options you desire.

Frames

▼ Wood is the most popular, and many would say the best, frame material. It's a good natural insulator, and lends a natural look indoors that metal and vinyl can't match. Most wood frames are available with metal or vinyl exterior cladding, which makes them virtually maintenance free.

▼ Vinyl is a less expensive alternative, and solid vinyl frames cannot rot. The best products have multiple-channel extrusions, which increase energy efficiency.

▼ Aluminum frames are durable, rot-proof, and more dimensionally stable than wood or vinyl. Quality examples have thermal breaks to reduce the metal's natural conductivity of heat and cold.

▼ Whichever material you choose for your window frames, buy the highest quality units you can afford. Features will include factory-installed weather-stripping systems, strong joints (finger joints for wood; welded, not screwed, corners for vinyl and aluminum, and heavy-duty, easy-to-operate hardware.

Glazing

▼ Windows have varying degrees of insulation efficiency. Insulation capability is measured by R-value. The higher the R-value, the better the insulation. Double glazing, which has an insulation value of R-2, is standard issue today; triple glazing, R-3, sometimes is used in northern locations, though it results in heavy, bulky windows. A newer alternative (and the wave of the future, according to industry experts) is low-E glass, which delivers R-3 to R-4 insulation value, yet costs only about 15 percent more than conventional double glazing.

▼ Low-E glass, which has a slight bluish tint, comes in different types designed to minimize heat loss and drafts in cold climates, or heat gain in warm areas; the latter can be combined with tinted glass to reduce air-conditioning needs even further. Another benefit of low-E glass is its ability to filter out the ultraviolet light that can fade furnishings.

▼ Check the guarantee on the seals of windows with insulating glass; the best carry 15- to 20-year warranties.

Ice Cream Parlor Flavor

Eating in this kitchen is like stepping back into turn-of-the-century America. And what could be more delicious than dining in a room inspired by an old-fashioned soda fountain?

▼ The metal bistro chairs with heart-shaped backs are straight out of an ice cream parlor. Their delicate shaping helps to fancy-up a simple, square table. Overhead, the colorful Tiffany-style hanging lamp adds a burst of color to the setting.

▼ In the kitchen work area, punched aluminum panels, inserted into the cabinet doors, are reminiscent of old pie safe doors.

▼ Country-style open pantry shelving suspended over an L-shape counter forms a pass-through dividing the work area from the eating area—a great look without the expense of wall construction.

▼ The off-white cabinetry and window frames stand out against the painted wood paneling. The side panels of the bay window open outward; the center window panel is stationary.

▼ Adding an interesting, eclectic touch is a floor covered in African slate. The entire kitchen has been designed to create a quaint, clean, airy room reminiscent of those sweet salons of days gone by.

K I T C H E N · I M P R O V E M E N T
C H E C K L I S T · T H R E E

Working with a Designer

Once you've selected a design professional to handle your kitchen remodel, you're ready to begin creating your "dream kitchen." Use these tips to help you focus on your specific needs.

1. Be prepared.

☐ Arrive at your first meeting with your list of priorities for your new kitchen *(see Determine Your Needs, page 5)*. Include everything you want the remodel to address.

☐ If you have visited showrooms and stores, bring along a list of them with your notes on what you saw.

☐ If you have worked with another designer, bring along sketches or plans the other designer provided.

☐ Be ready to discuss what you liked and didn't like about what you saw in the showrooms and in your work with other designers.

☐ If you're meeting outside your home, bring along a sketch of your present kitchen floorplan.

☐ Bring a pad and pencil. The designer may leave you with notes, but you also should take notes yourself.

2. Be cooperative.

☐ Your designer will ask you a lot of questions about your lifestyle, your needs, and your tastes. This will help her determine the direction her design should take. The more specific the information, the easier her job will be.

3. Be decisive.

☐ If you want to discuss design options with your spouse or family, the designer will understand, but don't take an unreasonably long time to make choices.

4. Be realistic about accepting a designer's budget.

☐ You don't have to hire a designer whose charges you feel are excessive. Once you've entered into an agreement with a designer, however, remember that the designer doesn't work for free.

5. Defer to the designer in appropriate matters of technical expertise.

☐ This is why you hired a designer! She probably knows more than you do about plumbing, wiring, construction, and so on. If you don't trust her judgment, don't work with her.

6. Appreciate the conceptual suggestions the designer brings to the project.

☐ Ideas that may sound outlandish at first can become real design solutions with a little modification. Work with the designer to hone an interesting idea into something you both feel is workable. Don't feel you have to accept an idea merely because the designer is in love with it, but don't just say "No" to everything you don't like. Tell the designer why you don't like something. This will help her stay on track.

7. Don't abuse the designer's time.

☐ Remember the designer is running a business, and her time is valuable. Your designer should be willing to talk, but keep in mind that she has other clients who also require her attention.

8. Remain calm and courteous during the actual work.

☐ Remodeling can be a very messy, stressful experience. Be prepared for noise, dust, and lots of workers tramping through your kitchen while the job is being done.

9. Fulfill your contractual obligations, and be fair and honorable to the tradespeople recommended or hired by the designer.

10. Be willing to function as a referral source for the designer's future clients.

ELEMENTS OF DESIGN

Fabulous Floors

There are a number of suitable materials you can use for your country kitchen floor. Most of the floors you'll see in this book are covered with vinyl flooring, wood, or ceramic tile. Here is some basic information about these three popular flooring materials.

Vinyl

▼ The most popular choice for kitchen flooring, vinyl is resilient, inexpensive, stain-resistant, and easy on the feet. Manufacturers offer a huge variety of colors, textures and designs to complement any decor. Most vinyl flooring requires low maintenance, and can be cleaned with everyday cleaners.

Wood

▼ When most people think "country," they visualize the warm glow of a wooden floor. Wood flooring is available in many tones and patterns, is easy to maintain, and can be refinished to look like new. Tough hardwoods are recommended for flooring because this surface gets a lot of wear and tear. In kitchens, where spills are a fact of life, many experts recommend using laminated wood flooring rather than solid boards. Laminated wood flooring is made of a thin top layer of hardwood glued to crossbanded layers of less expensive wood. This layering makes the flooring less likely to split or warp when it is exposed to moisture.

▼ Wood flooring must be covered with a protective coating, such as polyurethane, that prevents staining and wear. Depending on the flooring you choose, the protective coating may be applied at the factory, or on-site once the floor is laid. In general, you can choose between satin and high-gloss finishes. When exposed to direct sunlight for extended periods of time, polyurethane finishes may tend to yellow; some people think this adds to the beauty of the floor. To avoid yellowing, use a clear epoxy finish, or a polyurethane-based finish that is not photochemically reactive (affected by sunlight). This information should be printed on the can.

Tile

▼ Tile conveys a look of elegance and status, even when the project is relatively inexpensive. It is a good choice for southwestern and French country kitchens. There are several fundamentals you should know before you choose this beautiful and durable flooring material. The more porous quarry tiles and Mexican terra cottas require waxing, and will stain. Glazed ceramic tiles are easy to maintain, but their high-gloss finish makes them treacherous when wet; reserve these for countertops and backsplashes, and keep them off the floor. Nonporous, matte-glazed tiles may be the best choice for flooring. They don't show dirt as easily as porous tiles, and they're less slippery when wet than glazed tiles.

▼ When you shop for tile, you'll see that it is graded for various uses. Be sure to select tile that is recommended for use as flooring; some tile is not sturdy enough to take the wear. Also consider the type of grouting you will use. Grout is available in many colors—you can opt to blend or contrast it with your tile. Remember also that grouting stains, and can be difficult to clean.

▼ Tile offers tremendous creative freedom. The floors on pages 54 and 56 actually were designed by the homeowners. With some imagination and guidance, you can create a truly unique and beautiful tile floor for your kitchen. Before you tile, consider the overall effect of the project. Remember that tile is difficult to tear up and replace. If you're choosing an off-beat pattern or color, be prepared to live with it.

A·L·W·A·Y·S R·O·O·M
F·O·R O·N·E M·O·R·E

*Strange to see how a good dinner
and feasting reconciles everybody.*
—Samuel Pepys

Dining à la Française

Beautiful and functional, this eat-in kitchen is a natural gathering place for good conversation.

▼ Unlike the American farm kitchen, with its checkerboard patterns and light wood cabinetry, this French country style kitchen has a special glow that comes from polished copper, tile and glass. Everything here seems to reflect the warmth of the cooking fire.

▼ The work area is set off by white tiles, complementing the maple countertops and the cabinets finished in rich dark wood tones.

▼ Although there's a standard gas stove in the work area, a Belgian cooking stove, with a heavy-duty vent, adds warmth and charm to the room. Copper cookware, hung all in a row from simple pot racks, provides color, reflected light and ambience.

▼ The massive table, left uncovered to show off the patina of the wood, seats eight comfortably. Ladderback rush-seat chairs feature scalloped details that look more European than the straight-edged Shaker variety. A Tiffany-style stained glass lampshade hangs low from a chain attached to the tin ceiling.

▼ The tile floor is decorated with a border and pattern squares assembled from smaller tiles in different shades of blue and green.

ELEMENTS OF DESIGN
COPPER COOKWARE

Copper is ideal for stovetop cooking because it conducts and distributes heat evenly. Serving pieces made of copper will keep foods warm at the table.

▼ Its rich color makes copper a lovely kitchen accessory. If you display copper cookware, polish it regularly for best effect.

▼ Commercial copper cleaners will clean copper adequately. Or you can try these natural cleaners: Mix together flour, salt, lemon juice, and ammonia. Or make a paste of flour and vinegar. Rub the paste on your copper cookware. Wash the cookware in sudsy water, rinse it, and buff with a clean, soft cloth.

COUNTRY WAYS
Tiffany Lamps

The brilliant colored glass lamps created by Louis Comfort Tiffany remain America's most outstanding contribution to the Art Nouveau movement of the late 19th century. We have come to use the term "Tiffany" to describe virtually any lamp with a shade made of leaded panels of colored glass. However, real Tiffany lamps are regarded as artwork, and are found most often in museums, private collections, and prestigious auction houses. Even in their time, Tiffany lamps were considered luxury items and were quite costly.

▼ Tiffany lamps are distinguished by Tiffany's patented method of glass making and coloration known as *favrile*, or "by hand." Unlike centuries-old stained glass, which was colored by applying a tint to the surface of clear glass, Tiffany's favrile glass had color "baked" into it. While the glass was hot, it was sprayed with metallic vapors. The type of vapor, the temperature of the furnace, and the length of time the glass was heated determined the color that was produced.

▼ In creating his lamps, Tiffany took advantage of the new phenomenon of electric lighting that was rapidly replacing gas and oil lighting in homes. Although there are some examples of early Tiffany oil lamps, the remarkable colors of Tiffany's glass are shown to best advantage by the whiteness of electric light.

Tumbleweed Connection

Classic southwestern country style makes this lovely kitchen/dining room work. The furnishings were found by chance, and brought together by design.

▼ Talk about found treasures! The tongue-and-groove cedar paneled ceiling and Mexican double doors were salvaged from demolished buildings. The ceiling light came from an old courthouse. The commercial stove was purchased at a restaurant supplier, but the range hood was found—believe it or not—in a junkyard.

▼ At 9 feet in length, the pine dining table is perfect for this king-size room. The homeowner found the table on a hunt through flea markets and junk shops. Stately pine chairs evoke rugged yet regal Mexican style.

▼ The extraordinary gumwood cabinets, bought at auction, are from a turn-of-the-century tobacconist's shop. Their marble countertops echo the smooth coolness of the tile floor and adobe walls.

▼ The custom tile floor, designed by the owner, was a major expense. The adobe walls were painted to match—creamy white with a touch of pink, and a terra cotta stripe border all around.

▼ What you *don't* see is just as important as what you do see: there are no curtains on the doors or windows, no wall decorations, the items on the cabinets are utilitarian. It is this lack of ornamentation that further enhances the airy, Southwestern sparsity of the room.

ELEMENTS OF DESIGN
Ceiling Fans

A ceiling fan is an economical and attractive way to improve the air circulation in any room.

▼ To function efficiently, a ceiling fan must be mounted correctly. Mount a cooling fan so the blades are 8 to 9 feet above the floor. For recycling warm air, mount the fan within 12 inches of the ceiling. Never mount a fan less than 8 inches from the ceiling. If mounted closer, the air becomes trapped between the blades and the ceiling, and will not circulate.

▼ Ceiling fans are sold by diameter. A 42-inch fan serves a 200-square-foot room, and a 52-inch fan will handle a 400-square-foot room.

▼ Fans typically have four blades. The more blades, the less efficient the fan. A two-blade model provides the most air movement.

*The more a man knows, and the
farther he travels, the more likely he
is to marry a country girl.*
—George Bernard Shaw

A *Touch of Glass*

The dilemma: you love the country richness of dark wood, but don't want a dark dining area. The solution: choose a glass-topped table instead of a wood one to open up and brighten the area.

▼ Fresh from the patio, this glass-topped metal table looks light and breezy in a kitchen dominated by wood. To highlight the look, set the table with place mats instead of a tablecloth. A wipe with glass cleaner after every meal keeps the table sparkling.

▼ The stylish wood and metal chairs were purchased through a catalog. A cushioned window seat provides seating on one side of the table. Overhead, a skylight and a hanging fern add to the al fresco atmosphere; the white walls make the room as light-bright as possible.

▼ In the high-traffic area between the barsink and the table, a pretty Oriental rug protects the polished oak floor and adds a spot of brightness. Other more utilitarian scatter rugs are placed in front of the working sink and cooktop areas, where the floor gets the most wear.

▼ An overhead bartender's glass rack holds everyday glasses and barware in the bar area. The backsplash features a hand-painted tile mural.

COUNTRY WAYS
Company's Coming

Life in an Ozark Mountain cabin could be quite isolated and lonely, so the arrival of visitors was a special event. Ozark folks had plenty of ways to tell if visitors were going to "drop" in. In fact, dropping something — depending on what you dropped and how it fell — was thought to be a sign of unexpected guests.

▼ Dropping a piece of cutlery meant that a guest was on the way — a fork indicated a man, and a knife meant a woman.

▼ Dropping a dishrag meant that someone dirty was approaching the cabin. If the rag fell in a wad on the floor, the visitor would be a woman. If the rag fell spread out on the floor, the vistor would be a man.

▼ If the towel used for drying dishes fell to the floor, a stranger would arrive very soon. If the towel fell twice, the stranger would be hungry and ask to be fed.

Windows on the World

This gorgeous dining room has the great advantage of its wonderful windows. You can keep the interior design very simple when the actual countryside is surrounding you.

▼ Privacy wasn't a problem in this kitchen and dining area located at the back of the house. The woods behind the house were lovely to look at, so they became the inspiration for this remodel. Every one of these windows opens to let in the fresh forest air.

▼ Along the back wall, built-in cabinets provide storage and more. Take note of their color: painted a neutral shade, they provide a backdrop for showing off the wood and wicker dining set, without calling attention to themselves. One cabinet conceals an air conditioner, and two more encase stereo speakers.

▼ The knotty pine trestle table is matched with pretty wicker armchairs for an outdoorsy effect. The place mats pick up the soft green of the cabinetry. A crock of geraniums was brought over from the window sill to decorate the table. Perhaps next time one of the potted plants, or even the birdhouse, will be the centerpiece.

C O U N T R Y   W A Y S
Wild West Coffee

Here's one Texas cowboy's special recipe for coffee: Take one pound of coffee; wet it good with water; boil it over a hot fire for thirty minutes; pitch a horse shoe in and, if it sinks, put in some more coffee.

V·A·R·I·A·T·I·O·N·S
O·N A T·H·E·M·E

*I drink to the general joy of the
whole table.*
—William Shakespeare

Pioneering the Future

At first glance, this kitchen with its combination cooktop island/dinner table seems the epitome of modern living. But the idea of an all-purpose main room goes back to our pioneer foreparents—and it still makes good sense today.

▼ The unique shape of the six-sided central island offers almost unlimited options for the cook. Special features include a cooktop with a griddle/broiler, two electrical outlets on the eating side of the island, a spice drawer, lots of roomy cabinets and seemingly endless counterspace.

▼ By placing the sink on an angle in the corner, this truly becomes a "kitchen in the round." Traffic flows in a circular pattern.

▼ The monochromatic almond-toned cabinetry places the focus on the dining area. The lovely oak half-table easily seats four. Roomy Windsor chairs are cozied-up with contrasting tie-on chair seats.

▼ A modern fixture lights the area effectively and unobtrusively so it does not detract from the eye-catching copper range hood and pot rack. Recessed lights provide ambient lighting for the room.

▼ The pretty tile backsplash features hand-painted tiles scattered throughout. A woven grass window shade, potted bulb plants, the crock of kitchen utensils, and a big pottery jug full of beautiful blooms all add touches of country charm to a highly functional room.

COUNTRY WAYS
Country Kitchen Collections

For an instant country atmosphere, display your collectibles in the kitchen. Almost anything can be considered a collectible—a truly great collection primarily should reflect your personal taste—but you may enjoy focusing on items that are particularly appropriate to the kitchen.

▼ The items below are highly suitable for kitchen collectibles. Let this list inspire you, then let your imagination run wild!
  ▼ Baskets, old and new
  ▼ Demitasse cups and saucers
  ▼ Novelty salt and pepper shakers
  ▼ Advertising memorabilia, especially Coca-Cola, Campbell's Soup, Mr. Peanut (Planter's) and Ivory Soap
  ▼ Collectible tin canisters
  ▼ Sugar and creamer sets
  ▼ Mugs
  ▼ Pitchers
  ▼ Teapots
  ▼ Old-fashioned glass and metal juicers
  ▼ Metal cookie cutters and cake molds
  ▼ Pottery and china, especially blue-and-white ware, ironstone, majolica, and hand-painted ceramics
  ▼ Barnyard animal motifs made of ceramic, wood, or metal
  ▼ Cookbooks from all eras
  ▼ Decorative bottles and colored glass

▼ Best of all, because they're not necessarily fine or fancy, kitchen collectibles are relatively inexpensive. General merchandise stores, card shops, garden centers, and even supermarkets and drug stores usually sell pretty baskets and collectible tins for reasonable prices (remember, no one has to know where you found those pretty things). Common kitchen items, such as juicers and cookie cutters, can be found at flea markets and tag sales.

▼ Display your collection in a hutch, on open pantry shelves or on countertops, hanging on the wall, or anyplace that pleases your fancy. Use the tops of cabinets to display collections of baskets and large ceramic pieces.

ELEMENTS OF DESIGN

The Windsor Chair

You've seen it countless times — the graceful arched bowback chair with vertical spindles and a roomy, contoured saddle seat. It's the quintessential country chair for a country kitchen.

▼ A 17th century English design, the Windsor chair takes its name from the English town where King George I popularized the style. The chairs were simple yet attractive, easy and inexpensive to produce. The Windsor chair first was made in this country in Philadelphia around 1725. Over the next 100 years, it evolved into a uniquely American fashion.

▼ There are many variations of the American Windsor chair — furniture historians have numbered 45 different types. However, the basic characteristics of the Windsor chair are universal: a bowed, sack or hoop back, a carved saddle seat, and simply turned legs set at a slant or splay. The curved back is formed by using green wood, or by bending wood with steam, and is held in place with slender spindles starting from the rear of the seat. In the earliest American Windsor chairs, different woods were used for different parts of the chair, and the whole chair was painted — usually dark green or black.

▼ The Windsor chair's place in American history is firmly set. It is used in historic restorations throughout the country, such as Independence Hall in Philadelphia and Mount Vernon, George Washington's Virginia home. Today, Windsor chairs are available in any number of variations and price ranges — from a $60 armless maple chair to an 18th century chair worth several thousand dollars. With such a glorious history, and a reputation that never goes out of style, the Windsor is the ideal choice for a country kitchen.

The Safe Country Kitchen

Most home accidents occur in the kitchen. While safety is primarily a matter of good judgment and common sense, there are design features you can build into your kitchen to make it a safer environment.

Burns

▼ Burns are the most common kitchen accident. In a typical scenario, a pot slips out of your hand as you remove it from the cooktop. To minimize such accidents, provide a quick set-down spot for hot pans next to the cooking surface. This counter space should be at least 15 inches wide. For maximum safety, allow 15 inches on each side of the cooktop.

▼ Protruding pot handles are another common cause of burn accidents. Children are especially prone to bump into them. To reduce the chance of such collisions, routinely swivel pot handles out of the way of kitchen traffic. A 15-inch set-down space next to the cooktop will allow for such positioning.

▼ If you are remodeling to include an island or peninsula that will double as an eating area, it's better to locate the sink there, rather than the cooktop.

▼ Built-in ovens are both practical and attractive, but in many kitchens they are not positioned close enough to counters. It's just as important to provide a set-down spot for roasting pans coming out of the oven as it is for pots on the cooktop.

Fire

▼ The chance of a stove-top fire is remote. Nevertheless, mount a chemical-compound fire extinguisher near the cooking area for safety, because burning grease or fats cannot be extinguished with water. Or keep a large container of baking soda next to the cooktop; baking soda will smother grease fires.

ELEMENTS OF DESIGN

Chemicals

▼ Household chemicals are another potential danger. Too often they are stored under the sink in a cabinet that's accessible to children. Common sense dictates that rodent poisons, cleaning solutions and caustic substances should be kept out of children's reach.

Collisions

▼ Counters and floors should be planned with safety in mind. Avoid having sharp corners on countertops and islands, which tend to be at eye level for young children. Pick a flooring material that provides good traction when wet; wet shoes and an armful of groceries are a recipe for a fall if your kitchen floor surface is slick.

Wonderful Wicker

Wicker is not a material but a process. It is the art of weaving with reed, willow, or sea grasses. High-quality wicker always is woven of reed—thin poles of rattan split off from the solid section of the rattan vine.

▼ Rattan grows primarily in the Southeast Pacific. It looks like bamboo, but has a solid core that makes it strong enough to be used for furniture frames. The skin of rattan can be left on, showing its characteristic "marbleized" coloring and growing nodes. If the poles are peeled and sanded, the surfaces become pale and porous, good for staining and painting.

▼ The reed used for weaving wicker is porous, and will absorb stain readily and evenly, because it is composed entirely of material from the core of the plant. In addition to being woven to produce the wicker parts of furniture, reed can be wrapped around a rattan frame for decorative purposes.

▼ Cane is the skin of the rattan plant. Therefore, it is nonporous, and does not take stain or paint. It is peeled off the rattan plant, and used for wrapping and winding over hardwood or rattan frames. It also is woven into seats, and is used for surface texture in wicker designs.

Caring for Wicker

Wicker furniture is not necessarily delicate. If it is properly constructed of quality materials, and not subjected to abuse, wicker can last indefinitely. These tips will help you care for your wicker furniture.

▼ If the wicker is woven of natural material, it will dry out over a period of time in all but the most humid tropical climates. If a piece of wicker furniture appears to be brittle, hosing it down lightly should be enough to restore moisture and elasticity.

▼ To clean natural wicker, painted or not, gently rub it with a cloth using plain water or a mild detergent solution. Follow with a light hosing. Natural wicker usually is stained, or coated with clear varnish or lacquer. If the finish becomes dull, a light application of mineral oil should restore the sheen.

▼ To remove paint from wicker, it is best to consult a furniture stripping professional because stripping chemicals can damage the wicker severely. Reed, willow and rattan pieces can be dipped or hand-stripped by a pro. After the paint is removed, the piece should be washed, allowed to dry, and stained, painted or varnished to your liking. Oil-based glossy enamel is best for painting wicker; water-based latex paints will crack when used on wicker. Spray painting may coat wicker more effectively than brush painting.

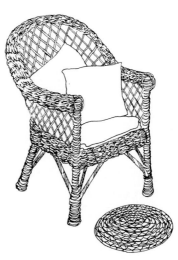

A Room with a View

For summertime dining, nothing compares with a screened porch. This Adirondack haven provides a beautiful eating area plus a comfy place to sit back and enjoy a glass of iced coffee on a summer's evening.

▼ There was no need for a major remodel of this space. The unfinished wooden peaked porch roof and supports create the perfect framework for an al fresco dining room. The look is rustic, yet cozy.

▼ An assortment of old wicker furniture is given a new lease on life with dark green and bright red paint. The seat cushions are covered with a cheery red, yellow and white print. The furniture stands out in colorful relief against the painted plank flooring.

▼ Blooming potted plants are the main decoration in this sylvan setting. With a stage as beautiful as this, there's no need for clutter. The table is spread with madras plaid napkins on a red print cloth. Multi-colored ceramic tableware and a pretty potted geranium completes the tablescape.

To rise at six, to dine at ten,
To sup at six, to sleep at ten,
Makes a man live for ten times ten.
—Victor Hugo

DO·IT·YOURSELF·DECOR

F·L·O·W·E·R·S F·O·R T·H·E T·A·B·L·E

Flowers are lovely; love is
flower-like;
Friendship is a sheltering tree.
— Samuel Taylor Coleridge

Picking Posies

▼ Cut flowers late in the evening. Bring along a clean, warm water-filled bucket, and put the flowers in the water immediately after cutting. Leave them in the water outside overnight; the stems will stiffen, and the flowers will turn up. When you take the flowers indoors, recut the stems before arranging them.

▼ For longer lasting bouquets, cut flowers just before they are in full bloom.

▼ Always cut flower stems on the diagonal; straight-cut stems do not take in water as well. Add an extra crosscut on iris, anemone, tulip, lantana, stock, clarkia, salvia, nasturtium, artemisia, astilbe, mums, globe thistle, peony, phlox and gladiolus.

A CENTERPIECE FOR EACH MEAL
Feeling creative? Try a different type of country centerpiece for breakfast, lunch and dinner.

Breakfast
- ▼ A wire egg basket filled with eggs
- ▼ Daisies bunched in a ceramic milk pitcher
- ▼ A cobalt glass bowl filled with oranges, lemons and limes
- ▼ Simple stuffed toys made from country calicos
- ▼ A flat clay flowerpot, lined with a cloth napkin and filled with freshly baked muffins

Lunch
- ▼ Pots of herbs arranged at the center of the table
- ▼ African violets grouped together in a decorative shallow bowl or basket
- ▼ A white ceramic bowl filled with artichokes
- ▼ Homemade cookies; use cookie cutters as napkin rings
- ▼ Lilacs bunched in an old glass milk bottle
- ▼ A "natural vase" made from a melon and filled with flowers *(directions, pages 74-75)*

Dinner
- ▼ A wooden duck decoy placed on a bed of cattails or wild grain stalks
- ▼ Single candlesticks with candles in different shades of the same color
- ▼ Sea shells and coral grouped in a basket or wooden bowl
- ▼ Freshly cut roses laid in a clean garden basket
- ▼ Ivy twined around the center of the table; use more ivy for napkin rings

MAKING ARRANGEMENTS
Beautiful bouquets are not nearly as difficult to make as you may think. Just follow this guide to flawless flower arranging.

▼ Almost anything can double as a flower holder, even if it doesn't hold water. Just line the vase-to-be with something waterproof, such as a plastic food container or glass bowl.

▼ Be creative when you pick flowers; don't be afraid to try unusual combinations. Go into the garden with a color scheme in mind, and mix different varieties of flowers into the scheme. Mix branches of tiny vegetables, such as baby tomatoes or peppers, into the bouquet to add texture and interest. Think of flowers as neutral — they don't have to match your room decor — and choose whichever colors you like.

▼ The best bouquets are formed right in your own hand. Start with a core of long-stemmed flowers, and add flowers around the core, one or two at a time. Turn the bunch as you go, so the shape and fullness are even all around.

▼ If you're arranging flowers in a vase, begin with an outline, using spiky flowers such as delphinium or larkspur to define the arrangement's height and width. Place heavier or clustered flowers, such as snapdragons or dianthus, closer to the bottom of the arrangement.

▼ Large or heavy flowers, such as gerbera daisies, zinnias, mums or clusters of phlox, create a heavy, dense arrangement. To lighten it, add airy stems of Queen Anne's lace, baby's breath, feverfew, asparagus fern, or maidenhair fern. Or use small-flowered marigolds — they're pretty and long-lasting.

▼ Don't forget to include foliage. Branches, twigs, and grapevine stems and leaves help to make an arrangement look full.

▼ Arrange flowers loosely enough so that you can see their individual shapes.

▼ Keep flower arrangements away from direct sunlight and drafts.

FLOWER POWER
The following are ways to help your cut posies
stay fresh looking and lovely.

▼ Strip off foliage that will be below the water level in the container. If the bouquet includes roses, be sure to remove the thorns as well.

▼ Use distilled water to hold and arrange flowers; fluoridated water can cause the petal tips of some flowers to turn brown.

▼ Although fresh water is fine to use, and many florists swear by it, some floral arrangers like to doctor water to stretch the life of their flowers. To do this, mix one part lemon-lime soda with two parts water. Add two drops of nonchlorine bleach to delay bacteria buildup.

▼ Change the water every day.

▼ Humidify flowers every day with the lightest spray from a plant mister; dry air can shorten floral staying power.

▼ To postpone petal fall-off, which is a big problem with poppies, tulips and crocuses, use an eyedropper to place a couple of drops of melted wax carefully inside each flower right at the base of the petals.

▼ When flower heads begin to droop, cut the stems again under water, and immerse the entire bouquet in a sink full of barely warm, not hot, water for a few hours. Soak roses for only one hour, as they are very fragile.

▼ These flowers, cut and placed in water, have the greatest staying power: black-eyed Susan, gaillardia, gladiolus, bachelor's button, clarkia, coreopsis, stock (the double-flowered variety), delphinium, rose, dianthus, chrysanthemum (especially Shasta daisy), marigold, daylily (each flower lasts a day, but the stems have many blossoms that open in succession), yarrow, phlox, calendula, snapdragon, peony and sweet pea.

▼ Certain flowers exude harmful juices after being cut that hinder a bouquet's health. Daffodil sap, for instance, keeps other buds from blooming. To de-sap daffodils, keep them in water for 24 hours before joining them with other flowers; don't recut the stems. Campanula, balloon flowers, lantana and heliotrope have a milky sap that hurts other posies, clouds the water, and may cause allergic reactions in some people. Desap these flowers by placing their stems in hot water overnight.

Country Kitchen Centerpieces

Fill one of the following kitchen items with beautiful blossoms to create a terrific table arrangement.

▼ Arrange grape hyacinth and *Buddleia* in a pretty ceramic teapot.

▼ Lay a hurricane lamp chimney flat on its side. Place a block of floral foam or sphagnum moss in the center, and arrange ferns and flowers inside.

▼ Use a copper colander or ring mold to hold fresh fruit and flowers. Line the colander with a bowl to hold moistened floral foam.

▼ Decorative bottles and jars from gourmet herbs and vinegars are perfect for holding just a few blossoms. Mix in some pussy willows in the spring, colored leaves in the fall, and holly in winter.

▼ Dry artichokes to use as perennial table decorations. Spread open the petals, and stuff them gently with newspaper so they stay open. Submerge the artichokes in sand or corn meal so they will keep their shape as they dry, and place them in a warm spot. To speed the drying process, keep the artichokes in the oven when it's not in use. The artichokes will dry in 1 to 2 weeks.

▼ Use an old wooden cigar box in a centerpiece to give your table an old-fashioned dry goods store feeling. Fill the box with lady apples, kumquats, dried flowers, or penny candy if you can trust yourself!

▼ An empty bear-shaped dispenser makes a centerpiece base that gives everyone a smile. Fill it with a nosegay of flowers, or sprigs of baby's breath.

FOREVER FLOWERS
Drying flowers needn't take up a lot of space. Some flowers can be arranged, freshly cut, in a container and displayed while they're drying.

▼ Place the freshly cut flowers in water in the display container, and let them absorb water for 2 days. Then empty the water from the container, wipe the stems and container dry, and rearrange the flowers in the container to air dry. Keep the flowers out of sunlight while they're drying.

▼ You can use this drying method with the following flowers:

Baby's Breath: Strip off the leaves

Statice: Don't handle it too much after it has dried; it tends to become brittle

Chinese Lantern (Physalis): Cut the stems when the lower seed pods are reddish in color

Money Plant (Lunaria): Remove the outer seed husks to reveal the attractive seed pods

Strawflowers: Their stems won't stand straight when dried; before drying, cut each stem to an ⅛-inch length, and insert a length of floral wire through the stem midway into the flower head

Yarrow: Strip off the leaves

Tansy

Queen Anne's Lace

Cattails

Eucalyptus

M·I·X & M·A·T·C·H
C·E·N·T·E·R·P·I·E·C·E·S

Choose an element from each column to create a one-of-a-kind centerpiece for your table. Place the focal point in or on the base. Then place the finishing touches within or around the focal point.

BASE (choose one)	FOCAL POINT (choose one)	FINISHING TOUCH (choose one or two)
Basket	Chunky candle	Nuts
Porcelain platter	Several candles of different heights	Red, green or golden apples
Crocheted doily	Fresh pineapple	Pomegranates
Decorated tray	Large bunch of perfect grapes	Small antique toys
Wooden bowl	Short floral bouquet	Ivy vines
Cutting board	Stemmed cake plate filled with cookies	Bunches of herbs
Low-lying wreath	Cut glass bowl with floating candles	Satin and lace ribbons
Quilted square	Wooden primitive or weathervane figure	Colored glass marbles

VASES FROM NATURE
Melons, squash, pumpkins, pineapples, and other shapely seasonal fruits and vegetables can be fashioned into whimsical vases with a few strokes of the knife.

Although you usually don't squeeze a vase before buying it, in this case you would be wise to do so. Choose a firm fruit or vegetable for your vase. Using a knife or an apple corer, cut a small slice off the top of your selection, and scoop out the seeds and pulp. Insert a slender container filled with water to hold the flowers, making sure its top is out of sight. Any type of jar will do, as well as a floral vial or throw-away vase. Then have fun creating a still life, fresh from your grocery bag.

ELEMENTS OF DESIGN
The Finishing Touch
The centerpiece should add the final, crowning touch to your table. The following will help you achieve perfect results every time.

▼ The centerpiece should complement the meal, not distract from it. Good food inspires good conversation, but only if your guests can see each other. Be sure the centerpiece is low enough for guests to see across the table.

▼ If you use a tall centerpiece, make it very tall. Place the bulkiest part of the arrangement above eye level on a pedestal. This treatment works best on very large tables.

▼ The centerpiece doesn't have to be in the center of the table. Try placing it at one end of an oval or rectangular table if no one will be seated there.

▼ The centerpiece doesn't have to be one unit. A few potted herbs grouped together or placed in a circle makes a lovely table arrangement.

▼ Use your imagination. The centerpiece doesn't always have to be flowers. Silver dollar or eucalyptus branches, dried thistles, pussy willows, or bare branches spray painted or left natural, all make lovely centerpieces.

▼ Instead of a single centerpiece, place a small bouquet at each place setting.

▼ Choose the tablecloth or place mats and napkins you want to use, and put the cloth on the table before arranging the centerpiece.

STAND-UP WATERMELON CENTERPIECE

Directions:
Cut a sliver from one end of a watermelon so the melon stands upright. Cut about 3 inches from the other end for the top opening. Draw a double zigzag line around the top, and 2 double scalloped rows below the bottom zigzag. Using a paring knife, cut out only the green part of the rind from between the lines, leaving scallops of green rind alternating with the cut out white sections. Using a melon baller, scoop out melon balls, leaving a 1½-inch-thick shell. Fill the shell with cut fruit and the melon balls.

WATERMELON BASKET

Directions:
Remove a sliver from one long side of a watermelon so the melon sits steady. Draw a 3- to 4-inch-wide basket handle across the center top of the melon. Draw a scalloped top edge for the basket. Cut along the lines. Remove the two large pieces to form the handle and top edge of the basket. Using a melon baller, scoop out melon balls, leaving the part under the handle intact. Draw decorative shapes along the handle. Cut out the shapes, removing only ⅛ inch of the rind. Scoop out melon balls from under the handle. Fill the basket with cut fruit and the melon balls.

STAR-SPANGLED WATERMELON

Directions:
Cut a sliver from one long side of a watermelon so the melon sits steady. Draw an oval opening on top. Draw star shapes on the watermelon. Using a small paring knife, cut out each star, removing ⅛ inch of the rind. Cut out the oval "lid" at a 45° angle. Using a melon baller, scoop out melon balls, leaving a 1½-inch-thick shell. Fill the melon with cut fruit and the melon balls.

Thou wast that all to me, love,
For which my soul did pine—
A green isle in the sea, love,
A fountain and a shrine,
All wreathed with fairy fruits
and flowers.
And all the flowers were mine.
—Edgar Allan Poe

A COUNTRY CENTERPIECE
The important thing to remember about making this centerpiece is that it will be viewed from all sides.

Materials: Mushroom basket; aluminum foil; floral foam; waterproof floral tape; floral preservative; 1 bunch of Baker or leatherleaf fern; variety of flower buds and blossoms: Statesmen button mums, daisies and small roses.

Directions:

1. If you are cutting flowers fresh from the garden, fill a bucket with warm water, and add 1 teaspoon of floral preservative for each quart of water. As you cut the flowers, place them in the bucket. Recut the stems at an angle under more warm water with floral preservative added. Place the flowers back in the bucket, and let them soak in the preservative solution for 12 hours, or as long as possible.

2. Cut a piece of floral foam large enough to fill the basket and extend above the basket rim. Soak the floral foam in the preservative solution for about 12 hours.

3. Line the basket with the aluminum foil. Secure the wet floral foam to the lined basket with the floral tape.

4. Cut each fern branch into two or three pieces; the top piece forms a point, and the lower, blunt-tip pieces form "angel wings."

5. Insert the fern points, angled downward, into the floral foam to cover the sides of the foam. Insert one or two long fern points, angled downward, at each side to define the length of the arrangement. Insert the "angel wing" fern pieces around the top of the foam.

6. Place some of the button mums at each side of the basket, making sure they extend out as far as the ferns. Push the mum stems up into the floral foam so the flowers droop down among the ferns.

7. Place one button mum on each side of the center top; this finishes the outline of a triangle shape for the arrangement. To keep the centerpiece from getting too tall, and preventing people from seeing each other across the table, put your elbow on the table, hold your lower arm straight up, and turn your palm parallel to the tabletop. Don't place top flowers any higher than your palm.

8. Fill in a skirt of smaller button mums around the sides of the arrangement. Sprinkle a few of the remaining mums among the ferns, placing the larger mums toward the center of the arrangement for weight, and using the smaller mums to define the outline. To avoid creating a formal look, distribute the mums unevenly.

9. Trim off most of the leaves from the daisies. Fill in spaces in the arrangement with the daisies; keep the original triangle shape in mind, but make it rounded by sloping from the top down the sides, and to the ends. To get a graceful curve at the edges and sides of the floral foam, insert the flower stems so the flower heads curve down. For a natural look, don't face all the flower heads outward. Turn some flowers at an angle, so only half of each face shows.

10. Place the small roses in various spots around the arrangement for surprise and color.

11. Check for and fill in any extra-large gaps, but don't fill in every space; let individual flowers be seen.

12. To create an airier arrangement, cut a few of the mum and daisy multiple flower stems into smaller groupings or singles.

ALL GOOD GIFTS
A deliciously lovely centerpiece.

▼ Stuff a large, handled basket with crumpled newspaper or folded towels. Cover the stuffing with a solid color cloth napkin.

▼ Place cookies and small fruits in small baskets; cherries, grapes and berries are good choices. Place the small baskets in the large, stuffed basket.

▼ Adjust the stuffing so the small baskets sit at varying heights in an attractive arrangement. Fill in around the small baskets with large fruits and flowers. Pack the large basket very full so that removing one piece of fruit will not leave a large hole in the arrangement.

ALTERNATE ARRANGEMENTS
Make the centerpiece a part of the meal.

▼ Place several loaves of bread on a cutting board, with pretty butter dishes on opposite corners. Add a few sprigs of greenery in a bud vase.

▼ Fill a basket with fruit to accompany cookies, cake, pie or cheese at the end of the meal.

▼ Set the coffee pot on a doily on a tray, and surround the pot with cups and saucers, a creamer, sugar bowl, small bottles of liqueurs, and small dishes of spices to flavor the coffee.

▼ Set out dessert plates with a single blossom on the top plate.

KITCHEN
C·L·O·S·E-U·P·S

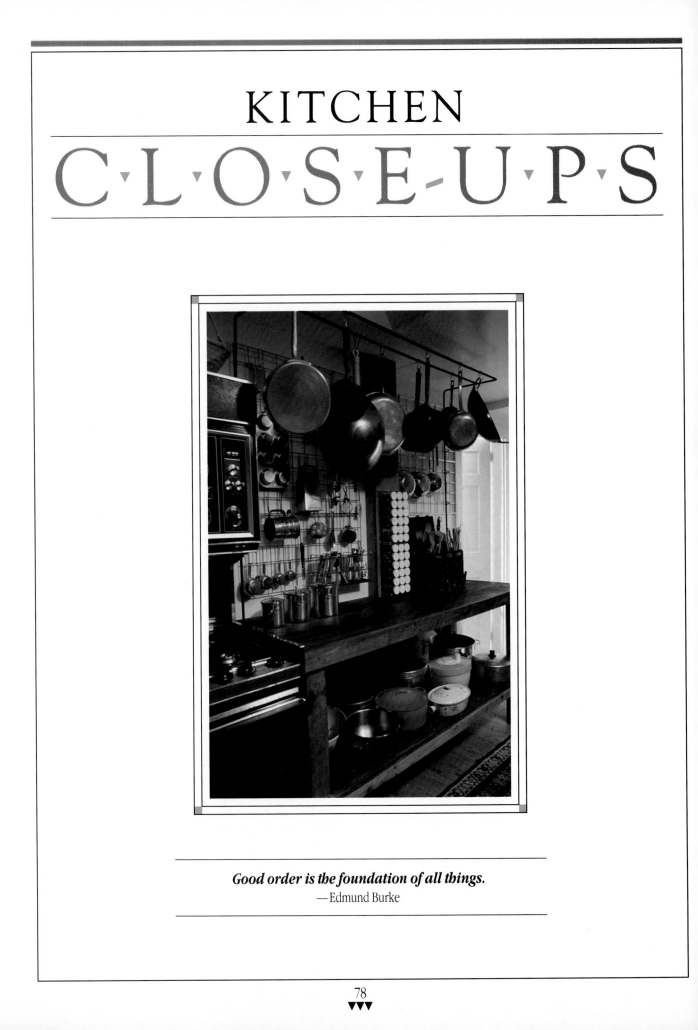

Good order is the foundation of all things.
— Edmund Burke

This chapter takes an in-depth look at the fine points of kitchen design—the details that really make a kitchen work for you.

We concentrate on five kitchen areas: the sink, pantry, kitchen corners, and under and above the counter. You'll learn how to maximize efficiency without sacrificing country charm.

▼ Change under-the-counter cabinets from a pot-and-pan purgatory to a paradise of organization.

▼ Use wall space and over-the-counter clearance to liberate your counters from appliance overload.

▼ Explore ingenious cabinet designs that capitalize on corner space.

▼ Tuck shelves in out-of-the-ordinary spaces to create an instant pantry.

▼ Turn an ordinary sink into a vision of beauty.

The key to a country kitchen is combining good sense and beauty—we show you how.

U·N·D·E·R
T·H·E C·O·U·N·T·E·R

Wherefore are these things hid?
—William Shakespeare

Under Agenda

The time-conscious cook wants to have the necessities right at hand when creating culinary masterpieces. Storing spices in a shallow drawer next to the cooktop with often-used pots, pans and bowls in the cupboard under the drawer is a country-clever use of space.

▼ There's no law that says you must keep your spices on a wall-hung rack. A "spice drawer" is an excellent alternative. This drawer has been fitted with angled inserts to keep the jars in order and easy to grab.

▼ The cabinet directly below the spice drawer has been made more efficient with the addition of two pull-out shelves to hold cookware and mixing bowls. This handy system maximizes the storage space.

▼ The bleached oak cabinetry features shiny brass hardware. The gray-black laminated countertop gives the impression of slate, with wipe-clean convenience.

COUNTRY WAYS
Country Catch-Alls

▼ For ease in cooking, keep your wooden spoons, wire whisks, and so on, in a decorative container next to the food preparation area. Pitchers and crocks are naturals for this purpose.

▼ For a different type of catch-all, use a clay flowerpot with a saucer underneath. As you wash and rinse utensils, just place them directly back into the flowerpot — the water will drain into the saucer below.

▼ Hanging baskets made of wire or natural materials are great for holding kitchen necessities. Hang one near the stove or sink.

COUNTRY WAYS
Put Time On Your Side

The country home is beautiful, but also is very practical. The wise homemaker knows that the demands of raising a family and keeping house leaves no time to waste. Clever arrangement of your cooking space and careful meal planning can create a kitchen that runs like clockwork.

▼ The rule of thumb for setting up your kitchen is the more often a utensil or appliance is used, the closer it should be kept to the preparation area. If a utensil or appliance is used infrequently, such as a waffle iron, store it in a back cupboard or pantry.

▼ Arrange food staples on your cupboard shelves according to cooking use: baking supplies, pastas, cereals, etc. If you use an item very often, such as salt or pepper, keeping it on the counter may be best. Remember, country kitchens frequently keep the everyday in plain sight. Keeping food staples on open pantry shelves near the preparation area creates a country look while maximizing the efficiency of a kitchen.

▼ Sunday evening, sit down and plan an entire week's worth of meals. Make a list of specialty foods you need to buy, and staple items you are low on.

▼ Shop in bulk; it saves time and money. Keep a notepad and pencil next to your pantry, and jot down an item before you run out of it. When you go to the store, keep an eye out for specials and stock up. Buy extras of non-cooking products that get used up quickly, such as toilet paper and paper towels, especially when they're on sale.

▼ Set aside one drawer for basic non-cooking supplies such as tape, pencils, notepaper, scissors, string, and a flashlight. Make a household rule that anything taken out of the "basics" drawer gets put back in!

The English never abolish anything. They put it in cold storage.
—Alfred North Whitehead

ELEMENTS OF DESIGN

Small Kitchen Smarts

Use your ingenuity when you're organizing a small kitchen. Clever use of space can save you a lot of headaches.

▼ Design areas to serve more than one function. For example, an island work area can double as a breakfast bar and provide storage underneath.

▼ Built-ins generally take up less space than freestanding pieces; banquettes and a small table tucked into a corner are far more space efficient than a table and separate chairs.

▼ Install banked floor-to-ceiling cabinets instead of the shorter standard units.

▼ Neatly organized objects take up less space than jumbled ones. Subdivide cabinet storage, with shelves, drawer dividers, and wire racks used as needed to maintain easy accessibility and good organization.

▼ If your ceiling is high enough, use a ceiling-hung pot rack, or a series of hooks screwed into the joists, to augment cabinet storage.

▼ Use empty wall spaces by hanging shallow, between-the-studs shelves to hold spice jars or single rows of glasses.

▼ "Frame" a window or door with shelves above and around it for added storage.

▼ Consider installing appliances that "disappear" when not in use, such as a pull-out range hood, a food processor on a lift-up shelf, or a built-in toaster.

▼ To preserve counter space, buy downsized small appliances if they meet your needs. Units that mount under upper cabinets also free counter space.

▼ If it meets your functional needs, consider installing an all-in-one appliance, which combines a stove, dishwasher, and refrigerator in a single compact unit.

▼ A 30- or 31-inch-deep American-style refrigerator eats up precious space, and projects awkwardly from standard-size cabinets. If you don't need all that fresh food storage, consider getting a flush-mount, under-the-counter model or, for more capacity, an 84-inch-tall, 24-inch-deep unit.

▼ A small kitchen is not a place for a pack rat. If possible, store infrequently used specialty items, such as a lobster pot, fondue set, or meat grinder in other parts of the home. Get rid of gadgets you never use.

Book Nook

If you're the kind of person who likes everything where you can see it, install open shelving under your counters instead of the standard cabinets with doors.

▼ These shelves are the perfect place for a cookbook collection. The books are close at hand for the cook's convenience, but do not take up valuable space on the countertops or walls.

▼ Other items to store under the counter on open shelves include condiments, spices, a collection of teas, and canisters of flour, sugar, and so on.

▼ The shelves shown above actually are part of an island with a cooktop and food preparation area on top. The island is tiled from top to bottom with beautiful French hand-painted tiles in farmyard motifs. Larger tiles run up the side and cover the work space. Smaller coordinating tiles frame the shelf area.

Straight and Narrow

Your kitchen drawers can perform a variety of functions. The drawers above provide storage for food wraps, utensils and kitchen linens.

▼ The flatware drawer has been fitted with a number of partitions to keep everything strictly in order. The shallow drawer below keeps aluminum foil, plastic wrap and plastic bags right at hand.

▼ Behind a cabinet door, a battery of white drawers holds kitchen towels, potholders and linens.

▼ The drawers and cabinets have beautiful mahogany fronts. A smooth granite countertop provides a wipeable work surface.

O·V·E·R
T·H·E C·O·U·N·T·E·R

*It is only in the country that we can
get to know a person or a book.*
— Cyril Connolly

Shingle Style

Create a marvelously textured wall treatment by attaching Shaker-style roof shingles to the wall.

▼ Placed above the cooktop, the shingles serve as a great backing for a lightweight wall grid. Cup hooks inserted directly into the wood hold a bamboo steamer and potholders.

▼ Everyday kitchen utensils are hung from the grid. This arrangement keeps ladles, measuring cups and spoons close at hand for the cook, and adds visual interest to the wall. Even food processor blades can be both convenient and eye-catching when hung in a row. Other necessary utensils are stored in a revolving countertop rack.

▼ A clever cookbook rack is anchored in the wall below the shingles. The cookbook is at the cook's eye level, but up above messy splatters.

A Place For Everything
(photo, page 78)

Be imaginative in your use of space; don't just think in terms of shelves and cabinets for storage. The wall shown on page 78 is a perfect example of how cookware arranged in the open can be both a practical and attractive storage solution.

▼ The metal grid wall unit is a catch-all for the smaller cooking items. For convenience sake, items such as the measuring cups are hung in size order. Cookware that is used less frequently, such as the sifter and the cupcake pan, are hung at a higher level. A space-saving rack stores spices at-the-ready on their side.

▼ Large handled pans and a wok are suspended from an overhead pot rack. Unlike most racks, which are ceiling hung, this one is anchored to the counter below and steadied with a ceiling hook.

▼ Here the traditional cabinet and countertop work area is replaced with a heavy-duty butcherblock table, complete with an indentation for knives. Under the work surface, there's plenty of room for covered pots and casserole dishes.

▼ A copper canister set adds a decorative touch. It has the same ready-to-work feeling as the copper cookware above it, but also lends charm to the area.

User Friendly

Every cook knows the frustration of spilling or spattering on their favorite cookbook. Or trying to prepare a recipe and having to run from counter to cooktop to follow the directions. The solution? Suspend the cookbook in a convenient location.

▼ This rack is mounted under the cabinets, above the preparation area. A special feature of this rack — it can be folded up and out of sight when not in use.

COUNTRY WAYS
Raised Eyebrows

In times gone by, facial features were thought to reveal not only people's personality traits, but even to predict the future. Yet sometimes the many interpretations of specific facial characteristics would contradict each other. For example, some folks believed that a woman whose eyebrows met at the center would marry someone close to home. Other folks swore by this rule: If your eyebrows meet across your nose, you'll never wear your wedding clothes.

COUNTRY WAYS

COUNTRY WAYS
Everyday Superstitions

Here are the roots of some of the best known, least understood superstitions.

▼ *Crossing your fingers:* Two intersecting lines always have been a sign of protection. When two fingers of the same hand cross, they are thought to bring good luck and make wishes come true.

▼ *Knocking on wood:* Ancient civilizations believed trees were the homes of gods. To pay homage to these deities, common folk made a habit of tapping on trees. Today, knocking on wood guards us against being overly optimistic.

▼ *"Gesundheit" or "God bless you":* It was believed at one time that one's soul resided in the head, and could be expelled by a sneeze. Reciting either of these phrases became a safeguard against the devil.

▼ *Tossing salt over your shoulder:* Salt, which once was scarce, was considered a symbol of life. When some was spilled, a pinch of it was cast over the left shoulder to blind the evil spirits lurking there (all *good* spirits resided on the *right* side). Now we believe spilling salt is bad luck, and so we do the same.

▼ *Broken mirrors:* The reflection seen in glass was thought to be another "self" or soul. Any damage done to that image would harm the original, and life would renew itself only after seven years. That's why we believe we're struck with bad luck for a 7-year period whenever we crack a mirror.

▼ *Black cat crossing your path:* In Norse legend, black cats drew a chariot bearing the goddess Frigga. After serving the goddess for seven years, the cats became witches. Now we change our course when a black cat (possibly a witch in disguise) crosses in front of us.

▼ *Friday the 13th/Unlucky 13:* The "devil's dozen" were 13 witches who met with the devil on Fridays. Now some people still stay home on Friday the 13th, and some building contractors still don't include a 13th floor.

Suspended Animation

This countertop area is a study in how to blend modern technology with country touches.

▼ Make a wall do double duty by installing a shelf above the countertop.

▼ By selecting all white appliances, the look is still clean and uncluttered even though space is limited. The combination toaster oven/microwave is a two-in-one space saver. The cordless, under-the-cabinet can opener has just enough clearance below it. A wall-hung aluminum foil and plastic wrap dispenser frees up drawer space, and the hanging dish drainer functions as a shelf for everyday dishes. The swing-out towel rack opens up when you need it, and folds flat when you don't.

▼ For a country touch, pretty painted pottery is displayed on the shelf and a colorful kitchen print is hung on the wall above the shelf. The wall itself is covered in a pastel vertical stripe to add visual height.

ELEMENTS OF DESIGN
The Great White Way

You might say that kitchen appliances have gone back to their roots in recent years. At one time, white was the only choice for everything from refrigerators to stand mixers. Later generations craved color — choosing from harvest gold, avocado, and copper brown for kitchen appliances. Today, white is back and more in demand than ever. You'll see some enthusiasm for bold contemporary colors, such as red, black, royal blue, and even forest green, but white is the most popular color for today's kitchen appliances.

▼ White appliances look clean and orderly. Best of all, because white blends with just about any color, it offers tremendous freedom in kitchen decor, and allows the homeowner to redecorate the kitchen without replacing appliances.

If white leaves you cold, look for appliances in almond, a warm beige tone that works as a neutral in any decor.

G·O·T
Y·O·U C·O·R·N·E·R·E·D

Houses are built to live in,
not to look on.
—Francis Bacon

Corner Wise

So often the corners of a kitchen are left as wasted space. Here, a corner is designed to provide valuable storage space and to double as a work space.

▼ This corner cupboard conceals an arsenal of kitchen appliances. The left-hand door slides into the wall, and the other door swings open to the side to provide easy access to the appliances.

▼ Below the counter, the corner cabinet door is hinged to fold open. Corner cabinets should be designed to work in harmony with the rest of the cabinetry; opening a corner cabinet should not prevent you from opening the cabinet or drawer adjacent to it.

▼ By extending the extra-large tile into the counter level area inside the corner cupboard, this becomes usable work space.

▼ The maple cabinet doors were bleached to achieve their distinctive pale yellow cast *(see Bleaching and Whitewashing, page 26)*. The upper tier cabinets in the rest of the kitchen were fitted with glass panels.

COUNTRY WAYS
The Corner Cupboard

A staple of country decor, the corner cupboard developed out of necessity. Before the era of built-in cabinets, a cupboard was an absolute must to provide storage for nonperishable foods and cookware.

▼ These storage pieces first appeared in America in the 1600's. Originally called a "cup board," the name referred to the construction of the piece: Several board shelves, left open, that were used to hold cups, plates and other dishes. Eventually, the shelves were framed with side pieces and doors were added.

▼ The standard cupboard consists of two separate sections. The top section contains three or four shelves that can either be left open or enclosed by doors. The bottom section often contains drawers or cabinets. Although the two pieces are built to be taken apart (for ease in moving), they were always built together to insure a stylistic match.

▼ Although they usually are freestanding pieces, some cupboards are built-in.

▼ The "corner" cupboard came into vogue during the 1700's. The wedge-shaped back allowed this piece to easily fit into the corner of a room. The "parlor," used for entertaining and receiving of company, was the room in which these cupboards most frequently appeared. The corner cupboard generally is more ornate than a standard square cupboard. These fancier types of cupboards were used to display fine china or porcelain.

▼ Corner cupboards eventually were built-in to the room itself. When the room was designed, the designer would add decorative cornice moldings and baseboards for the cupboard that matched those of the room. The corner cupboards were then painted to blend with the room's decor.

COUNTRY WAYS
Ant Control

To keep ants out of the house, place some whole garlic cloves along the entryways, under the sink, and in cabinets. A sprinkle of talcum powder or paprika works, too.

KITCHEN · IMPROVEMENT CHECKLIST · FOUR

Determine Your Electrical Needs

Electrical appliances and gadgets are great, but does your kitchen have enough power to run them all? Older houses are notoriously short of electrical power (another good reason to remodel). Newer houses are better equipped electrically, but you still may blow a fuse when your kitchen is running full throttle. Don't assume your contractor will provide you with sufficiently wired circuits automatically. You must tell him what you need. Here's how you'll know.

1. Building codes specify minimum electrical requirements for the kitchen. These are:

☐ Two 20-amp circuits for small appliances, including the refrigerator. This usually is enough to run an average kitchen.

☐ An outlet receptacle above any kitchen or dining room counterspace wider than 12 inches.

☐ A permanently installed light fixture, controlled by a separate switch.

2. Measure your appliance electrical usage to determine how much extra power you need.

☐ Note the amperage (power required) of every appliance in your kitchen. You'll find it stamped on the appliance itself, or listed in the instruction manual. The total amps for all your appliances will tell you how much power you must have for those occasions when you use the appliances simultaneously.

3. Make a list of how and when you use appliances.

☐ Which appliances do you tend to use at the same time? (Don't forget appliances that must run continually, such as the refrigerator.)

☐ How many amps must you have to run your appliances together? Your kitchen should be wired to handle your most electrically demanding meal, such as Thanksgiving dinner.

4. Consider where you use your appliances. This will help you decide the placement of electrical outlets.

☐ Which appliances are best placed near the sink?

☐ Which are best place near the stove or cooktop?

☐ Which need the most room?

☐ Which appliances can be mounted on the wall or under a cabinet?

5. Think about your lighting requirements (*see page 15*). This will help you determine the most convenient placement of light switches.

☐ Which lights will be used most often?

☐ Where will you need task lighting?

☐ Where will you place ambient lighting?

☐ Can less frequently used lights be wired to individual switches to save power?

☐ What type of lamps will you use? Incandescent? Fluorescent? Halogen?

☐ How much power will they need?

6. Once you have determined your power requirements, you can decide how best to meet them.

☐ Will it be necessary to add a third 20-amp circuit to your kitchen wiring? Discuss the available options with your contractor or electrician.

7. Examine your kitchen's electrical needs from a practical standpoint.

☐ Sketch a floorplan of your kitchen, and mark the areas where you will need a power source.

8. Examine your needs from an aesthetic standpoint.

☐ What types of outlets do you want? Double outlets, called duplex receptacles, are mounted in metal or plastic boxes recessed into the drywall. The receptacles are relatively large, and grouping several together can detract from the decorative effect of the wall or backsplash.

☐ What options do you have? One alternative is surface-mounted wire track, which contains many outlets, spaced about a foot apart, and is mounted directly on the wall or backsplash. The wire track is connected to the kitchen electrical system through one duplex receptacle.

☐ What types of switches do you want? Visit a home center or hardware store to see what's available.

☐ Will you use dimmer switches? They can be quite effective in the dining area. There are dimmer switches that slide vertically, and others that are pushed to turn on the light and turned clockwise to dim it. A trip to your local home center will help you decide.

☐ Must the outlets and switches be mounted on the walls? Is it possible to mount them on the cabinetry instead? This method has the advantage of clearing wall space, and placing outlets out of the direct line of vision. In a busy work area, however, cords plugged into a waist-high outlet may get in your way.

A *Fresh Angle*

Put your cooktop in the corner? Why not! This sunny arrangement lets you enjoy the view while you cook, and makes great use of an often overlooked area.

▼ An easy-to-clean tile backsplash lines an extra-deep built-in shelf that is within reach of the cook but high enough to avoid excess heat and spatters.

▼ Often used pots and pans are stored in the cupboards directly below the cooktop.

▼ Overhead, a shelf edged with crown molding runs all around the kitchen.

▼ A solution when the light is good but the view isn't: fit the window with glass shelves to display a variety of plants and herbs.

*You cannot fly like an eagle
with the wings of a wren.*
—William Henry Hudson

Just Around the Corner

By creating a unit of cabinets and shelves that extends from the corner on either side, this kitchen uses the available space fully and still maintains its 1830's country charm.

▼ Two hanging cabinets with glass paneled doors are connected by open pantry shelving, bringing to mind an old-fashioned corner hutch. On the shelves, within easy reach, are everyday dishes, frequently used serving pieces and glassware. Behind the glass doors, away from dust, are kept the special dishes that are used less often.

▼ The panel door cabinets below are modern reproductions in a classic style chosen to reflect this home's authentic 19th century heritage. White paint and simple white ceramic knobs give a clean, bright look to the room.

▼ Fluorescent lighting mounted under the cabinets transforms a dark corner into a useable work space. Three electrical outlets make this area highly efficient.

▼ The wood grain countertops actually are easy-to-clean formica with a wooden molding behind them.

▼ On the windows, a lower tier curtain ensures privacy while the unadorned upper window lets in light.

▼ Wood tone and white are the predominant colors here. A subtle counterpoint of blue and white china on the shelves echo the curtain's windowpane check.

ELEMENTS OF DESIGN
Adding a Touch of Country

Not everyone has the time or resources to remodel or redecorate their kitchen in country style. So we compiled a list of those elements that add a country touch to even a standard tract house kitchen. Try adding one piece to your kitchen to give a little country flavor, or pick and choose several favorites to create a more complete look.

▼ Wooden cupboards, standard or corner-style, for displaying country collectibles, china and decorative crockery
▼ Open pantry shelving
▼ Blanket chests or trunks
▼ Ladderback or Windsor chairs
▼ Wood, brick, stone, or other natural flooring
▼ Pine furniture, cabinetry or flooring
▼ Shaker-style furniture
▼ Wicker furniture
▼ Rocking chairs
▼ Wooden tables
▼ Butcherblock countertops or tables
▼ Tile countertops or backsplashes
▼ Stenciling on walls, curtains or furniture
▼ Peg racks, pot racks, plate racks
▼ Patchwork: quilts, table runners, wall hangings, place mats, and so on
▼ Calico prints, checks, plaids and other homespun fabrics
▼ Rag rugs, stenciled rugs
▼ Blue and white spongeware and china, alone or mixed together
▼ Decorative plates, jelly and candy molds, and antique utensils
▼ Ironstone pottery
▼ Majolica serving pieces
▼ Copper cookware
▼ Baskets
▼ Weathervanes
▼ Heart motifs on sconces, boxes, candy molds
▼ Wildflowers
▼ Dried herb and flower wreaths

COUNTRY WAYS
Lucky Codfish

Superstitious seamen carried the "ear stones" of a codfish for good luck. Most fish have such small, white, stone-like pieces (found under the gill cover behind the eye in a sac near the internal ear), but codfish ear stones were believed to be especially lucky and to give protection at sea. The superstition grew out of the belief that because the ear stones keep codfish afloat, the stones would do the same for a person who carried them.

A Space in the Sun

This arrangement takes advantage of the glorious sunlight provided by two corner windows—perfect for plants, wonderful for work.

▼ The roomy new cabinets in this kitchen were made from old pumpkin pine, giving an antique look to modern units.

▼ A narrow shelf, also of pumpkin pine, runs around the room above the countertop. Clear glass jars hold flour, sugar, legumes, cereal, coffee—in short, everything a busy cook needs to have at hand. The jars are a great alternative to a canister set, particularly when arranged on the shelf to catch the light.

▼ A slab of marble covers the hole left when a sink was removed. This makes the corner particularly valuable as a baking preparation area.

▼ Rather than shut out any of the sunlight that makes this corner special, the windows have been left curtainless. Even the Maidenhair fern has been hung in the corner so it gets plenty of light but doesn't block the windows.

COUNTRY WAYS

Tater Talk in the Ozarks

Folks in the Ozark Mountain regions of Arkansas and Missouri had some very definite ideas about when and how to plant potatoes.

▼ It was believed that vegetables that grew underground, such as potatoes, were best planted by the "dark of the moon," that is, during the period from the full moon to the new moon, when the moon was waning.

▼ Ozark farmers also considered the signs of the zodiac before planting. It generally was believed that potatoes grew best if the moon was in Pisces—around mid-March. This superstition may have been "rooted" in the idea that the sign of Pisces governs the feet, according to astrologers.

▼ Some farmers believed that potatoes should be planted on the hundredth day of the year—April 10 (9 in Leap Year)—regardless of weather conditions or astral considerations.

▼ Most farmers agreed that potatoes should be dug by the light of the moon (between the new moon and the full moon) to prevent the potatoes from rotting.

S·H·E·L·V·E·S
A·N·D P·A·N·T·R·I·E·S

Infinite riches in a little room.
—Christopher Marlowe

Showcase Shelves

To make a kitchen corner more cozy, or create extra drama in your dining room, try adding a hutch, corner cupboard or simple shelf unit. Then showcase your decorative china pieces and kitchen collectibles.

▼ Here, favorite plates line the back wall of a hutch. The combination of blue and white porcelain pieces of various designs and origins, and blue on white spongeware on the same shelves as colorful majolica pieces lends an eclectic country charm to the collection. Shapely bowls and cups are placed in front of the plates. Cup hooks screwed into the ends of the shelves allow for a row of hanging mugs, making the arrangement visually interesting, and adding needed storage space.

▼ Experiment with different arrangements, and change them as often as you like—with the seasons, perhaps. The soft pink blossoms bunched in a unique majolica pitcher hint that spring has sprung. In summertime, the shelves might be lined with white doilies and decorated with sea shells found at the beach. For autumn, the showcase could feature mini pumpkins and gourds in a spatterware bowl, or branches of autumn leaves arranged in the pitcher. Come December, the shelves can be draped with evergreen garlands and holly branches.

COUNTRY WAYS
Majolica
With the current passion for Victoriana, majolica ceramics are enjoying a renaissance.

▼ The colorful, molded, lead-glazed earthenware first was produced in the 1850's in England and the United States.

▼ The name majolica comes from 15th century Spanish/Moorish pottery called "maiorca," or "maiolica" in Italian, that was produced on the island of Majorca. The reason the name was given to the Victorian earthenware is unclear, because Victorian era majolica bears no resemblance to the maiorca produced individually by artists and craftsmen. Victorian majolica seems frivolous by comparison. Perhaps that is why few majolica producers endowed their pieces with the traditional maker's mark.

▼ Victorians surrounded themselves with majolica. The whimsically-shaped dishes not only adorned the dining table, but were found throughout the house as urns, flower pots, and even umbrella stands. Shapes ranged from fish to straw hats, but the most common (and those most often reproduced today) had leaf, flower, fruit, or vegetable motifs. Despite its tremendous initial popularity, majolica was out of favor by about 1900.

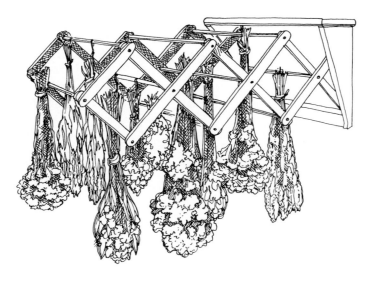

COUNTRY WAYS

Display the Everyday

Don't limit yourself to traditional paintings or wall hangings when decorating your kitchen. The charm of country decor is in its varied beauty and devotion to the practical side of life.

▼ If you have the wall space, try hanging and arranging everyday utensils so they remain accessible for cooking, are out of the way, and add visual interest to the room. Serving trays, colanders, woks, ladles and spoons are excellent candidates for display.

▼ If you wish, you can integrate a calendar or bulletin board into your arrangement to make it all the more functional.

▼ Add a framed picture or poster to create a more artistic, collage-like effect.

▼ In the entryway or foyer, hang a mail basket, hats, raincoats, satchels, umbrellas, and whatever else you need to grab while going into or out of the house.

▼ How to hang all these accoutrements of everyday living? Hardware stores carry a wide assortment of hooks and hangers. Picture hooks are rated by the amount of weight they can support, and are fine for hanging anything to which you can attach a wire or string loop.

▼ Coat hooks and peg racks project farther from the wall, and in most cases should be secured to wall studs, or to wooden boards attached to wall studs.

▼ To attach a hook or hanger of any sort to a hollow wall, use toggle bolts, or plastic or lead wall anchors.

▼ If you favor rotating your hanging scheme, consider using a wire or wooden rack that has movable hooks to hold a range of large and small objects.

Baker's Secret

Lightweight metal bakery shelving is an easy way to expand kitchen storage. The freestanding metal framework blends with any style, but its no-frills practicality makes it perfect for country decor.

▼ This unit tucks neatly into a corner. Adjustable shelving holds a wide variety of items.

▼ Here the most frequently used items—creamers, pitchers, a butter tub, and so on, are placed on the center shelf. The least used items are placed on the highest and lowest shelves.

▼ Other items to store on these sturdy shelves include appliances, pots, pans, canned foods, wines, cookbooks, frequently used dishes and glasses.

COUNTRY WAYS

A Tisket, A Tasket . . .

No country household could have functioned without a collection of baskets. Hand-woven baskets were used as clothes hampers, drying racks for fruit, sieves, and even baby cradles. A typical country household probably would have had single-handled baskets for gathering eggs, large two-handled field baskets for transporting fruits and vegetables from the fields, and oblong or oval covered market baskets.

▼ The majority of American baskets were, and still are, made of splint—thin, flexible strips of wood from oak, ash, hickory, or poplar trees. Willow is another popular basketry material, and there are baskets made from straw, vines, and even cornhusks.

▼ Baskets were considered inexpensive and commonplace, so they usually were not signed or marked by their creators. Most baskets did not enjoy long lives because they were naturally fragile and frequently used. Few examples of antique baskets survive, and they largely are not functional.

▼ You'll find fine baskets in virtually every kind of store you can think of—gift shops, craft shops, even discount stores and supermarkets. Use baskets as serving pieces, wastebaskets, plant holders, and more. New or old, baskets woven of natural materials belong in a country home.

Behind the Curtains

If you want a change from open pantry shelving, and are tired of your cabinet doors, try a fabric face-lift. Easy to make, easy to change and inexpensive too—what more could the country homemaker want!

▼ Here a blue and white cotton floral brings the charm of Dutch delftware to a kitchen pantry. The fabric was shirred and gathered to add softness to the kitchen. The curtains were suspended below the tops of the cabinets to hide the contents of the lower shelves, while leaving the top shelves visible to reveal decorative pieces of china.

▼ A second shirred and gathered curtain conceals the bottom of an old double sink.

▼ Window curtains in the same fabric and a complementary wallpaper complete the look.

ELEMENTS OF DESIGN
Cantilevered Shelving

If you don't like the look of shelf hardware, try using shelves with no visible means of support. The trick is to encase the supports within the shelves, which in turn are fastened to metal brackets that are embedded in the wall studs and hidden inside the wall.

▼ Notch out the wall studs to accept the metal brackets. The front of each bracket should be flush with the front face of the stud.

▼ One-quarter-inch square metal tongues project from the brackets perpendicular to the wall (hardwood dowels also can be used, but must be of larger dimension than the metal tongues to provide the necessary support). The length of the tongues is determined by the depth of the shelves; the tongues project at least halfway into the shelves.

▼ The tongues fit into mortises in the shelves. Use a drill and chisel to cut the mortises into solid wood shelves. Or build up shelves from smaller pieces of wood, leaving gaps that become the mortises.

Something Old, Something New

Not an inch of space is wasted in this remodeled kitchen. The wall bumpout, which divides the kitchen from the dining area, has been custom built with open shelving to hold necessities. The hutch next to the bumpout is homemade; the ideal showcase for a collection of pewterware.

▼ Modern living calls for modern convenience—even in a country home. So a special inset was built into the wall bumpout to hold a television with access to the wall outlet. The stationary shelf is only as deep as the TV, allowing free play for the wires behind. Hanging a large decorative platter above calls attention away from the ultra-modern entertainment area.

▼ An ingenious tall, shallow pantry was created on the side of the bumpout. A plain wooden door with interior hinges can close to be flush with the bumpout wall. Inside the pantry, all the shelves are adjustable, and the uppermost and lowest shelves are deeper than those in the center.

▼ A pull-out shelf holds canned beverages—no digging to the back of the cabinet to find what you want. The overhead shelves hold cookbooks, lined up at the edge for easy reaching.

S·I·N·K·S·C·A·P·E·S

*Human felicity is produced not so
much by great pieces of good fortune
that seldom happen,
as by little advantages
that occur every day.*
—Benjamin Franklin

White On White

White is the great *trompe l'oeil* — it "fools the eye" by making small spaces visually enlarge. That's the trick to this sink area, and an important point to keep in mind when you want a country look in a small area.

▼ A plain tile border in bright white makes the single porcelain sink seem larger than it is. The sink is undermounted for easy counter clean up.

▼ A 34-inch-deep countertop leaves room for a behind-the-sink shelf to hold frequently used dishes and glasses. The backsplash shelf is covered with the same tile that surrounds the sink. This arrangement puts necessities within easy reach, and cuts down on the frequent opening and closing of cabinet doors.

▼ The bright white of the tile is reflected in the paint used around the paned windows. The windows are curtainless to let in the sunlight.

▼ Off-white countertops and cabinets offset the bright white of the tile.

▼ Open pantry shelving adjacent to the sink area is kept neatly organized.

ELEMENTS OF DESIGN
Backsplashes

The area directly behind your sink or stovetop area, a backsplash should be easy to clean as well as pleasing to the eye. Tile is always a popular choice for a country kitchen, but there are many others. Keep the following tips in mind when shopping for backsplash material.

▼ Whatever material you decide to use should be water-resistant and easy to clean. For aesthetic appeal, extend the backsplash to cover the entire vertical surface, from the top of the counter to the bottom of the cabinet above.

▼ Post-formed, one piece counter and backsplash constructions are best avoided. Though inexpensive and easy to install, they are made with thin, vertical-grade laminate that is not designed for use as a countertop surface.

ELEMENTS OF DESIGN
Super Shelves!

If you wish to have wall-mounted shelves made of a heavy material, such as marble or heavy-gauge steel, you must take extra care when mounting the shelves, especially if you plan to store heavy objects on them. Here are some guidelines.

▼ Mounting brackets should be screwed directly into the wall studs behind the drywall or plaster. Use an electronic stud finder to make the location of studs easier.

▼ Use mounting screws long enough to have a solid grab in the studs. Two-inch wood screws work well in most situations.

▼ If the mounting location has only one stud available for the shelves' support, install a mounting cleat for each shelf and attach the shelf to it. Make the cleat by cutting a piece of 1 x 3-inch pine to the same length as the shelf. Screw the cleat into the wall at the single stud using a 3-inch wood screw. Then use a molly bolt to attach the cleat to the drywall where no stud is available. Screw the shelf onto the cleat. The shelf weight will be distributed over the length of the cleat, insuring secure installation.

▼ Do not attempt to screw shelves directly into drywall or plaster where there are no studs. The weight of shelves can make even plastic screw anchors pull loose from a wall.

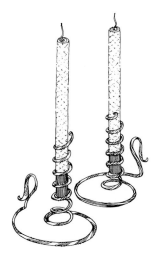

A Sunken Garden

A sunken tiled area between the three-bowl sink and the bay window lets a potted herb garden flourish year round. Designed with herbs in mind, the garden area has a built-in drain to make watering a breeze.

▼ The stainless steel sink features a central draining bowl ideal for food preparation with a bowl on either side for washing and dish draining.

▼ The backsplash was tiled in a subtle checkerboard pattern of soothing light and dark ecru shades. The design allowed for a shelf area behind the sink and in front of the herbs.

▼ To remain true to the design of this New England colonial house, a border of unique leaded glass panes was installed above the new bay window.

▼ Ceramic and wooden mortar and pestle sets, used to grind dried herbs, are useful and decorative. Small aluminum molds hung on the window frame become kitchen wall art.

COUNTRY WAYS
Make a Soap Scrubber

Country sense dictates a disdain of waste, and this includes leftover bits of soap. The solution? Collect the leftover slivers of bar soap and place a handful of the slivers in the center of a square of nylon netting. Fold up the netting so there are several layers of net around the slivers, tuck in the netting ends like a package, and sew all around the edges with heavy thread. Use the soap scrubber for scrubbing collar stains before laundering, or for cleaning hands after gardening or painting.

*L*et There Be Light

An ordinary kitchen window was enlarged and transformed into a breathtaking masterpiece of brilliant, sparkling light. By adding see-through cabinets above the sink, the resulting look is modern with country overtones.

▼ Custom cabinets with glass doors and glass shelves are fitted to the window itself. The dishes and glasses inside camouflage the view somewhat, but let in the light. White wooden handles are centered on the bottom of the cabinet doors, instead of on the side, making them easier to reach.

▼ The multi-paned backsplash glass panels are antique English flint glass.

▼ With such dramatic windows, the cabinets and sink must take a back seat. The simplest design is best. Red granite was used for the countertop. The sink is undermounted. Two dishwashers cut down on after-meal clean up time.

▼ Way up top, splashes of color come from onyx and agate sculpture. A newly installed molding adds visual interest. Tucked in the corners are stereo speakers.

I remember, I remember
The house where I was born,
The little window where the sun
Came peeping in at morn.
—Thomas Hood

DO·IT·YOURSELF·DECOR

B·U·I·L·D A
K·I·T·C·H·E·N I·S·L·A·N·D

Oh! it's a snug little island,
A right little, tight little island!
—Thomas Dibdin

KITCHEN ISLAND
(52 x 57½ x 35½ inches)

Materials: Two 24 x 36-inch base kitchen cabinets (available at home centers and some department stores); BB exterior-grade plywood: ¾ x 48 x 72 inches, ½ x 48 x 48 inches and ¼ x 48 x 96 inches; 10 feet of 2 x 3 lumber *(see chart below for dimensions of wood pieces)*; four 2½-inch-long carriage bolts with washers and nuts; 1½-inch-long No. 9 flathead wood screws; ¾-inch-long screws; wood glue; 1 multiple electrical outlet strip; two 18¾ x 25¼-inch wire grids *(see* FIG. III, 1, *page 110)*; seventy-two 6-inch square tiles; thirty-four 6-inch bullnose-edge tiles and four 90° corners; tile cement; tile grout; sandpaper; tack cloth; primer; black paint; paint for cabinets in color desired; paintbrushes; lattice strip or cardboard; power or hand saw; fine-toothed saw; drill with assorted size bits and expandable bit; countersink and screwdrill set; hammer; clamps; straight-edge; tape rule; square; toothbrush; sponges; clean rags; notched trowel, and rubber trowel or squeegee.

Code	Pieces	Size
A	(2)	24" x 36" Base cabinets
A1	(4)	2½" Carriage bolts
B (PLY)	(2)	¼" x 34½" x 47" End panels
C (PLY)	(2)	¼" x 4" x 42" Kickplates
D (PLY)	(1)	¾" x 51¼" x 48" Top
D1 (PLY)	(1)	¾" x 9" x 37¼" Top
D2 (PLY)	(1)	¾" x 9" x 14" Top
D3 (2 x 3)	(2)	1" x 1⅝" x 57" Side rails
E (PLY)	(2)	½" x 14½" x 48" Top ends
E1 (PLY)	(2)	½" x 6½" x 48" Top ends
F	(1)	Multiple elec. outlet strip
G	(2)	18¾" x 25¼" Med. wire grids

Directions:

1. Do not order precut ¼-inch plywood end panels for the A base cabinets. Cut the two one-piece B end panels, and the other wood parts, to size. Rip the D3 side rails to 1 x 1⅝ inches from the 2 x 3 lumber.

2. Assemble the A base cabinets following the manufacturer's directions. Clamp the A cabinets together back-to-back. Select a drill bit that is the same diameter as the shank of the A1 carriage bolts. Drill four holes through the back of the A cabinets, one at each top and bottom corner *(see* FIG. III, 1*)*. Insert each A1 bolt, place a washer and nut on the end, and tighten. Remove the clamps.

3. Cut 2¼ x 4-inch kickplate notches in the bottom corners of the B end panels *(see* FIG. III, 1*)*.

4. Place the A cabinets on one end. Apply glue to the up end. Place a B end panel on the cabinet end, with one edge of the panel in the slot at the sides, and bend the plywood so it will slip in the opposite side slot. Shift the pieces so their top and bottom edges are flush. Place heavy objects on the end panel until the glue sets. Repeat at the opposite end with the other B end panel.

5. Glue and clamp the C kickplates to the bottom of the B end panels *(see* FIG. III, 1*)*. Sand the cabinets smooth, and wipe off all the sawdust with the tack cloth. Paint the cabinets; paint the kickplates black.

6. Drill a ⅝-inch-diameter hole 1¾ inches below the top edge of one of the B end panels, ½ to 1 inch clear of the metal corner brace. Use the square to mark lines joining the hole edges to the top edge of the panel. Cut out the notch with the fine-toothed saw. Attach the F multiple outlet strip to the end panel *(see* FIG. III, 1*)*. Drill a hole in the cabinet shelf and bottom big enough for the multiple outlet cord plug to pass through. Pass the outlet cord through the notch and holes to the floor. The cord will plug into an outlet placed in the floor in the middle of the kitchen under the island; hire an electrician to install the floor outlet.

7. Glue and clamp the E top end pieces to each other flush all around. Repeat with the E1 top end pieces.

8. Place the D1 and D2 top pieces on a flat surface, good sides down and butt ends together. Place the E top end on D1/D2, flush at one long edge and centered side to side. D1/D2 overlap E by 1⅝ inches at each side. E overlaps D1/D2 by 5½ inches at one long edge. The D top piece will fit in this space. Pencil mark at the overlaps. Take the pieces apart, apply glue, and attach the pieces with the flathead wood screws, using four screws through E into D2, and six screws through E into D1.

9. Using the flathead wood screws, glue and screw the D3 side rails to the bottom edges of the D top piece, flush at the edges and at one side. The rails will extend 9 inches beyond D. Place the D1/D2/E assembly on the extended ends of the D3 rails. Apply glue to the mating edges, and to the top of E where it meets the bottom of D. Screw through D1/D2 into the D3 rails. Screw through the bottom of E into the bottom of D *(see* FIG. III, 1*)*. Using the ¾-inch screws, glue and screw the E1 top end to the bottom of D, flush at the opposite end between the D3 rails.

10. Place the top assembly on the cabinets. The cabinets fit into the recess between E, E1 and D3. The longest overhang E is at the multiple outlet end *(see* FIG. III, 1*)*. Attach the top assembly to the cabinets

(Continued on page 111)

▼▼▼

FIG. III, 1   KITCHEN ISLAND

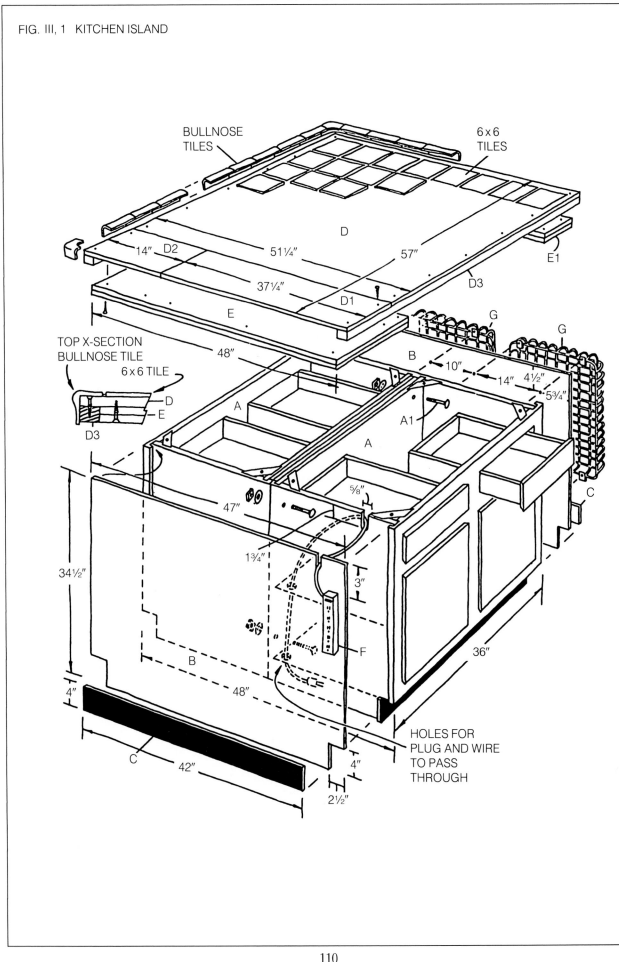

BULLNOSE
TILES

6 x 6
TILES

D

14"   D2   51¼"   57"   E1

37¼"   D3

D1

E

TOP X-SECTION
BULLNOSE TILE

6 x 6 TILE

D
E
D3

48"

G

B   10"

14"   4½"

5¾"

G

A

A1

A

5⁄8"

C

47"

1¾"

3"

34½"

B

F

36"

48"

4"

HOLES FOR
PLUG AND WIRE
TO PASS
THROUGH

C   42"

4"

2½"

Kitchen Island (continued)

with the flathead wood screws through the holes provided in the cabinet metal corner braces *(see* FIG. III, 1*)*.

11. Prime the top and edges of the island top. Place the square tiles flat on the top, and the bullnose-edge tiles along the top's edges. Equalize the spacing between the tiles. Make a spacer from the lattice strip or cardboard that is the thickness of the spaces between the tiles.

12. Cement the bullnose-edge tiles in place first, then the square tiles. Remove four to five tiles at a time, and apply the tile cement with the notched trowel held at a 45° angle. Press the tiles in place firmly with a slight twisting motion. Using the spacer, align the tiles so all the joints are uniform and straight. Clean off excess cement on the faces of the tiles immediately. Let the tiles dry in place for about 24 hours.

13. Mix and use the grout following the manufacturer's directions. Work the grout into the joints with the rubber trowel or squeegee. Wash off excess grout with a wet sponge. To shape the grout lines in the tiles, strike the joints with the handle of the toothbrush. Clean the tiles and dress the joints with a damp sponge. When the grout is dry, polish the tiles with a clean rag.

14. Place the island in position over the floor electrical outlet. Plug in the multiple outlet cord. Attach the G wire grids to the opposite side of the island from the multiple outlet strip *(see* FIG. III, 1*)*.

ELEMENTS OF DESIGN
Dishwashers

▼ A top-of-the-line model dishwasher is a good investment. One with a built-in water heater also is more energy efficient, allowing you to keep your house's hot water supply at a lower temperature, such as 120° or 130°.

▼ Two dishwashers are a worthwhile splurge for many homeowners. One can be used for dishes and glassware, the other for pots and pans, to eliminate the time and bother of hand-washing and make entertaining easier.

ELEMENTS OF DESIGN
Sinks

▼ A multiple-bowl sink allows more than one task to be done at the same time, such as rinsing salad vegetables and draining pasta. A second sink, located on a work island or adjacent counter, is recommended if people must cross the cook's path to get water, or if the main sink's location forces the cook to stray too far from other task areas.

▼ A stainless steel sink is the easiest to maintain, but presumes the use of chrome fixtures. A white porcelain or fiberglass sink allows more decorating freedom.

▼ Regardless of the sink material chosen, an undermounted sink is recommended *(see photos, pages 103 and 107)*. An undermounted sink rests below the countertop, so you can wipe directly into the sink without going over the bump of a sink rim. Not all sinks can be undermounted; those with flatter rims work best. Successful undermounting depends largely on the ability and creativity of the carpenter doing the installation.

KITCHEN
C·R·A·F·T·S

*There is nothing better than that a man should
rejoice in his own works.*
—Ecclesiastes

C ountry crafting is purposeful; no room bears this out so well as the kitchen. Even the most artistic handcrafts, such as Amish table runners or crocheted tablecloths, put function before fashion. In this chapter, you'll find a wonderful collection of projects designed to be used, not just admired.

From small-scale projects perfect for weekend crafting to more elaborate items that will satisfy your desire for challenging handwork, we provide you with an abundance of beautiful projects. For the seamstress or crocheter, there are cushions, tablecloths, an apron and table runner. For the woodworker, there is a plate rack, china showcase, Pennsylvania Dutch corner cabinet, and more.

We even show you how to revitalize your entire kitchen from top to bottom with step-by-step instructions on stenciling.

K·I·T·C·H·E·N
H·E·L·P·E·R·S

*Enough, if something from our
hands have power
To live, and act, and serve
the future hour.*
—William Wordsworth

ROSEBUD APRON & MITT

Materials: 1 yard of 45-inch-wide white polyester/cotton fabric; 1 yard of bright yellow fabric; ¾ yard of green calico fabric; scraps of bright red calico fabric; white, green and bright yellow threads; ⅓ yard of synthetic batting; tracing paper; dressmaker's carbon; tracing wheel; cardboard.

Directions:

1. Apron: Cut a 9½ x 33-inch front panel from the white fabric.

2. Enlarge the vine appliqué design in FIG. IV, 1 onto tracing paper, following the directions on page 241. Using the dressmaker's carbon and tracing wheel, trace the design, centered, onto the panel.

3. Trace a leaf, bud, and bud leaf from the vine onto the cardboard, and cut them out. Using the cardboard patterns, cut out five buds from the red calico. Cut out nine leaves and five pairs of bud leaves from the green calico. Baste all the pieces in place on the panel. Using the green thread and a machine zigzag stitch, sew two rows, one on top of the other, for the stems, and once around all the calico pieces.

4. Cut a 2½ x 9½-inch strip from the yellow fabric. Sew one long edge of the strip to the top edge of the panel on the wrong side. Press, and turn the strip to the right side of the panel. Turn under the strip's raw edge to make a 1-inch binding, and topstitch the strip edge to the panel. Cut two 2½ x 34-inch strips from the yellow fabric, and bind them in the same way to the long edges of the panel.

5. Cut two 16 x 24-inch side panels from the green calico, and make a narrow hem on one long edge of each panel. Gather a short end of each side panel to 8 inches, keeping one hemmed edge to the right and the other to the left of the front panel. Cut two 3½ x 36-inch strips from the yellow fabric, and pin one edge of each strip to the gathered end of a side panel so that the strip extends from the hemmed edge for a tie. Finish the ties in the same way as the front panel binding in Step 4, turning under each end.

6. Place the long raw edges of the side panels ½ inch in on the wrong side of the front panel's side bindings, with the panels right side out, waist bands on top, and bottom edges even. Topstitch the panels together along the outer edges of the side bindings. Turn up 2 inches at the bottom for a hem.

7. Cut two 18 x 2½-inch strips from the yellow fabric for the neck ties. Fold each strip in half lengthwise, turn under the raw edges, and topstitch near the edges. Insert one end of each strip into the top of the front panel binding, and stitch it on. Hem the tie ends.

8. Mitt: Enlarge the mitt pattern and rosebud appliqué in FIG. IV, 1 onto tracing paper. Cut four mitts from the white fabric and four mitts from the batting. Using the dressmaker's carbon and tracing wheel, trace the rosebud appliqué onto one fabric mitt. Using the cardboard patterns, cut out a bud from the red calico. Cut out two leaves and a pair of bud leaves from the green calico. Appliqué the calico pieces onto the fabric mitt following the directions in Step 3.

9. Sandwich two batting mitts between two fabric mitts, right sides out, and baste the layers together along the edges. Repeat. Place the mitts right sides together and overcast the edges, leaving the wrist edge open. Stitch a seam just inside the overcast edges. Turn the mitt right side out. From the green calico, cut a 3-inch-wide bias strip long enough to bind the wrist edge. Stitch one edge of the bias strip inside the mitt, then turn the binding over the wrist edge to the outside of the mitt, turning under the raw edges of the binding. Cut a 2 x 8-inch strip from the green calico. Turn under the raw edges, fold the strip in half lengthwise, and slipstitch the edges together *(see Stitch Guide, page 240)*. Fold the strip and stitch the ends to the inside of the mitt for a hanger loop.

1 SQ. = 1"

FIG. IV, 1
ROSEBUD
APRON & MITT

PENNSYLVANIA DUTCH BREAD BOX & CORNER CABINET

Materials: General Materials for Stencil a Country Kitchen *(page 151)*; unfinished bread box; unfinished corner cabinet; sandpaper; tack cloth; acrylic paints: soft black and mustard brown, and paints for stencil designs in colors of your choice; satin polyurethane; paintbrushes; No. 0000 steel wool *(optional)*; small white enamel knob for cabinet.

Directions:

1. Sand the bread box and corner cabinet smooth, and remove all the sawdust with the tack cloth. Paint a soft black base coat on the bread box. Paint a mustard brown base coat on the corner cabinet.

2. Enlarge the stencil designs in FIGS. IV, 2A and 2B *(page 118)* onto paper, following the directions on page 241. Also enlarge one woman figure and the tulip heart in FIG. IV, 2B to half size, using a ratio of 1 square = ½ inch. Trace and cut a stencil for each design, following the instructions in Stencil a Country Kitchen, Steps 1 and 2.

3. Using stencil brushes, and following Stencil a Country Kitchen, Steps 2, 5 and 6, stencil the bread box and corner cabinet with the multicolor stenciling technique or, if you wish, use another stenciling technique *(stenciling techniques are shown on pages 155-156)*. Build color with two or three light coats of paint; avoid heavy paint build-up. Use the photo at right of the bread box and cabinet as a color and design placement guide, or create your own design layout.

4. Clean and store the stencils and brushes following Stencil a Country Kitchen, Step 7.

5. When the stenciled designs are dry, use a paintbrush to apply two protective coats of the polyurethane to the bread box and cabinet. If you wish to create a handrubbed look, rub the bread box and cabinet with No. 0000 steel wool between coats. Attach the enamel knob to the cabinet door as shown in the photo at right.

C O U N T R Y   W A Y S

Tree of Life

Parents used to plant a tree to mark the birth of a child because trees, especially evergreens, are symbolic of long life. This charming custom still is practiced by many folks today.

C O U N T R Y   W A Y S

Dutch Treat

Famed for their decorative art, the Pennsylvania "Dutch" were not Dutch at all. They were Germans, or "Deutsche."

▼ With William Penn as their leader, the Pennsylvania Dutch began to emigrate to America from the Rhineland and Switzerland as early as 1863. They settled in the farming regions to the north and west of Philadelphia.

▼ The Pennsylvania Dutch are credited with bringing the art of decorative Fraktur painting to America. Fraktur painting stems from the art of manuscript illumination practiced in the Middle Ages, and includes both colorful motifs and elaborate Gothic lettering.

▼ In the early 19th century, Fraktur painting was often taught in the Pennsylvania German schools. It was used on important documents, such as birth and marriage certificates. Eventually the colorful art made its way onto home furnishings, pottery and tin.

PENNSYLVANIA DUTCH BREAD BOX & CORNER CABINET STENCILS

FIG. IV, 2A   1 SQ. = 1″   FIG. IV, 2B   1 SQ. = 1″

BASKET O' BLOSSOMS DOORMAT

Materials: 14 x 24-inch woven seagrass doormat; red, blue, light blue and green cotton fabrics; yarn needle with ½-inch eye.

Directions:

1. Cut or tear each cotton fabric across its width into 1½-inch-wide strips. To thread each fabric strip through the needle, fold the strip widthwise until it fits through the needle's eye.

2. Mark the horizontal center row of the mat. Each square in the chart in FIG. IV, 3 represents one cross stitch over one woven mat square.

3. Following the chart, and using the yarn needle and fabric strips, work the basket design in cross stitch, starting at the center row *(see Stitch Guide, page 240)*. When starting a new strip, leave a 3-inch tail of fabric at the back of the mat, and work four or five cross stitches over it. When the basket design is finished, overcast stitch around the edge of the mat with red.

COUNTRY WAYS

Versatile Sassafras

A native of North America, sassafras is a member of the laurel family. The tree has an aromatic bark, leaves with two or three finger-like lobes, and small, blueish fruits. Sassafras has been popular for generations, both as a flavoring and to make dye.

▼ In 18th century Philadelphia, people made good use of the local sassafras trees. The leaves of the trees were used to make an aromatic tea, and the bark was the basis of a dye for wool.

▼ A naturalist of the period noted that wool was colored with sassafras dye in a brass boiler. Urine was used as a fixative to keep the dye from bleeding and to aid its absorption into the wool. The fine orange color produced by sassafras dye was prized for its ability to remain fast when exposed to sunlight.

FIG. IV, 3 BASKET O' BLOSSOMS DOORMAT

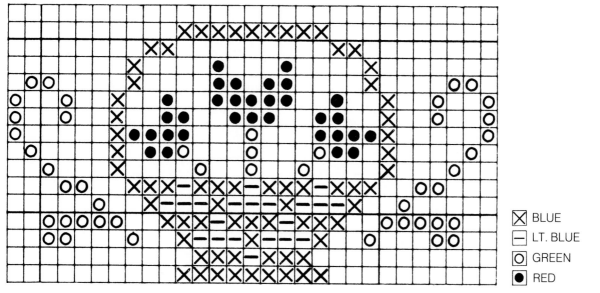

⊠ BLUE
— LT. BLUE
○ GREEN
● RED

"BLESS THIS HOUSE" RUG
This hooked rug is made with strips of wool fabric.

Materials: 1 yard of 50-inch-wide burlap fabric; tracing paper; dressmaker's carbon; tracing wheel; 16 x 18-inch or larger rug frame intended for rug hooking; strong fabric to cover rug frame; new or used tightly woven wool fabrics *(see photo for shades needed, and Step 1 for amounts)*: 3 shades of solid blue, 2 to 3 shades of solid gold, shades of solid wine, shades of brownish pink, bright pink tweed, solid bright pink, palest, light, medium, dark and darkest solid green, green tweed, solid orange rust, solid khaki, medium and dark solid brown, and solid natural; primitive rug hook (not latch hook); 3¾ yards of 1½-inch-wide twill tape; matching thread; sharp scissors; tacks or stapler; long or T-pins.

Directions:

1. To figure the amounts of the wool fabrics needed, estimate that 5 square feet of fabric are needed for 1 square foot of rug; each hooked area is covered with five layers of fabric. If you are using old clothes, rip out the seams and hems. Remove linings, interfacing and padding. Cut out button holes, and remove buttons, zippers, hooks and eyes.

2. Wash every wool fabric, new or old, before using it to remove any fabric sizing, and to make the wool softer and easier to manage. Machine wash the fabrics in cold water on the delicate cycle; wash dark, medium and light colors separately. Line-dry fabrics that feel thick after being washed. Dry the remaining fabrics in the dryer on the delicate setting. Washing sometimes shrinks loosely woven or basketweave fabrics enough to make them usable. If they remain too loose after washing and drying, try shrinking them in a hot dryer.

3. Enlarge the design in FIG. IV, 4 onto tracing paper, following the directions on page 241. Using the dressmaker's carbon and tracing wheel, transfer the design onto the burlap, leaving excess burlap all around the design. If this is your first hooked rug, leave enough space between the design edges and burlap edges to practice the hooking stitch.

4. Fold in the end of the twill tape about ½ inch. Pin one edge of the tape to the burlap along the outside edges of the design, with the tape extending in toward the center. Hand- or machine-stitch the tape to the burlap about ⅛ inch from the design's outside edges. Press the tape back.

5. Assemble the rug frame, and wrap the four sides with 2-inch-wide strips of the strong fabric; the corners do not have to be covered. Use the tacks or staples to hold the beginning and end of each strip in place.

6. Place the burlap over the frame; the area you wish to work should be in the center of the frame. Use about six long or T-pins to pin one side of the burlap firmly to the frame. Pull the burlap firmly across the frame, and pin the other side. Pin the top of the burlap, pulling firmly as you work. Then pin the bottom, again pulling firmly so the burlap is taut. If the burlap loosens while you are hooking, pin it again.

7. Cut each fabric into ¼-inch-wide strips along the straight of the fabric; strips cut on the bias will break.

8. If this is your first hooked rug, practice the hooking stitch before starting to hook the design. Learn how to hook curves and straight lines in all directions. Hold a fabric strip in one hand, between your thumb and forefinger, touching the underside of the burlap. Hold the rug hook's wooden handle in the palm of your other hand, with your thumb and forefinger pointing to the shank of the hook. From the topside, push the hook down through the burlap and pull up the end of the strip to the topside. The succeeding stitches will be loops pulled about ¼ inch above the burlap. As each loop comes through the burlap, pull it slightly toward the previous completed loop; this helps achieve a uniform height. If you pull a loop too high, pull it down from underneath. The hand on the top of the

rug is your working hand. The hand below the rug guides the strip on the bottom, and feeds the strip through your thumb and finger. All the strips should start and end on top. Cut off the strips even with the tops of the loops. The finished rug should be springy and soft; a hard rug is the result of packing the loops too close together. The loops should cover the burlap and touch each other, but not be crowded. At first, pull a loop through every second mesh until you get the feel of what you are doing. Then you may want to pass over more spaces, or hook closer. Keep the underside of the rug neat; do not let the strips twist. When you need to move from one spot to another, cut the strip on top and start again in the new spot.

9. Begin hooking the rug near the center of the design, following the chart in Fig. IV, 4 and using the photo as a color guide. Outline each motif, then hook its interior. After each section is hooked, hook two rows of background around it. After the design is finished, hook two straight rows around the edges of the rug, then fill in the remaining background with gentle curving rows. Include your initials, if you wish.

10. When the rug is finished, cut the burlap 1 inch from the stitching line all around. Fold the twill tape to the back of the rug, covering the excess burlap, and slipstitch the tape to the back of the rug *(see Stitch Guide, page 240).*

FIG. IV, 4 "BLESS THIS HOUSE" RUG   1 SQ. = 2"

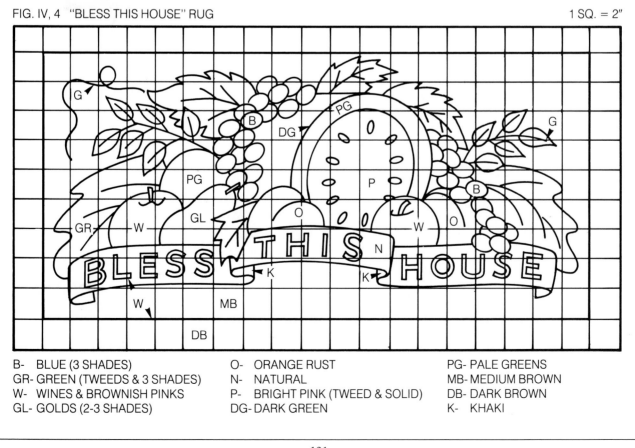

B-	BLUE (3 SHADES)	O-	ORANGE RUST	PG-	PALE GREENS
GR-	GREEN (TWEEDS & 3 SHADES)	N-	NATURAL	MB-	MEDIUM BROWN
W-	WINES & BROWNISH PINKS	P-	BRIGHT PINK (TWEED & SOLID)	DB-	DARK BROWN
GL-	GOLDS (2-3 SHADES)	DG-	DARK GREEN	K-	KHAKI

ENGLISH PLATE RACK

Materials: Pine: three 1 x 10 x 36-inch pieces for sides and top *(see Note below)*, and six 1 x 3 x 36-inch pieces for center and bottom shelves, and hanging cleats; scrap board; twelve 36-inch-long ½-inch-diameter wooden dowels; thirty-two 1½-inch-long flathead wood screws for assembly; four 2-inch-long flathead wood screws for hanging, with wall anchors to fit, if necessary; wood glue; wood putty; sandpaper; tack cloth; paintbrush; satin polyurethane; No. 000 steel wool; combination saw, sabre saw or circular saw; backsaw; miter box; power drill with assorted bits; clamps; screwdriver; level; nail.

Note: *The actual size of a 1 x 10 pine board is ¾ x 9¼ inches.*

Directions:

1. Measure, mark, and cut the plate rack parts to the dimensions shown in FIG. IV, 5A *(page 124)*. Cut the dowels to size using the backsaw and miter box.

2. Mark the placement for the dowel holes in the rack top and shelves, following the measurements in FIG. IV, 5B *(page 124)*. Drill ⁹/₁₆-inch-diameter holes through the two center shelves. To avoid chipping the shelves, clamp the scrap board to each shelf, and drill through the shelf into the scrap board. Drill ½-inch-diameter holes in the bottom shelves and rack top.

3. The rack top, sides, shelves and hanging cleats are butt joined. Drill all the screw holes before gluing the parts together. Position the shelves, rack top and cleats against the rack sides, and clamp them in place. Drill pilot holes for the screws, slightly smaller than the screws' diameter, through the rack sides into the edges of the shelves, top and cleats *(see FIG. IV, 5A)*. Drill additional pilot holes through the rack top into the top cleat, and through the bottom cleat into the back bottom shelf *(see FIG. IV, 5C, page 124)*. Drill counterbore holes to recess the screws beneath the wood surface.

4. Slip the dowels through the holes in the center shelves. Glue and screw the center shelves to the plate rack sides.

5. Glue and screw the bottom shelves to the rack sides. Glue and screw the rack top to the sides, fitting the dowels in their holes. Do not use glue on the dowels.

6. Drill two hanging holes through each cleat *(see photo)*. Glue and screw the cleats to the rack sides, then to the rack top and back bottom shelf.

7. Fill all the screw holes with the wood putty, and sand them smooth. Sand the entire rack, and remove all the sawdust with the tack cloth.

8. Using the paintbrush, apply two coats of the polyurethane, rubbing down with the steel wool between coats.

9. With a helper, hold the plate rack where you want to hang it, and place the level on the rack top. When the plate rack is level, tap a nail through each cleat hanging hole.

10. If the rack is to hang from studs, drill pilot holes for the hanging screws. Or drill holes in the wall for the screw anchors, and insert the anchors. Slip the hanging screws through the cleat hanging holes. Raise the rack into position, and find the pilot holes or anchors with the screw ends. Screw the rack in place.

COUNTRY WAYS
Old-Fashioned Sparkle

Long before automatic dishwashers and fancy detergents, resourceful homemakers devised their own ways to get dishes clean. The following is a kitchen hint, circa 1888, from the National Farmer's and Housekeeper's Cyclopedia.

▼ In washing dishes, fill a dish-pan half full of very hot water, and put to the quantity a half cup of milk. It softens the hardest water, gives the dishes a clear, bright look, and preserves the hands from the rough skin or chapping which comes from the use of soap.

FIG. IV, 5A   ENGLISH PLATE RACK

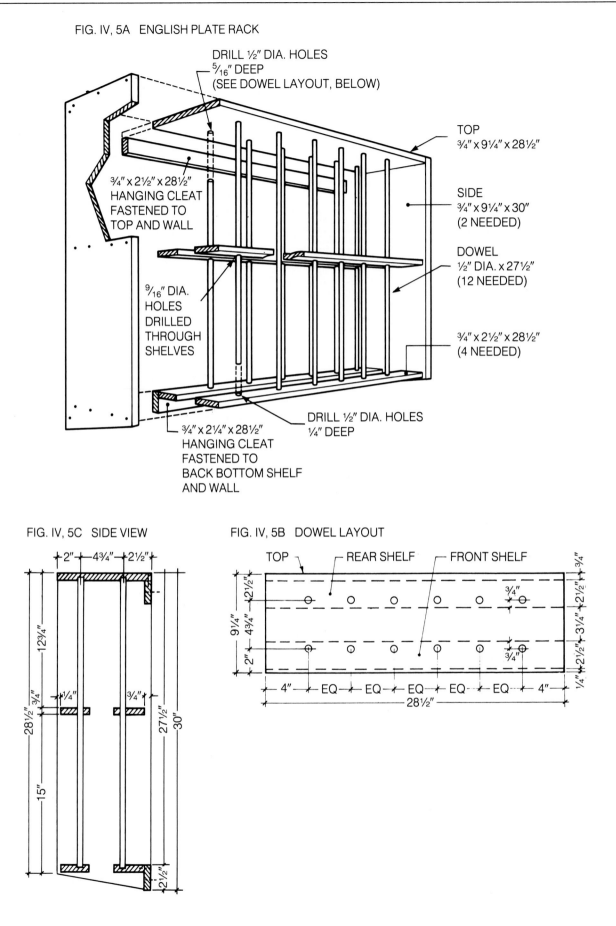

DRILL ½" DIA. HOLES
5/16" DEEP
(SEE DOWEL LAYOUT, BELOW)

TOP
¾" x 9¼" x 28½"

¾" x 2½" x 28½"
HANGING CLEAT
FASTENED TO
TOP AND WALL

SIDE
¾" x 9¼" x 30"
(2 NEEDED)

DOWEL
½" DIA. x 27½"
(12 NEEDED)

9/16" DIA.
HOLES
DRILLED
THROUGH
SHELVES

¾" x 2½" x 28½"
(4 NEEDED)

DRILL ½" DIA. HOLES
¼" DEEP

¾" x 2¼" x 28½"
HANGING CLEAT
FASTENED TO
BACK BOTTOM SHELF
AND WALL

FIG. IV, 5C   SIDE VIEW

2"   4¾"   2½"

12¾"

28½"   ¾"   ¼"   ¾"   27½"   30"

15"

2½"

FIG. IV, 5B   DOWEL LAYOUT

TOP   REAR SHELF   FRONT SHELF

¾"

9¼"   2½"   4¾"   2"

2½"   3¼"   2½"

¼"   3¾"   3¾"

4"   EQ   EQ   EQ   EQ   EQ   4"
28½"

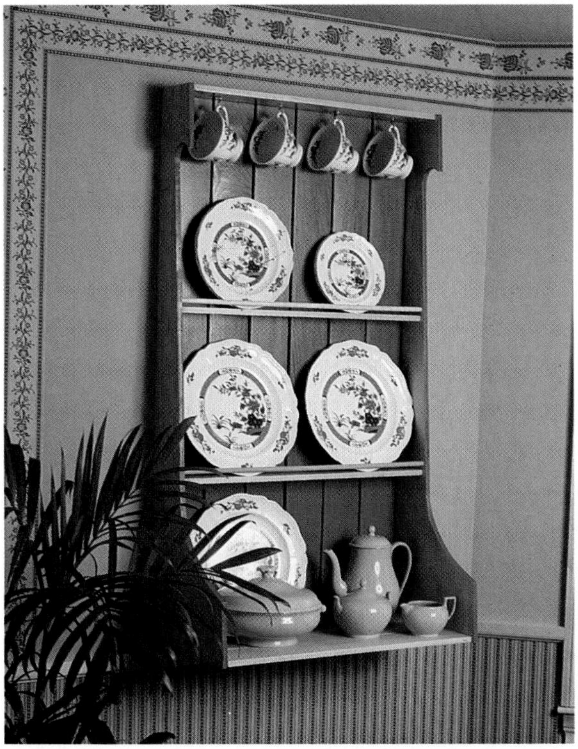

China Showcase

Materials: One ½-inch-thick 2 x 4-foot quarter panel of AA Int. grade birch plywood, with grain running the length; 32 feet of ½ x 3½-inch lattice; 4 feet of ⅜-inch-diameter wooden dowel; 1¼-inch-long wire brads; 4 cup hooks; wood glue; sandpaper; tack cloth; slate blue paint; paintbrushes; satin polyurethane; paper; graphite paper; stylus or old ballpoint pen; power saw or cross cut saw; jigsaw or coping saw; power drill with ⅜-inch bit; hammer.

Code	***Pieces***	***Size***
A (LAT)	(6)	½" x 3½" x 40½" Back slats
B (LAT)	(1)	½" x 3½" x 22" Top
C (LAT)	(3)	½" x 3½" x 22" Bottom shelf slats
D (LAT)	(1)	½" x 3½" x 22" Lower shelf
E (LAT)	(1)	½" x 2½" x 22" Upper shelf
F (PLY)	(2)	½" x 11¼" x 40½" Sides
G (DOW)	(2)	⅜" dia. x 22½" Rails

Directions:

1. Enlarge the pattern for the F sides in Fig. IV, 6B onto paper, following the directions on page 241. Using the graphite paper and stylus or old ballpoint pen, transfer the pattern to the plywood. Cut out the F sides with the jigsaw or coping saw.

2. Cut the lattice and dowel parts to size following the chart above. Sand all the parts, and wipe off all the sawdust with the tack cloth.

3. Paint the A back slats slate blue.

4. Glue and nail the A back slats to the B top and to one C bottom shelf slat, flush at the ends of B and C *(see* Fig. IV, 6B*)*. Space the A back slats 3/16 inch apart *(see* Fig. IV, 6A*)*.

5. Glue and nail the D lower shelf to the A back slats 11¼ inches above the C bottom shelf slat. Glue and nail the E upper shelf to the A back slats 12 inches above the D lower shelf *(see* Fig. IV, 6A*)*.

6. Drill two ¼-inch-deep ⅜-inch-diameter blind holes in each F side for the G rails *(see* Fig. IV, 6B*)*. Glue and nail one F side to the A/B/C/D/E case assembly *(see* Fig. IV, 6A*)*. Check that the shelves are square. Insert the G rails in their holes. Place the remaining F side in position. If all the parts fit together well, glue and nail the remaining F side to the case assembly.

7. Glue and nail the remaining two C bottom shelf slats in position; space the bottom slats 3/16 inch apart *(see* Fig. IV, 6A*)*.

8. Paint the front edges of the F sides slate blue.

9. Sand the china case, and wipe off all the sawdust with the tack cloth; sand lightly over the painted areas. Using a paintbrush, apply two coats of the polyurethane to the entire china case, sanding lightly between coats. When the polyurethane is dry, attach the four cup hooks, evenly spaced, to the B top.

FIG. IV, 6A CHINA SHOWCASE

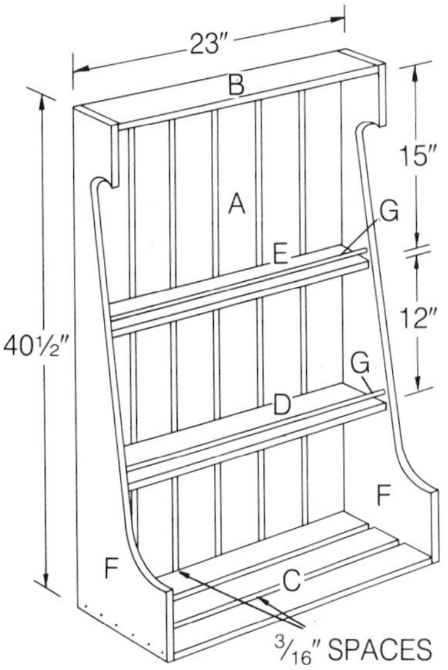

FIG. IV, 6B
SIDE PATTERN

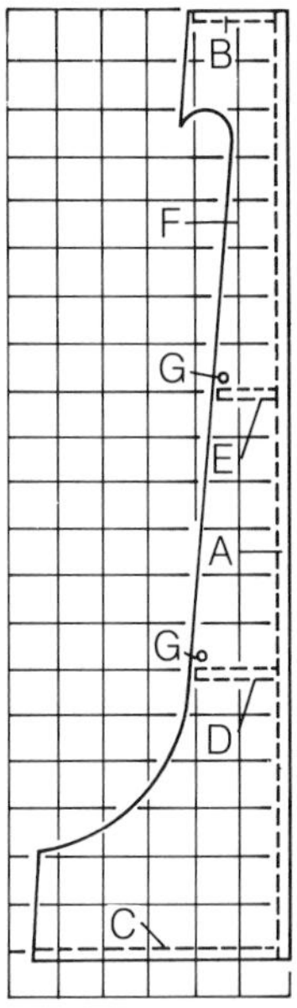

1 SQ. = 2"

T·A·B·L·E
T·O·P·P·E·R·S

*Spread the table
and contention will cease.*
—English Proverb

FRENCH COUNTRY TABLE SETTING
(52-inch-wide table runner; 13 x 19-inch place mats; 17-inch square napkins)

TABLE RUNNER
Materials: Zweigart 53-inch-wide Sondrio cross stitch fabric in white; matching thread; DMC embroidery floss: No. 797 Royal Blue; embroidery hoop; tapestry needle.
Directions:
1. Purchase the fabric according to the length of your table; include enough yardage for about a 10-inch drop at each end. Cut the fabric about ¾ inch outside the diamonds on all sides. Machine-stitch ¾ inch from the raw edges on all four sides. Fringe the edges to the stitching lines.
2. The fabric is woven to form alternating plain and patterned diamonds. The cross stitch motif is worked in every other plain diamond *(see photo)*, and in each corner of the runner. The motif can be worked this way just on the drop, or across the entire runner and along the top edges. Using the tapestry needle, embroidery hoop and two strands of embroidery floss, center and cross stitch the motif in FIG. IV, 7 in every other plain diamond *(see Stitch Guide, page 240).*

PLACE MATS
Materials: Hamilton Adams Imports 45-inch-wide Flax Tweed 50 fabric in white; matching thread; DMC embroidery floss: No. 797 Royal Blue; embroidery hoop; tapestry needle.
Directions:
1. For each place mat, cut a 13 x 19-inch fabric rectangle with three diamonds centered across it. Cut ¾ inch outside the diamonds on all sides. Machine-stitch ¾ inch from the raw edges on all sides. Fringe the edges to the stitching lines.
2. Using the tapestry needle, embroidery hoop and two strands of embroidery floss, center and cross stitch the motif in FIG. IV, 7 in each diamond of the place mat *(see Stitch Guide).*

NAPKINS
Materials: Royal blue linen; matching thread.
Directions:
For each napkin, cut an 18-inch linen square. Press under ¼ inch twice on each side. To miter each corner, open out the folds at the corner. Fold the corner under diagonally at the point where the inner side folds cross. Cut off the corner ¼ inch above the diagonal fold. Refold the sides as before, forming the miter. Edgestitch the side hems in place along the inner folded edges.

FIG. IV, 7 FRENCH COUNTRY TABLE SETTING CROSS STITCH MOTIF

COUNTRY MORNING BREAKFAST SETTING

General Directions:

A small print floral bed sheet with a border design is used to make the curtains (the border design is the curtains' bottom edge), and the place mats and napkins. The remainder of the floral sheet and a coordinating bold stripe bed sheet are used to make the ruffled pillows and the berry basket lining. Use the photo as a guide in coordinating bed sheets to use as the fabrics.

COUNTRY CURTAINS

Materials: Small floral print unfitted bed sheet with border design; matching thread; curtain rod.

Directions:

1. Install the curtain rod at the top of the window, or in the middle for café curtains. Measure from the top of the rod to the sill, and add 4¼ inches for the length. Measure the width of the window. Cut two rectangles of this length and width from the bed sheet, placing the sheet's border design so it is at the bottom edge of each rectangle.

2. Turn under ½ inch at each side edge of the rectangles, and stitch. Hem each rectangle's raw top edge ¼ inch. At each top edge, turn a 2-inch hem to the back, and stitch over the ¼-inch sewing line. Stitch again down the center of each hem to make a rod casing and heading. Slip the curtains over the rod.

SCALLOPED PLACE MAT

Materials: Small floral print bed sheet remaining from Country Curtains; matching machine quilting thread; double-fold bias tape in complementary color; matching thread; thin synthetic batting; scalloped plastic place mat or brown paper; tailor's chalk; ruler; sharp hard-lead pencil.

Directions:

1. Use the scalloped plastic place mat as the pattern. Or make your own pattern by cutting a 15 x 22-inch rectangle from the brown paper, and folding it in quarters to 11 x 7½ inches. Draw three and a half evenly spaced scallops freehand along the open top, and two and a half scallops along the open right side; start the half scallops at the top left and lower right edges. Cut out the folded rectangle along the scalloped edges, and open the paper for the full pattern.

2. Place the plastic or paper pattern on the sheet. Using the tailor's chalk, trace a mat top and bottom. Cut out the traced shapes. Place the plastic or paper pattern on the batting, and cut around the pattern.

3. Fold the mat top in quarters, and mark the centerpoint at the corner of the inside fold. Unfold the top. Using the ruler and sharp hard-lead pencil, draw radiating lines lightly from the centerpoint to the inside curves where the scallops meet; these are the quilting lines.

4. Place the mat bottom, wrong side up, on a flat surface. Place the mat batting and the top, right side up, on the mat bottom. With all edges even, pin the layers together.

5. Using the machine quilting thread and close ⅛-inch stitches, and working from the center out, machine-quilt along the radiating lines.

6. Bind the mat's edges with the bias tape; turn in the tape's raw ends ½ inch, and overlap the tape 1 inch where the ends meet.

SCALLOPED NAPKIN

Materials: Small floral print bed sheet, double-fold bias tape and matching thread remaining from Scalloped Place Mat; brown paper; tailor's chalk.

Directions:

1. Cut a 10-inch square from the brown paper. Scallop the square's top edge and right side following the directions in Scalloped Place Mat, Step 1.

2. Cut a 20-inch square from the bed sheet. Fold the fabric square in quarters to a 10-inch square, with the two open sides at the top and right. Place the paper pattern on the folded fabric so the left and bottom edges of the pattern are flush with the folded fabric's left and bottom edges. Using the tailor's chalk, trace the scallops onto the folded fabric. Keeping the fabric folded, cut out the scalloped edges. Unfold the fabric.

3. Bind the edges of the napkin with the bias tape, following the directions in Scalloped Place Mat, Step 6.

Curly locks, Curly locks,
Wilt thou be mine?
Thou shalt not wash dishes
Nor yet feed the swine;
But sit on a cushion
And sew a fine seam,
And feed upon strawberries,
Sugar and cream.
— Nursery Rhyme

RUFFLED SQUARE PILLOW
(about 18 inches square, plus ruffle)

Materials: Small floral print bed sheet remaining from Scalloped Napkin *(page 128)*; coordinating bold stripe unfitted bed sheet; matching threads; 18-inch square knife-edge pillow form, or synthetic stuffing.

Directions (½-inch seams allowed):

1. Use one of the bed sheets for the pillow front and back, and the other bed sheet for the ruffle. Cut two 19-inch fabric squares for the pillow front and back. Cut a 4 x 216-inch strip, pieced as necessary, for the triple-fullness ruffle.

2. Stitch the short ends of the ruffle strip together to make a loop. Fold the loop in half lengthwise, wrong sides together, and press the fold. Divide the loop in half at the seam, and pin mark at the opposite raw edge. Halve the loop again, and pin mark at the quarters; the pin marks denote the four corners of the pillow. Using the longest machine stitch and leaving long thread ends at the beginning and end, sew a gathering row around the loop between the marks ½ inch from the raw edges. As you reach each mark, lift the presser foot and pull the ruffle away to create 8 inches of slack in the thread. Resume sewing ⅛ inch from where you left off. Repeat ¼ inch outside the first gathering row. Gather the ruffle evenly to 18 inches between the beginning and the first mark by pulling up on the bobbin threads. Secure the gathers by wrapping the threads in a figure "8" around a straight pin inserted at a right angle to the ruffle edge. Cut the first slack thread 4 inches from the first mark, and wrap the thread around the pin to secure it. Repeat between the remaining marks until the entire ruffle is gathered to fit an 18-inch square.

3. Pin the ruffle to the pillow front right sides together, matching the quarter marks to the pillow corners, and baste. Sew on top of the inner gathering stitchline. Remove the thread ends, pins and basting.

4. With right sides together and the ruffle between, sew the pillow back to the pillow front around three sides and four corners. Turn the pillow right side out, and stuff it. Turn in the open edges, and slipstitch the opening closed *(see Stitch Guide, page 240)*.

COUNTRY WAYS

Healthful Honey

Natural honey, produced by bees from flower nectar, is widely recommended by folk doctors for a variety of ills. Some folk "cures" are grounded more in superstition than fact, but the revived interest in herbal medicine has revealed that many old-fashioned remedies actually are medically sound.

▼ Depending on the kinds of flowers used to make the honey and the type of soil in which they grew, honey can be rich in minerals and some vitamins.

▼ One Vermont folk doctor noted that honey can have a gentle sedative effect on high-strung people. It can help relax the body, soothe the stomach, and act as a mild laxative. Honey even has been known to relieve pain from arthritis.

▼ The same Vermont doctor recommended honey, along with regular toilet training, to prevent bed-wetting in children. The doctor held to a common theory of the time that bed-wetting often occurred in children who were nervous by nature; honey's sedative effect helped calm them. In addition, levulose, the type of sugar found in honey, is known to attract moisture (that's why breads and cakes made with honey remain moist for long periods). According to the doctor, feeding a child a teaspoonful of honey before bedtime would help the child retain the fluid in his body throughout the night.

BERRY BASKET

Materials: Small floral print bed sheet, coordinating bold stripe bed sheet and matching threads remaining from Ruffled Square Pillow *(page 130)*; thin synthetic batting remaining from Scalloped Place Mat *(page 128)*; 8-inch-high round woven basket.

Directions (½-inch seams allowed):

1. Measure the basket's girth (G) at the widest part. Measure the basket's height (H). Add 1 inch to G and 2 inches to H, and cut two floral print rectangles with those measurements for the lining. Cut a bold stripe rectangle measuring G plus 1 inch by H for the cover. Also cut a 1 x 24-inch floral print strip for the bow.
2. Sew the floral print rectangles right sides together along the top edge. Sew the short ends together to make a pocket. Turn the pocket right side out, and slide a layer of the batting into the pocket to make a padded lining. Edgestitch the raw bottom edges of the lining together to enclose the batting.
3. Press the top and bottom edges of the bold stripe rectangle ½ inch to the wrong side. Sew the short ends right sides together to make a loop. Turn the cover right side out, and slip it over the lining, stopping 1 inch below the lining's top edge. Slipstitch the cover to the lining along the cover's top and bottom edges *(see Stitch Guide, page 240)*.
4. Fold a ¼-inch hem along both long edges of the floral print strip, and press. Fold the strip in half lengthwise, and topstitch along the long edge and short ends. Make a bow with the strip, and tack it below the outer top edge of the lining *(see photo, page 129)*. Tuck the covered lining into the basket.

C O U N T R Y   W A Y S

The History of Baskets

Functional in design and pretty to look at, the rustic appeal of baskets represents the elements of country style at its best.

▼ According to many experts, the making of baskets is one of the oldest crafts in America. Native Americans wove baskets long before the arrival of the first European immigrants. Early settlers brought baskets with them from Europe, or obtained them through trade with the Indians. Eventually the colonists began crafting their own baskets, making them out of grasses, twigs, wood splints and roots. By the beginning of the nineteenth century, baskets were made for commercial use.
▼ The Shakers were renowned for their beautiful, well-made baskets. By 1837, the Shakers were selling more than 70 varieties of baskets outside their own communities.
▼ The most widely produced baskets in the 1800's were splint baskets woven from ash, oak and hickory.
▼ Colonial settlers used powdered pigments mixed with oil or buttermilk to color their baskets. This homemade paint provided more than color — it protected baskets from damp weather and wear and tear.

ENGLISH COTTAGE TEA COZY

Materials: 36-inch-wide fabric: ¼ yard of white calico and ½ yard of yellow calico; scrap of red calico fabric; ½ yard of lining fabric; matching threads; synthetic batting; embroidery needle; embroidery hoop; embroidery floss: Black, Light and Dark Pink, Red, Yellow, Gold, Blue, Light Green, Medium Green and Dark Green; tracing paper; dressmaker's carbon; tracing wheel.

Directions (½-inch seams allowed):
1. Cutting: From the white calico fabric, cut a cottage Front and cottage Back, each 6 inches high and 12 inches wide. Also cut two 5 x 9-inch Gables. Fold each Gable in half lengthwise to 2½ x 9 inches. Starting 4 inches from the bottom of each, draw a slightly curved line to the top of the center fold, cut on the drawn line, and open. **From the yellow calico fabric,** cut a 14 x 15-inch Roof. **From the red calico scrap,** cut a 5 x 8-inch Chimney. Cut a batting piece to match each cottage piece. Baste each batting piece to the back of its cottage piece, except for the cottage Front. **From the lining fabric,** cut two 8 x 16-inch pieces.

2. Embroidery: On tracing paper, draw a 4 x 10-inch rectangle. Draw a seam allowance ½ inch above the top long edge. Using the photo as a design and placement guide, draw a door at the center, resting on the bottom line. Draw two windows. Draw vines, with leaves that are up to ½ inch long. Using the dressmaker's carbon and tracing wheel, trace the embroidery lines onto the cottage Front, centered between the ends, with the top edge matching the top line. Place the cottage Front in the embroidery hoop. Using the embroidery needle and six strands of embroidery floss, outline the door and windows in Black, and fill in with Black long and short stitches *(see Stitch Guide, page 240)*. Work the vines in Dark Green stem stitch, and the leaves in Light and Medium Green satin stitch. Work the flowers in Light and Dark Pink, Red and Yellow lazy daisy stitch, with Yellow French knot centers *(see photo)*. Scatter Blue French knots around the vines and leaves. When the embroidery is finished, baste the matching batting piece to the back of the cottage Front.

3. Roof Seam: Right sides together, sew the Roof to the cottage Back and Front, stopping ¾ inch from each end *(see* FIG. IV, 8*)*. Turn under 2½ inches at each seamed edge of the Roof, and stitch across the ends. Bring in each side of the Roof to match the side of the attached cottage piece *(see* FIG. IV, 8*)*; the extra fabric

will form a pleat at the top edge of the cottage piece. Stitch down the side edges through all layers. Stitch across the top edges through the pleats.

4. Chimney: Fold the Chimney in half, right side in, to 2½ x 8 inches, and sew the ends and long edge, leaving an opening for turning. Turn the Chimney right side out, turn in the open edges, and slipstitch the opening closed *(see Stitch Guide)*. Sew the ends of the Chimney, 2 inches apart, to the center of the Roof to make a handle *(see photo)*.

FIG. IV, 8   ENGLISH COTTAGE TEA COZY

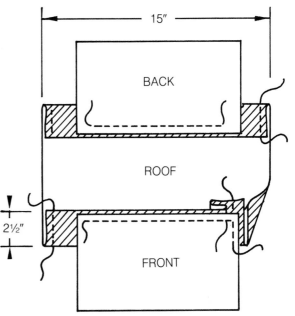

5. Gables: Sew a Gable at each end of the cottage, matching the Gable's center to the center of the Roof. Turn the cottage right side out.

6. Lining: With right sides together, sew the lining pieces together at the short ends and one long edge. Turn up 1½ inches at the bottom edge of the cottage. Slide the lining inside the cottage, with a lining side seam at the center of each Gable. Turn in the lining's raw edge, and slipstitch the lining to the cottage around the bottom.

Thank God for tea! What would the world do without tea? — how did it exist? I am glad I was not born before tea.

—Sydney Smith

TILED TRAY & TRIVET

TRAY

Materials: 6 feet of ½ x 2⅝-inch lattice; ¼ x 13 x 18 inches of plywood; ¾-inch-long wire brads; 1-inch-long wire brads; six ½ x 5⅞-inch square tiles; tracing paper; graphite paper; stylus or old ballpoint pen; wood glue; wood putty; sandpaper; tack cloth; wood stain; wax; hot glue gun or countertop cement; cross-cut saw; rip saw; sabre saw; miter box; hammer; nail set.

Code	Pieces	Size
A (PLY)	(1)	¼" x 12¼" x 17⅛" Bottom
B (LAT)	(2)	½" x 2" x 17⅝" Sides
B1 (LAT)	(2)	½" x 2⅝" x 12¾" Ends
C	(6)	½" x 5⅞" x 5⅞" Tiles

Directions:

1. Cut the A bottom to size. Cut a ¼-inch square rabbet in the lattice *(see* FIG. IV, 9B*)*. Miter-cut the B sides and B1 ends to size *(see* FIG. IV, 9A*)*. Rip the B sides to 2 inches in width.

2. Enlarge the handle pattern in FIG. IV, 9B onto tracing paper, following the directions on page 241. Using the graphite paper and stylus or old ballpoint pen, transfer the pattern to the B1 ends. Cut out the handles with the sabre saw.

FIG. IV, 9A   TILED TRAY

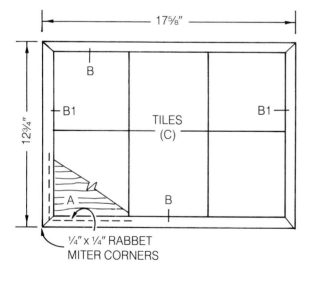

¼" x ¼" RABBET
MITER CORNERS

FIG. IV, 9B   TILED TRAY

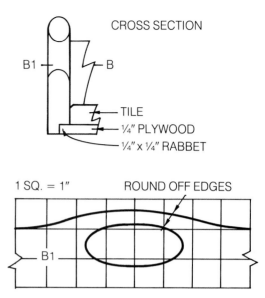

CROSS SECTION

B1   B

TILE
¼" PLYWOOD
¼" x ¼" RABBET

1 SQ. = 1"   ROUND OFF EDGES

B1

3. Using 1-inch wire brads, glue and nail the B sides to the B1 ends.

4. Using ¾-inch wire brads, glue and nail the A bottom to the B/B1 assembly *(see* FIG. IV, 9B*)*.

5. Set the nails. Fill the nail holes with wood putty, and sand them smooth. Sand the entire tray, and round off the edges. Remove all the sawdust with the tack cloth. Stain the tray. When the stain has dried, wax the tray.

6. Glue the C tiles in place with the hot glue gun or countertop cement.

TRIVET

Materials: 3 feet of ¾ x 1¼-inch pine; one ½ x 5⅞-inch square tile; 1½-inch-long finishing nails; wood glue; wood putty; sandpaper; tack cloth; wood stain; wax; hot glue gun; cross-cut saw; miter box; hammer; nail set.

Code	Pieces	Size
A	(4)	¾" x 1¼" x 7⅞" Frame
B	(1)	½" x 5⅞" x 5⅞" Tile

Directions:

1. Cut a ¼ x ⅜-inch rabbet in the pine strip *(see* FIG. IV, 9C*)*. Miter-cut the A frame pieces to size.

2. Glue and nail the A pieces together to form the frame *(see* FIG. IV, 9C*)*. Set the nails. Fill the nail holes with the wood putty, and sand them smooth. Sand the entire trivet, and round off the edges. Remove all the sawdust with the tack cloth. Stain the trivet. When the stain has dried, wax the trivet.

3. Glue the B tile in place with the hot glue gun.

FIG. IV, 9C TRIVET

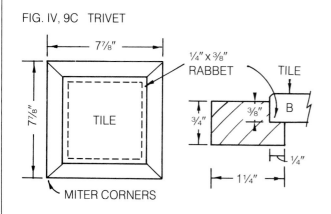

And I will make thee beds of roses
And a thousand fragrant posies.
—Christopher Marlowe

FIG. IV, 10 PRETTY POSIES EMBROIDERED NAPKIN

PRETTY POSIES EMBROIDERED NAPKIN

Materials: Polyester/cotton napkin; transfer pencil; tracing paper; embroidery floss: 1 skein each of Red, Orange Rust, Pale Green, Dark Blue Green, Pink and Light Salmon; No. 6 or 7 embroidery needle; embroidery hoop; ¾-inch-wide cotton lace trim; iron; sewing machine; terry cloth towel.

Directions:

1. Using the transfer pencil, trace the full-size half design in FIG. IV, 10 onto folded tracing paper. Then trace the tracing on the other side of the paper. Unfold the paper for the full design.

2. Place the tracing, pencil side down, on the napkin at a corner *(see photo, page 132)*. Set the iron on the cotton/polyester setting, and transfer the design with the iron.

3. Place the napkin in the embroidery hoop. Using the photo as a color guide, and following the stitch key in FIG. IV, 10, embroider the flowers, stems and leaves with the embroidery needle and three strands of embroidery floss *(see Stitch Guide, page 240)*. Work a border of Dark Blue Green backstitches around the napkin ¼ inch from the edges *(see Stitch Guide)*.

4. Machine-stitch the lace trim edging to the napkin. Press the finished napkin, right side down, on the terry cloth towel.

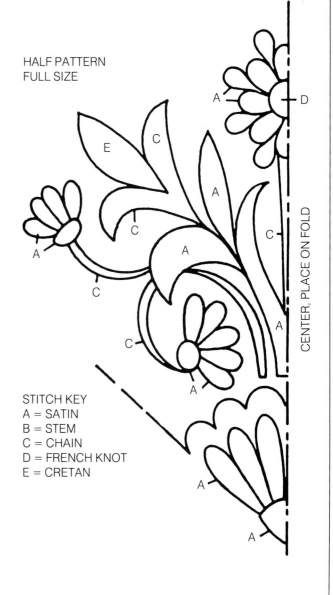

HALF PATTERN
FULL SIZE

CENTER, PLACE ON FOLD

STITCH KEY
A = SATIN
B = STEM
C = CHAIN
D = FRENCH KNOT
E = CRETAN

COUNTRY WAYS
Fingernailing the Future

It was said that you could tell a lot about people by the size and shape of their fingernails.

▼ People with short, stubby fingernails were thought to be gossips and tattletales. Children who bit their nails would not grow tall. People with long fingernails would enjoy a long life.

▼ There even was a formula, carried over from medieval times, for telling your fortune according to the day your nails were trimmed:
"Cut them on Monday, you cut them for news,
Cut them on Tuesday, a new pair of shoes.
Cut them on Wednesday, you cut them for health.
Cut them on Thursday, you cut them for wealth.
Cut them on Friday, a sweetheart you'll know.
Cut them on Saturday, a-journey you'll go.
Cut them on Sunday, you cut them for evil,
For all the next week, you'll be ruled by the devil."

*For everything that's lovely is
But a brief, dreamy kind delight.*
—William Butler Yeats

LOVELY AS LACE TABLECLOTH
(about 61 x 98 inches at the widest and longest dimensions of the oval)

Materials: Phildar Relais 8 or Perle 8 cotton thread: 21 balls of White or Ecru; size 1 mm crochet hook, OR ANY SIZE HOOK TO OBTAIN GAUGE BELOW.

Gauge: 52 sts or 17 holes = 4 inches; 17 rows = 4 inches.

Stitches Used:

Picot: Ch 3, sc in first ch.

Treble Mesh Pattern, Row 1: Ch 3 (counts as first tr), * ch 2, sk 2 sts, tr in next st; rep from * across. **Row 2:** Ch 3 (counts as first tr), * ch 2, tr in next tr; rep from * across. Repeat Row 2 for tr mesh pattern. **To Form Motifs of Filled Squares in Tr:** Work 2 tr in each ch-2 space, and tr in each tr on each side of ch-2. Any 2 adjacent filled squares share 1 tr and have a total of 7 tr. **Inc in Tr at End of Row:** After the last tr, work ** yo 3 times, insert hook at base of last tr, yo and draw up a lp, (draw yarn through 2 lps) 4 times; rep from ** for each inc required. **Inc at Beg of Row:** At the end of the previous row, ch 3 for each mesh to be inc, turn, ch 3 (for beg tr), then continue in tr mesh in ch.

Directions:

1. Tablecloth: Ch 70. Using the chart on page 242 as a guide, work the tablecloth in treble mesh pattern. To work the open spaces, ch 3 for each mesh skipped plus 1 ch. To fill the open spaces, 3 tr for each mesh filled plus 1 tr.

2. Edging, Round 1: Sc in next st, * ch 7, work in sc in the appropriate st to allow the ch 7 to lie flat loosely, not tautly; rep from * around, end sl st in beg sc, ch 1. **Round 2:** 7 sc in ch-7 sp, * sc in sc, 7 sc in ch-7 sp; rep from * around, join with sl st to beg ch 1, ch 1. **Round 3:** * Ch 7, sc in next sc; rep from * around. **Round 4:** Rep Round 2. **Round 5:** * Ch 9, sc in next sc; rep from * around. **Round 6:** * (Sc, hdc, dc, 2 tr, picot, 2 tr, dc, hdc, sc) in ch-9 sp, sc in next sc; rep from * around. Fasten off.

3. Finishing: Press the tablecloth on the wrong side with a damp cloth and warm iron.

The firm, the enduring, the simple,
and the modest are near to virtue.
—Confucius

FLYING GEESE AMISH TABLE RUNNER
(48 x 18 inches)

Materials: 45-inch-wide solid color fabric: 1½ yards of red, ⅝ yard of purple, and ½ yard of black; matching threads; white thread; 22 x 52 inches of synthetic batting; clear plastic template material (available in quilting and some sewing supply stores) or crisp cardboard; sharp white pencil; masking tape; quilter's or safety pins; darner or milliner's needle; between needle; black quilting thread; quilting hoop.

Directions (¼-inch seams allowed):

1. Patterns: Trace or transfer the patterns for patches A, B, C and D in FIG. IV, 11A *(page 140)* onto the clear plastic template material or crisp cardboard. Also draw a 2½ x 3½-inch rectangle for patch E. Cut out the patch templates carefully; the templates include the ¼-inch seam allowance. Use the sharp white pencil to trace around each template on the wrong side of the fabric. Use common edges when tracing to avoid wasting fabric.

2. Cutting: From the red fabric, cut a 22 x 52-inch quilt back. Then mark and cut sixteen E patches, six B patches, and two D patches. Flip the D template, and cut two more D patches. *From the purple fabric,* cut four 18½ x 3½-inch strips. Then cut eight B patches, and sixteen E patches. *From the black fabric,* cut four C patches, twenty-four A patches, sixteen E patches, and two B patches.

3. Center Block: Following the diagram in FIG. IV, 11B *(page 141)*, and using the photo as a color guide, sew the patches together to make the center block.

4. Triangle Panels: Sew the long edge of a black A patch to each short edge of the six red and remaining six purple B patches. Alternating purple and red units *(see photo)*, sew them to make two strips of six B patches each. At each long edge of each strip, sew a long purple strip. Using the photo as a placement guide, sew the triangle panels to the center block.

5. Border Strip: Sew each black E patch between a purple and red E patch at the long edges to make a three-patch unit. Sew eight units together to make a border *(see photo)*. Repeat. Sew a border to each long edge of the quilt top.

6. Basting: Spread the red quilt back, wrong side up, on a table and tape down the corners. Center the batting and the quilt top, right side up, on the quilt back. Using the quilter's or safety pins, pin together the three layers, from the center outward, straight to each edge and diagonally to each corner. Using the darner or milliner's needle, single lengths of the white thread and long stitches, baste through the three layers in the same directions you pinned. Baste additional horizontal and vertical rows 4 inches apart.

7. Quilting: Place the quilt in the quilting hoop, starting at the center of the quilt. Using the between needle and quilting thread, sew even running stitches through all three layers ⅛ inch from each seam.

8. Binding: Trim the batting flush with the quilt top. Trim the quilt back 1 inch outside the quilt top. At each outside edge of the quilt back, turn up ½ inch, then ½ inch again, and slipstitch the fold to the quilt top *(see Stitch Guide, page 240)*. Remove the basting.

COUNTRY WAYS
Bees and Change-Work

Most of us are familiar with the old-time quilting bee, where the women of a village or farming community would gather to work together on a quilt for one of the families. Many hands at work helped to complete the complex project in a relatively short time. The demands of farm and family left little time for gaiety, so a bee was an ideal way for folks to combine a social occasion with a practical purpose.

▼ Bees were a common practice for women and men. Both husband and wife would attend, even if only one was working. Stories of old-time New England include tales of husking bees, when farmers would enlist the help of friends to strip the husks from Indian corn, and logging bees, where men would work together to clear land on which a neighbor was going to build. A bee usually was an all-day affair accompanied by good food, and sometimes followed by music and dancing.

▼ Change-work was another way that country folks make their chores more bearable. If two friends were planning to make soap or apple butter, or carry out some other large-scale task, one would spend the day at the other's home and help get the work done. In a day or two, the favor would be returned, and both friends would have their work finished with only half the strain. Many people still practice this country custom, particularly for spring cleaning and holiday baking.

FIG. IV, 11A   FLYING GEESE AMISH TABLE RUNNER
ALSO CUT PATCH E (2½″ x 3½″)

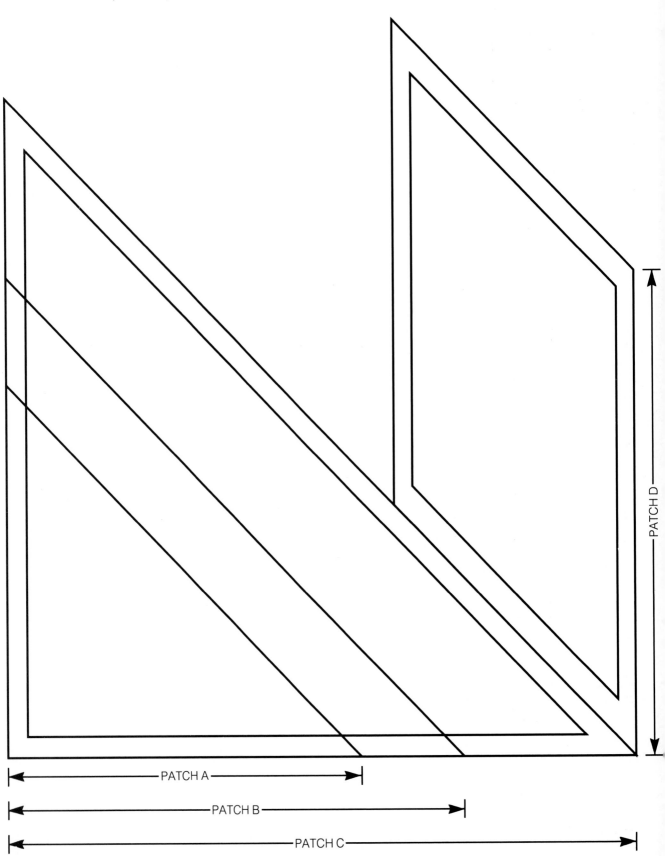

PATCH D

PATCH A

PATCH B

PATCH C

FIG. IV, 11B CENTER BLOCK, RUNNER

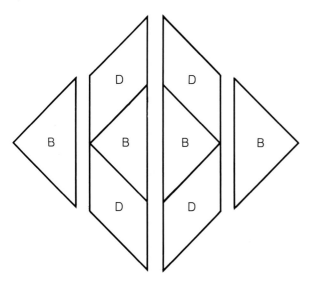

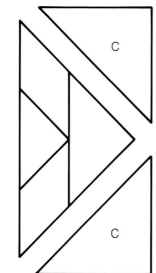

COUNTRY WAYS
The Plain Folk
"Plain and simple" are the hallmarks of the Amish, members of a religious sect characterized by its absolute reliance on biblical authority.

▼ Religious persecution in Europe forced the Amish to emigrate to Pennsylvania as early as 1727. There virtually are no Amish in Europe bearing the original name and upholding the traditional principles.

▼ The Beachy Amish (named for their leader Moses Beachy) split from the original order in 1927 when they decided to use automobiles. The Old Order Amish maintain the strict ways of their ancestors, avoiding the use of cars and electricity, and living chiefly by farming.

▼ The Amish often relied on nature for inspiration when making quilts; the "flying geese" pattern was so named because the lines of triangles resemble these wild birds flying in formation. It was also common for the Amish to deliberately stitch a flaw into a small section of their quilts. The "God's patch" is an Amish symbol of human imperfection to show that only God is perfect.

COUNTRY WAYS
Baby Talk
Superstitions, especially those connected to birth or babies, are as common among the Amish as they are in any other ethnic group.

▼ If a baby's baptismal water is saved and given to her when she is a bit older, she will become a first class singer.

▼ If a baby is born in a thunderstorm, he will die by lightening.

▼ If an old diaper is put on a baby at birth, she will become a thief.

▼ A baby must be carried on the left side when first nursing, or he will be left-handed.

▼ If a baby is weaned early in the spring, she may become permanently gray-haired.

▼ Nailing a horseshoe to a baby's crib will bring good luck, but it must be nailed convex side up so the luck won't run out.

DINING AL FRESCO: TABLECLOTH & CUSHIONS

Materials: Unfitted bed sheet; matching thread; matching piping; high loft synthetic batting; Scotchgard® *(optional).*

Directions:

1. Tablecloth: Measure the length and width of the tabletop. From the bed sheet, cut a rectangle that is 30 inches wider and 30 inches longer than the tabletop measurements.

2. Stitch a ¼-inch hem along each long edge, then hem each long edge again with a ½-inch hem. Hem the short ends the same way. The tablecloth will overhang the tabletop by about 14 inches at each edge and end.

3. Bench Cushions: Measure the length and width of one bench seat. From the sheet, cut four rectangles, each 6 inches wider and 6 inches longer than the bench seat measurements.

4. Pin the piping around all sides of two rectangles, right sides together, raw edges even, and ends overlapping. Cut eight 16-inch lengths of piping, and remove the cords. Pin a pair of lengths on opposite sides, under the pinned piping, 12 inches from each short end of each rectangle, for ties. Stitch the piping to the rectangles around all sides.

5. With right sides together, and the piping and ties in between, stitch each cushion top to a cushion bottom around three sides and four corners, leaving a 24-inch opening on the fourth side. Turn each cushion right side out through the opening.

6. Fold the batting to the desired thickness, and stuff it into the opening in each cushion, pushing the batting evenly into the cushion corners. Turn in the open edges on each cushion and tie, and slipstitch each opening closed *(see Stitch Guide, page 240).* Tie the cushions onto the benches under the seats *(see photo).*

7. If you wish, treat the tablecloth and cushions with Scotchgard®, following the manufacturer's directions.

COUNTRY WAYS
Weather Lore

Country folk in Early America were, by necessity, close to the ways of nature. By observing the weather and its effect on living things and everyday objects, the colonials attempted to predict fair and foul weather to come. Some of the observations below are mere superstition, while others are grounded in scientific fact.

▼ When ants travel in a straight line, expect rain; when they scatter, expect fair weather.

▼ A tough apple skin means a hard winter.

▼ If corn husks are thicker than usual, a cold winter is ahead.

▼ Cobwebs on grass are a sign of frost.

▼ When the scent of flowers is unusually prominent, rain is coming.

▼ When sunflowers raise their heads, rain is on the way.

▼ When floor matting shrinks, dry weather can be expected; when it expands, rain is coming.

▼ When milkweed closes at night, rain will follow.

▼ When birdsongs stop, listen for thunder.

▼ Geese fly higher in fair weather than in foul.

▼ Fish swimming near the surface and biting avidly means rain.

▼ If the barometer and thermometer both rise together, fine weather will follow.

▼ The bigger the moon's halo, the closer rain clouds are, and the sooner rain will fall.

LACE-EDGED TABLE LINENS

TOWEL EDGING

Materials: Phildar Perle 5 cotton thread (40-gram ball): 1 ball of White; size 9 steel crochet hook, OR ANY SIZE HOOK TO OBTAIN GAUGE BELOW; towel.

Gauge: Edging width = about 1½ inches.

Directions:

1. Edging: Begin with a chain slightly longer than the width of the towel, or the desired length. **Row 1:** Sc in 2nd ch from hook and in next 3 ch, * ch 5, sk next 4 ch, dc in next 5 ch, ch 5, sk next 4 ch, sc in next 7 ch; rep from * across for width of towel or desired length, ending with 4 sc instead of 7 sc. Cut off remaining ch. Ch 1, turn. **Row 2:** Sc in first 3 sc, sk next sc, * ch 5, dc in last ch of lp, dc in next 2 dc, ch 3, sk next dc, dc in next 2 dc, dc in first ch of lp, ch 5, sk next sc, sc in next 5 sc, sk next sc; rep from * across, ending with sc in last 3 sc. Ch 1, turn. **Row 3:** Sc in first 2 sc, sk next sc, * ch 5, dc in last 2 ch of lp, dc in next dc, sk next 2 dc, ch 5, sc in next ch-3 sp, ch 5, sk next 2 dc, dc in next dc, dc in first 2 ch of lp, ch 5, sk next sc, sc in next 3 sc, sk next sc; rep from * across, ending with sc in last 2 sc. Ch 1, turn. **Row 4:** Sc in first sc, sk next sc, * ch 5, dc in last 2 ch of lp, dc in next dc, sk next 2 dc, ch 5, sc in next ch-5 lp, ch 7, dc in next ch-5 lp, ch 5, sk next 2 dc, dc in next dc, dc in next 2 ch of lp, ch 5, sk next sc, sc in next sc; rep from * across. Turn. **Row 5:** Sl st in first 4 ch of lp, ch 3, dc in next ch, dc in next 2 dc, * sk 2 dc, ch 5, sk next ch-5 lp; holding back on hook the last lp of each tr, make 3 tr in the next ch-7 lp, yo and draw through all 4 lps on the hook—**cluster made**; (ch 5, sc in 5th ch from hook, make cluster in same ch-7 lp) 4 times; ch 5, sk next sc, ch-5 lp and next 2 dc, dc in next dc, dc in first 2 ch of ch-5 lp, skip next sc, dc in last 2 ch of ch-5 lp, dc in next dc; repeat from * across, ending with a dc in the last dc and following 2 ch. Fasten off.

2. Finishing: Place the edging on a padded ironing board, and steam press it flat. Position the edging on the towel, and stitch along the edging's sides and top edge. Tack the edging in a few spots to hold it in place.

FILET DIAMOND EDGING

Materials: Phildar Perle 5 cotton thread (40-gram ball): 1 ball of White; size 6 steel crochet hook, OR ANY SIZE HOOK TO OBTAIN GAUGE BELOW.

Gauge: Edging width = about 4½ inches.

Directions:

1. Edging: Starting at the narrow end, ch 46. **Row 1 (right side):** Tr (yo 2 times) in 5th ch from hook (counts as 2 tr), tr in each of next 8 ch; ch 2, sk 2 ch, tr in next ch—**1 sp made**; 1 sp; tr in each of next 3 ch—**1 bl made**; work 2 sps, 1 bl, 3 sps, tr in each of last 6 ch. Turn. **Row 2:** Ch 3 (counts as first tr); tr in next 3 tr—**1 bl over bl made**; ch 2, sk 2 tr, tr in next tr—**1 sp over bl made**; ch 2, sk 2 ch, tr in next tr—**1 sp over sp made**; 1 sp over sp; 2 tr in next ch-2 sp, tr in next tr—**1 bl over sp made**; 1 sp over bl, 1 bl over sp, 1 sp over sp, 1 sp over bl, 1 sp over sp, 1 bl over sp, tr in each of next 6 tr, do not work rem 3 sts. Turn. **Note:** Hereafter, the general term "bl" will refer to bl over bl, or bl over sp, and "sp" will refer to sp over bl, or sp over sp, as explained above. **Row 3:** Sl st across to 4th tr, work 3 bls, 1 sp, 3 bls, 1 sp, 1 bl, 2 sps, 1 bl. Turn. **Row 4:** Ch 3 (counts as first tr throughout), work 1 bl, 1 sp, 5 bls, 1 sp, 1 bl, 1 sp, 1 bl; do not work last 3 sts—**1 bl dec made at end of row**. **Row 5:** Sl st across to 4th tr—**1 bl dec made at beg of row**; ch 3, work 3 bls, 1 sp, 3 bls, 1 sp, 2 bls. Turn. **Row 6:** Ch 3, work 1 bl, 1 sp, 1 bl, 1 sp, 5 bls, 1 sp; * yo hook 3 times, insert hook in base of last tr worked, yo and draw up a lp, work off lps on hook 2 at a time; rep from * twice—**1 bl inc made at end of row**. **Row 7:** Ch 5, tr in 4th ch from hook, tr in next ch, tr in first tr—**1 bl inc made at beg of row**; 2 bls, 1 sp, 3 bls, 1 sp, 1 bl, 2 sps, 1 bl. Turn. Starting with Row 8, follow the chart in FIG. IV, 12A through Row 9. Then rep Rows 2 to 9 for the pattern, until the edging is the desired length. Fasten off.

2. Finishing: Place the edging on a padded ironing board, and steam press it flat. Pin and sew the long straight edge to the edge of a piece of linen.

GEOMETRIC EDGING

Materials: Phildar Perle 5 cotton thread (40-gram ball): 1 ball of White; size 6 steel crochet hook, OR ANY SIZE HOOK TO OBTAIN GAUGE BELOW.

Gauge: Edging width = about 5½ inches.

Directions:

1. Edging: Starting at the narrow end, ch 25. **Row 1 (right side):** Tr (yo 2 times) in 5th ch from hook (counts as 2 tr), tr in each of next 2 ch—**beg bl made**; * tr in each of next 3 ch—**1 bl made**; rep from * across—7 bls made. Turn. **Row 2:** Ch 5, tr in 4th ch from hook, tr in next ch, tr in first tr—**1 bl inc made at beg of row**; * ch 2, sk 2 tr, tr in next tr—**1 sp over bl made**; rep from * 6 times more. Turn. **Row 3:** Ch 5 (counts as first tr and ch-2), sk 2 ch, tr in next tr; ch 2, sk 2 ch, tr in next tr—**1 sp over sp made**; 1 sp over each of next 2 sps; 2 tr in next ch-2 sp, tr in next tr—**1 bl over sp made**; 1 bl over each of next 2 sps, 1 sp over bl; * yo hook 3 times, insert hook in base of last tr worked, yo and draw up a lp, work off lps on hook 2 at a time; rep from * twice—**1 bl inc made at end of row**. Turn. **Row 4:** Work 1 bl inc at beg of row, 1 sp over bl, 1 bl over sp; tr in each of next 3 tr—**1 bl over bl made**; work 1 bl over each of next 2 bls, 1 bl over sp, 1 sp over each of next 3 sps. Turn. Starting with Row 5, follow the chart in FIG. IV, 12B through Row 8. **Note:** Hereafter, the general term "bl" will refer to bl over bl, or bl over sp, and "sp" will refer to sp over bl, or sp over sp, as explained above. **Row 9:** Ch 3 (counts as first tr), work 4 bls, 1 sp, 1 bl, 1 sp, 4 bls, 1 sp, 1 bl; do not work last 3 sts—**1 bl dec made at end of row**. Turn. **Row 10:** Sl st across to 4th tr—**1 bl dec made at beg of row**; ch 3, work 1 bl, 1 sp, 2 bls, 1 sp, 3 bls, 1 sp, 2 bls, 1 sp. Turn. Continuing with Row 11, follow the chart in FIG. IV, 12B through Row 26. Then rep Rows 15 to 26 for the pattern, until the edging is the desired length. Fasten off.

2. Finishing: Place the edging on a padded ironing board, and steam press it flat. Pin and sew the long straight edge to the edge of a piece of linen.

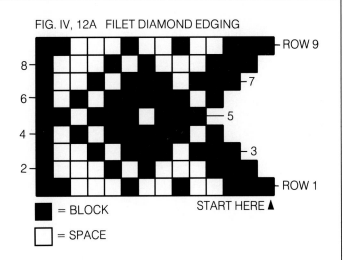

FIG. IV, 12A FILET DIAMOND EDGING

■ = BLOCK

□ = SPACE

START HERE ▲

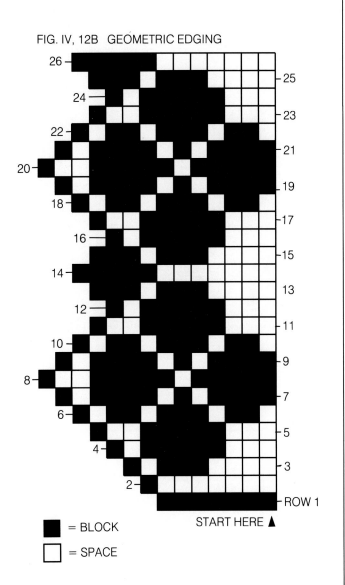

FIG. IV, 12B GEOMETRIC EDGING

■ = BLOCK

□ = SPACE

START HERE ▲

Among the several kinds of beauty
the eye takes most delight in colors.
—Joseph Addison

CHERRY-BRIGHT NAPKINS & PLACE MATS

Materials for Two Place Mats and Napkins:

45-inch-wide fabric: 1¼ yards of white polyester/cotton and ½ yard of red-and-white ⅛-inch check gingham; 8 yards of green double-fold bias tape; 4 yards of red single-fold bias tape; green and red threads; embroidery needle; embroidery hoop; embroidery floss: 1 skein each of Red, Deep Rose, Emerald and Leaf Green; tracing paper; dressmaker's carbon; tracing wheel; sewing machine.

Directions:

1. Napkins: For each napkin, cut an 18-inch square from the white fabric. Using the red thread and a machine zigzag stitch, bind the edges of each square, going around until the edges are cord-like *(see photo)*.

2. Trace the full size cherry design in FIG. IV, 13 onto tracing paper. Using the dressmaker's carbon and tracing wheel, transfer the design to a corner of each napkin *(see photo)*. To embroider each napkin, place it in the embroidery hoop. Using a single strand of embroidery floss doubled in the embroidery needle, work the stems and leaf veins in Emerald whipped stem stitch. Fill in the leaves with Leaf Green split stitch. Work the cherry highlights in Deep Rose split stitch, and fill in with Red split stitch *(see Stitch Guide, page 240)*. Begin at the edge of the design, and work toward the center.

3. Place Mats: For each place mat, cut an 18 x 12-inch rectangle from the gingham. From the green bias tape, cut two 20-inch and two 14-inch strips. Unfold the green strips, keeping the fold in the center, and press them. Sew each strip to an edge of the gingham rectangle, with the fold of the strip facing the center of the rectangle, and all raw edges even.

4. Cut two 20-inch and two 14-inch strips from the red bias tape. Open the red strips and sew them, right side facing down and fold on one side, over the green strips, with a red raw edge even with two green and a gingham raw edge.

5. Cut two 20 x 1½-inch and two 14 x 1½-inch strips from the white fabric. Place one long edge of each white strip even with same-length red, green and gingham raw edges, and sew. Open the white, red and green strips outward to make bands of color surrounding the gingham. Press, and miter the corners by hand. Sew down the loose edge of the red bias strips. Place the gingham mat right side up on the remaining uncut white fabric. Baste the mat to the white fabric near the mat edges, and cut off the excess white fabric. Bind all the edges of the mat with the remaining green bias tape.

FIG. IV,13 CHERRY-BRIGHT NAPKINS & PLACE MATS

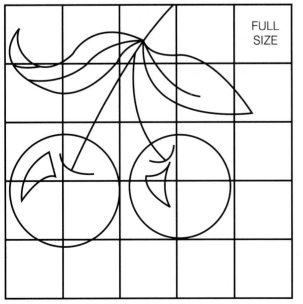

FULL SIZE

COUNTRY WAYS
Sewing Superstitions

The slightest deviation in daily routine could be deemed significant to superstitious country folk. In the Ozarks, there were superstitions governing all household chores, even sewing.

▼ If a woman sewing a new garment for herself broke a needle in the process, it was thought she wouldn't live to wear it out.

▼ A woman who sewed after sunset would be poverty-stricken all her life.

▼ Basting inadvertently left in a newly made garment was also a sign of poverty. Some people believed that it meant the cloth had not been paid for.

▼ It was considered bad luck to button a newly made garment before it had been worn, and a new shirt was supposed to be buttoned first on the person for whom it was made.

DO·IT·YOURSELF·DECOR

S·T·E·N·C·I·L IT
B·E·A·U·T·I·F·U·L

Better do it than wish it done.
—Anonymous

STENCIL A COUNTRY KITCHEN

Stenciling is a wonderful way to custom decorate your country kitchen. All the stencil projects shown in the photos on pages 150 and 153 were created from the stencil on page 152. The general directions for stenciling are below. Specific stenciling techniques are shown on page 154.

General Materials: Mylar® (available at craft supply stores), acetate sheets (available at art supply stores) or acetate report covers (available at office supply stores); acrylic paints, in tubes, jars and bottles, or spray cans; stencil brushes; natural sponges *(optional)*; toothbrush *(optional)*; masking tape; transparent tape; paper; tracing paper; black fine-point permanent felt tip pen; craft or utility knife; cardboard, piece of glass with edges taped, or piece of acrylic (available at home centers); paper toweling; palette knife *(optional; available at craft or art supply stores)*; cotton rags *(optional)*; rubbing alcohol *(optional).*

General Directions:

1. Cutting a Stencil: Cut a piece of the Mylar or acetate a few inches larger than the stencil design. Tape the acetate over the design with masking tape. Trace the design onto the acetate with the black felt tip pen. Using the cardboard, piece of glass with taped edges, or piece of acrylic as a cutting board, cut out the traced stencil sections with the craft or utility knife. Pull the knife toward you, and cut in a continuous motion. If the design needs to be turned, turn the acetate rather than the knife. Once the knife tip has pierced the acetate, do not lift the tip again until you have finished cutting the line or curve. If you make a mistake or the acetate tears, repair the spot with a piece of transparent tape.

2. Partial Stencils: Choose one part of the stencil design, such as the leaves or basket, and make a separate acetate stencil just of that part. Or cover the unwanted portions of the full stencil with masking tape and paper, and paint through the open spaces only.

3. Border Stencils: Make several tracing paper tracings, or photocopies, of one part of the stencil design. Draw or tape a guideline on the cutting board. Tape the copies, evenly spaced, against the guideline until you have an easy-to-handle length. Create a different border by turning every other copy upside down *(see window and curtain borders, page 153)*. Trace and cut a continuous acetate stencil.

4. Corner Stencils: Use the same method to make a quarter stencil for a four-sided border *(see table top, page 153)*. Tape one or two copies of the stencil part

to one corner of the table, so the copies create a mitered or squared-off corner. At the center of each of the corner's two edges, tape another copy of the stencil part. Tape additional copies, evenly spaced, between the center and corner copies; place all the copies the same distance from the table edges. Tape all the copies to each other, so you can move the single, L-shape border from the table to the cutting board. Trace and cut a continuous, L-shape acetate stencil. Place the acetate stencil at each corner of the table, matching the centers of the table edges to the stencil's centers.

5. Stencil Paints: Use acrylic paints to stencil. They are fast-drying, need only a quick water clean-up, and come in a wide variety of colors. Use a different stencil brush, or sponge, for each color you use. If you are doing a large stenciling project, clean the stencils when the paint starts to build up on them, to prevent paint build-up from distorting the stencil designs. Wrap the brushes or sponges in plastic wrap, or self-sealing plastic bags, to prevent the paint from drying on the brushes or sponges before you are finished.

6. Mixing Paint Colors: Any acrylic paint color can be used directly from a tube, jar or bottle, or mixed with other colors. Colors can be mixed with a stencil brush or palette knife. If you are doing a large stenciling project, mix a large quantity of the desired color at one time, because acrylic colors are difficult to match after they have dried. Acrylic colors dry darker than they appear to be when wet.

7. Cleaning Stencils, Brushes and Sponges: Clean stencils with cotton rags or paper toweling soaked in soapy water or rubbing alcohol. Pat the stencils dry. Store stencils flat or between layers of cardboard. Clean stencil brushes or sponges with soap and water until the rinse water runs clear. Let the brushes or sponges dry completely before using them to stencil again.

8. Projects: The chairs and table *(page 153)* were stenciled with the basic pouncing technique. The unfinished table was given a pine stain and coat of varnish first, and a coat of satin polyurethane spray after stenciling. Its border is the stencil central flower motif. The cabinets, window border and curtains *(page 153)* were stenciled with the dry brush technique; the window border is the stencil basket, the curtain border is the stencil leaf border. The window shade border *(page 153)* was made with the cut out technique, using the stencil central flower motif. The unfinished jelly cupboard *(at left)* was painted contrasting colors inside and out, and stenciled with the multicolor technique.

FIG. IV, 14   STENCIL A COUNTRY KITCHEN

FRONT OF STENCIL

STENCILING TECHNIQUES

Basic Pouncing Stenciling

For solid, one color images. Tape down the stencil. Holding the stencil brush like a pencil, dip it into acrylic paint. Using an up-and-down pouncing motion, pounce the brush on folded paper toweling to remove excess paint. Pounce the almost dry brush on the stencil cut outs, starting at the cut edges. Continue pouncing in circles until the cut outs are filled in with solid color.

Spray Stenciling

Produces soft-edged, blurry results. Tape down the stencil. Cover the surface beyond the stencil with newspaper. Apply fast-drying acrylic spray paint lightly with a back-and-forth motion, filling the stencil cut outs. Remove the newspaper after the paint dries.

Ombre Stenciling

Shades from one color into another. Pounce the bottom of the design in one color. As you move up the design, mix white gradually into the first color. When the color is almost pure white, start pouncing the second color, full strength.

Cut Out Stenciling

Gives a see-through design. No paint is necessary. Ideal for window shades, large lamp shades, and other stiff materials. Tape the stencil to the item. Using a pencil, trace the stencil cut outs onto the item. Cut out the traced design with a craft or utility knife.

Dry Brush Stenciling

Gives the faded look of very old stenciling. Excellent for walls and fabric. Dip the stencil brush into acrylic paint. Pounce the brush on folded paper toweling to remove as much paint as possible. Pounce the brush very lightly in circles on the stencil cut outs.

Sponge Stenciling

Creates an iridescent effect. Dip a natural sponge in acrylic paint. Dab the sponge on folded paper toweling until the sponge is almost dry. Pounce the sponge gently in circles on the stencil cut outs. Pounce two or three light coats of paint, or until the desired effect is achieved; let the paint dry between coats.

Multicolor Stenciling

For a colorful design. Tape the stencil at the top only. Mask off the cut outs to be used for other colors by taping paper under them. Pounce in the first color, and let the paint dry. Mask off those cut outs. Remove the paper from the cut outs for the second color, and pounce in that color. Continue until all the stencil cut outs are colored.

Spatter Stenciling

For a mottled look. Cover the surface beyond the stencil with newspaper. Dilute different colors of acrylic paint with water until they are the consistency of heavy cream. Dip a toothbrush in the first color. Aiming at the stencil, draw your thumb across the brush for a fine spatter, or tap the brush on your wrist for a broad spatter. Continue with the next color.

Dimensional Stenciling

Achieves a 3-D illusion. Select or mix a dark, medium and light shade of one color. Pounce the medium shade through the entire stencil, and let the paint dry. Pounce the light shade, over the medium shade, on the cut edges of some sections of the stencil. Pounce the dark shade on the remaining cut edges.

KITCHEN
G·A·R·D·E·N·S

Who loves a garden still his Eden keeps,
Perennial pleasures plants, and wholesome
harvest reaps.
—Amos Bronson Alcott

Fresh flowers, herbs and vegetables—the mainstays of the country kitchen. From a simple plot outside the back door to a clay pot on the window sill, we provide you with planting strategies and growing advice to help you reap a bountiful harvest every time.

Fresh herbs are essential to country cooking and making potpourri. With our raised-bed and window garden techniques, you can have a flavorful variety of herbs no matter where you live.

The taste of vegetables picked at their peak is incomparable. We make it easy for you to have your own supply by suggesting planting methods, natural pesticides, types of vegetables to grow—even the best method for canning your home-grown produce.

Wouldn't you love to see posies on your window sill in winter? Our tips for forcing bulbs will yield a bouquet of springtime magic for your home!

The most flavorful herbs come from your own garden. Our raised-bed gardening method guarantees a great harvest.

H·E·R·B·S I·N·D·O·O·R·S
A·N·D O·U·T

*Oh, better no doubt is a dinner
of herbs,
When season'ed by love, which
no rancor disturbs.*
—Owen Meredith

Window Herb Garden

Plant a fragrant selection of fresh herbs in your kitchen; their pots take up very little space, and you'll always have herbs right at hand for cooking.

▼ Tuck small pots of parsley, basil and chive plants on a window sill. Hang a pot of thyme from the ceiling, and brighten up the kitchen table with a decorative container filled with lemon balm and sage. Be creative in your use of space: Install shelves across a window to hold potted herbs, or brackets along the sides or top of a window frame to suspend hanging baskets.

▼ Basil, sage, thyme and chives will thrive if given some direct sunlight. Parsley and lemon balm can manage in bright indirect sun.

▼ Mist the herbs, except sage, with water daily to help raise the humidity level and discourage insects.

▼ If insects appear, run the plants under tepid water.

▼ Herbs need fresh air, so even in wintertime, crack open the kitchen window for a few minutes each day.

NATURE'S BEAUTY
Pots of fresh herbs can make marvelous natural centerpieces.

▼ Place individual pots of herbs in pretty baskets or group several pots together in a larger piece of decorative pottery.

▼ Snip fresh herbs and group them in bunches. Arrange the bunches in a glass vase or brandy snifter in place of flowers.

▼ To further the theme, twist and tie raffia around small bunches of herbs, and place the bunches at each individual place setting for decoration.

I·N·D·O·O·R H·E·R·B G·R·O·W·I·N·G G·U·I·D·E

Herb	Water	Feed	Special Tips
Basil *Ocimum basilicum*	1	A	Discard plants that cease to be productive
Chives *Allium schoenoprasum*	1	A	Start plants from bulbs offered by grocers
Lemon balm *Melissa officinalis*	1	A	Tolerates some shade
Parsley *Petroselinum crispum*	1	A	Tolerates shade, discard plants that cease to be productive
Sage *Salvia officinalis*	2	A	Pinch back stems for use as seasoning whenever they become large
Thyme *Thymus*	1	A	Excellent in hanging baskets

Water: 1 = keep evenly moist. 2 = keep barely moist. **Feed:** A = monthly in winter, bi-weekly the rest of the year.

Raised-Bed Herb Gardening

An outdoor herb garden is a sweet-smelling complement to the country kitchen, and makes your garden more than just a charming spot of green. The harvest will yield ample fresh herbs for cooking, plus plenty of herbs to dry for a tasty reminder of your garden all year long (see How to Dry Herbs, page 163).

Contrary to popular belief, herbs don't do very well in poor soil—they do better in moderately enriched soil. If you live in a poor soil area, our raised-bed herb garden, shown on pages 158-159, may be the perfect planting method for you. Follow the general directions for raised-bed gardening at right, then the specific directions for an herb garden below, to create a garden similar to the one pictured.

▼ Clear a 14 x 14-foot plot of grass and weeds.
▼ Nail 2 x 4's together to make 4-foot square frames. Place the frames 2 feet apart to allow for pathways between the beds.
▼ Set three or four varieties of herbs per bed, spacing the plants to keep them from crowding. Keep the soil moist for the first 2 weeks as the plants become acclimated. After you have planted the beds, cover the pathways with wood chips.

HERB LORE

The word "herb" comes from the Latin "herba," meaning grass. At one time, herb was spelled without the "h" and pronounced just as it was spelled. After the 16th century, the "h" was added to the word, but the pronunciation remained the same until the 1800's, when the English added the "h" sound. Today, both pronunciations are acceptable.

▼ Herbs are the leaves of aromatic plants and shrubs. Known for thousands of years, herbs are used to add flavor to foods, as well as for their fragrance and medicinal properties.
▼ Most herbs are classified into one of three families. The mint family *Labiatae* includes basil, lavender, marjoram, the mints, rosemary, sage, savory and thyme. The composite family *Compositae* includes tarragon, chamomile and yarrow. The umbel family *Umbelliferae*, which is characterized by feathery or finely cut foliage and flowers born on umbels, includes anise, angelica, caraway, chervil, cilantro, dill, fennel and parsley.

RAISED-BED GARDENING

Whether you're planning an herb garden or a vegetable garden, planting in raised beds can help if you live in a poor soil area, or if you just want to increase your crop yield. This is because the raised-bed method enriches the soil before you begin to plant. In addition, the soil stays loose, the roots grow deeper, and the plants are healthier because you don't walk on the beds. Best of all, raised-bed gardens need less weeding than ground-level gardens.

▼ Till or turn over the soil in the areas where the raised beds will be.
▼ Mark off the dimensions of the beds with twine.
▼ The pathways between the beds should be at least 1½ feet wide so you have enough room to move freely around the beds.
▼ Cut pressure-treated lumber, landscape timbers or railroad ties to the beds' dimensions, and frame the beds with the wood.
▼ Fill the beds to within 4 inches of their tops with the most fertile soil available.
▼ Add at least 2 inches of compost, such as well-rotted leaves, grass clippings or manure, or peat moss combined with vermiculite or perlite. Dig the compost or peat mix into the top few inches of soil. The beds now are ready for planting.
▼ After you have planted the beds, cover the paths between the beds with wood chips, small stones or pine needles, or plant the paths with grass.

**Who loves a garden
loves a greenhouse too.**
—William Cowper

COUNTRY WAYS
Meetin' Seed
In early New England, people referred to fennel, dill and caraway seeds as "meetin' seed."

▼ During the summer, women and children brought bunches of the ripe seeds to Sunday "meeting," or church services. It was believed that nibbling the seeds helped the parishioners stay awake during the lengthy prayers and sermons.

▼ Some historians speculate that the New Englanders chewed the seeds to keep from getting hiccups during church services. Hiccups were thought to be the product of a conflict between the flesh and spirit. Chewing the seeds helped keep the parishioners' minds on spiritual matters.

The Rules of Herbs

Whatever size or kind of herb garden you have in mind, these general rules will apply.

▼ Herbs must be set in soil that drains well. This means careful preparation of the plot before planting, but the results will be worth it.

▼ To improve drainage in ground-level gardens, dig the soil well to a depth of 8 to 10 inches, breaking up clods of earth. Work in a 1- to 2-inch layer of organic material, such as compost.

▼ Except for chives, dill and thyme, herbs planted in the ground don't need extra watering unless you live in a very hot and dry climate.

▼ When planting herbs in containers, use a good packaged potting soil or a soilless medium, which is lighter in weight.

▼ Since most herbs are destined for use in cooking, don't spray them with chemical pesticides or fungicides. To keep your herb garden naturally pest-free, see our tips for Old-Fashioned Pest Control on page 167.

SAVING SEEDS

Before sowing seeds you saved from last year, test them. Place 10 seeds between pieces of damp paper toweling, put the paper toweling in a plastic bag, and set the bag in a warm spot for 5 to 10 days. If at least 8 seeds germinate, you should get good results in the garden.

**When I am in the country
I wish to vegetate like the country.**
— William Hazlitt

HOW TO DRY HERBS
All herbs can be dried except chives, which should be frozen.

▼ Herbs to be dried should be picked on a clear morning after the dew has evaporated.

▼ Tie the stems together in small bunches, and hang the bunches upside down out of direct sunlight in a closet, attic, or the kitchen.

▼ When the herbs are dry, in about 2 weeks, place them on a clean piece of paper, and rub the stems between your palms until all the leaves have fallen off. With thyme, rosemary and oregano, strip the leaves from the stems by running your thumb and forefinger down the stems.

▼ Discard the stems.

▼ Rub the leaves through a fine mesh strainer to remove any remaining stem bits.

▼ Store the dried herbs in clearly labeled, screw-top glass jars.

V·E·G·E·T·A·B·L·E
G·A·R·D·E·N·I·N·G

Raised-Bed Vegetable Gardening

Vegetable gardens, like herb gardens, derive many benefits from the raised-bed method of planting. Raised-bed gardening doubles the yield of vegetables because the plants are set closer together in wide rows, instead of in the single-file rows of ground-level gardens. Use half your harvest fresh, and freeze or can the rest to have home-grown vegetables year-round. Follow the general directions for raised-bed gardening on page 162, then the specific directions below.

▼ Make the beds 3 to 4 feet wide, and any length you choose. Five 4 x 6-foot beds will provide space for 10 vegetables.

▼ Read the charts on pages 165 and 168-169 for specific information on planting each type of vegetable.

▼ Keep the vegetable seedlings that you start indoors well lighted after germination. Place them in a south window with full sun, and turn the plants regularly so they grow straight. Or place them 10 to 12 inches below one cool and one warm fluorescent light for 12 to 15 hours daily.

▼ A week after germination, give the seedlings weekly doses of 5-10-5 or 10-10-10 fertilizer diluted to one third the strength recommended on the label.

▼ Transplant seedlings started in flats to individual pots when the second pair of true leaves appears (the first pair to appear are the germination leaves; the next pair are the first true leaves).

▼ A week before transplanting or sowing corn, cucumbers, peppers, pumpkins, tomatoes, winter squash, zucchini, or other heat-loving vegetables outdoors, mulch their beds with black plastic or black biodegradable peat paper. This warms the soil, which speeds up plant growth, and prevents weeds.

▼ Right after planting beans, peas, broccoli, carrots, cauliflower or other vegetables that grow best in cooler soil, mulch their beds with dried grass clippings or shredded leaves.

▼ Stake or cage tomatoes, and grow cucumbers or peas on trellises.

VEGETABLE VARIETY

To plan your vegetable garden, check out the varieties of vegetables listed below. Most of them freeze well, especially asparagus, corn, okra, peas, peppers, spinach, puréed tomatoes, and zucchini and summer squash. Beets, cabbage, cucumbers, pumpkins, sweet potatoes, tomatillos, and whole tomatoes have a firmer texture when canned. Then check the Vegetable Growing Guide (pages 168-169), or Vegetables for Freezing and Canning (page 165), for the amount of space each mature plant needs in the garden.

▼ *Asparagus:* Mary Washington
▼ *Beans:* Blue Lake, Buttergreen, E-Z Pick, Kentucky Wonder, Keygold, Purple Pod, Royalty
▼ *Beets:* Detroit Dark Red, Formanova, Red Ace, Ruby Queen
▼ *Broccoli:* Green Comet, Premium Crop
▼ *Brussels Sprouts:* Jade Cross E
▼ *Cabbage:* Ataria, Emerald Cross, Savoy Ace
▼ *Carrots:* A Plus, Nantes Half Long, Red Cored Chanteny
▼ *Cauliflower:* Ravella Self-Blanching
▼ *Corn:* Butterfruit Bi-Color, Honey 'N Pearl
▼ *Cucumbers:* Pickle-Dilly
▼ *Okra:* Burgundy
▼ *Peas:* Green Arrow, Sugar Snap
▼ *Peppers:* Anaheim Chili, Cayenne, Golden Summer, Gypsy, Jalapeño, Pimiento, Purple Bell, Ruby King, Sweet Banana, Sweet Chocolate
▼ *Pumpkins:* New England Pie
▼ *Spinach:* Tyee
▼ *Squash, Zucchini/Summer:* Buccaneer, Butterblossom, Butterstick, Gold Rush, Green Magic; *Winter:* Sweet Dumpling
▼ *Sweet Potatoes:* New Jewel
▼ *Tomatillos:* Tomatillo
▼ *Tomatoes, Paste:* Bellstar, Mamma Mia; *Beefsteak:* Celebrity, Lemon Boy; *Cherry:* Sweet 100

V·E·G·E·T·A·B·L·E·S F·O·R F·R·E·E·Z·I·N·G A·N·D C·A·N·N·I·N·G

Vegetable	Planting Schedule	Sowing Schedule	Days to Germinate	Preserving Methods	Notes
Asparagus	4 weeks before FF through spring	SI 12 weeks	10 to 21 days	Can or freeze	Space mature plants 2 square feet apart. Use tender, tight-tipped spears in preserving
Beans, Snap	1 week after FF through July	SO	4 to 5 days	Can or freeze	Whole, or cut into 1-inch pieces
Beets	2 to 4 weeks before FF through summer	SO	7 to 10 days	Can	Can plain or pickled beets
Broccoli	6 weeks before FF to 1 week after	SI 6 to 8 weeks	3 to 10 days	Freeze	Freeze in varied sizes
Brussels Sprouts	2 weeks before FF to 3 weeks after	SI 5 to 8 weeks	3 to 10 days	Freeze or can	Maintain better color when frozen
Cabbage	6 weeks before FF to 2 weeks after	SI 6 to 8 weeks	3 to 10 days	Freeze or can	Freeze cabbage rolls; can sauerkraut
Carrots	2 weeks before FF through summer	SO	10 to 16 days	Freeze or can	Select carrots 1 to 1¼ inches in diameter
Cauliflower	6 weeks before FF to 1 week after	SI 6 to 8 weeks	3 to 10 days	Can or freeze	Great for pickles
Corn	FF to 6 weeks after	SI or SO 3 to 4 weeks	6 to 10 days	Can	Shuck ears, and freeze on the cob
Cucumbers	FF to midsummer	SI or SO 3 to 4 weeks	3 to 7 days	Can	Make into relishes, pickles
Okra	FF to midsummer	SO	5 to 9 days	Can or freeze	Use in vegetable soup and freeze
Onions (seed)	FF to 8 weeks after	SI 6 weeks	6 to 11 days	Freeze	Chop or slice; freeze in small quantities
Peas	2 to 6 weeks before FF	SO	6 to 12 days	Freeze	Don't shake or press down in packing
Peppers	1 week after FF	SI 6 weeks	6 to 14 days	Freeze or can	Chop or slice; freeze in small quantities
Pumpkins	FF to 2 weeks after	SO	7 to 10 days	Can	Don't mash; cube
Spinach	3 weeks before FF to 3 weeks after	SI or SO 4 to 6 weeks	6 to 14 days	Freeze	Wash thoroughly
Squash, Zucchini/Summer	FF to 8 to 10 weeks after	SI or SO 3 to 4 weeks	4 to 7 days	Freeze	Trim ends, but don't peel
Squash, Winter	2 weeks after FF	SI or SO 3 to 4 weeks	5 to 10 days	Can	Should have hard rind, stringless pulp
Tomatillos	FF to 2 weeks after	SI or SO 4 weeks	8 to 12 days	Can	Space mature plants 2 square feet apart. Adds great flavor to Tex-Mex sauces
Tomatoes	1 week after FF	SI 6 to 10 weeks	5 to 14 days	Can or freeze	Freeze purée or juice

KEY: FF = final frost. SI = start indoors; number of weeks before setting out indicated. SO = seed outdoors directly in the garden.

COUNTRY WAYS

Secrets of Champion Gardeners

Get the most from your vegetable garden with these tips from "green thumb" experts

▼ Before transplanting seedlings grown in flats or peat pots to the garden, dip the seedlings and containers into a 5-gallon pail filled with a solution of Miracle-Gro® fertilizer. The moisture helps loosen soil, so seedlings are easier to remove from flats, while the fertilizer reduces transplant shock.

▼ To get plants off to a quick start in the spring, keep the soil warm. Water the garden in the morning, and the sun will raise the soil temperature by evening.

▼ Proper watering is crucial no matter where you live. Water plants deeply early in the season to encourage the development of deep root systems. Light waterings keep roots near the soil surface, where they are most easily damaged by hot or dry weather. To water many rows of vegetables at one time without wetting the foliage or causing soil runoff, install a drip irrigation system of plastic hoses and drippers. Some systems have timers that shut off the water automatically.

▼ To get more tomatoes per plant, remove suckers. These tiny sprouts appear above branches on the main stem, or from below ground near the base.

▼ Get double pleasure from root vegetables, such as beets, carrots or turnips. As soon as they're big enough, pick some to eat as "baby" vegetables. Doing this also thins out the crop, allowing what is left in the ground to mature to perfection.

WATER WORKS

Gardens need at least 1 inch of water a week. If you get a dry spell, here's an effective—and easy—way to provide water.

▼ Install a do-it-yourself drip irrigation system. Dig a hole next to each plant, and insert a plastic jug with holes punched in its bottom. Fill the jugs with water as needed. Water will drip down to reach the deepest roots.

▼ To fertilize the plants, add a water-soluble 5-10-5 or 5-10-10 fertilizer to the water in the jugs.

FROST GUARDS

These anti-frost measures extend the growing season from early spring into fall.

▼ Use row covers. Tinted covers, such as shade cloths, also guard young lettuce plants from the sun's scorching rays during the summer.

▼ Shield individual plants, such as tomatoes or cabbages, with plastic "cloches." Cut off the bottoms of 1-gallon plastic jugs. At night, place a jug over each plant. Remove the jugs during the day so the sun doesn't bake the plants.

O, it sets my heart a-clicking'
like the tickin' of a clock,
When the frost is on the punkin
and the fodder's in the shock.
—James Whitcomb Riley

COUNTRY WAYS

Old-Fashioned Pest Control

Instead of using chemical remedies, try these natural pesticides in your vegetable or herb garden.

▼ Build good soil. Use fertilizers developed from plant and animal sources that decompose over time. They'll enrich soil with the nutrients plants need to flourish, and hardy plants are best able to withstand disease and insect attacks.

▼ Choose disease-resistant plants. Breeders have been very successful in developing hardier varieties that are more resistant to disease. Check plant labels for this information:
Tomatoes (with VFNT) that are resistant to verticillium and fusarium wilts, nematodes, and tobacco mosaic virus.
Beans that are rust resistant.
Cucumbers that are resistant to mosaic virus, scab and powdery mildew.
Peas that are resistant to powdery mildew and fusarium wilt.
Peppers that are resistant to tobacco mosaic virus.

▼ Rotate crops. Don't plant the same crop in the same spot more than 2 years in a row. This will reduce problems caused by nematodes, fungus diseases, and other soil-borne problems. These pests stay in the soil over the winter, so when you plant the same crop in the same soil the following year, the pests already are there. Rotating crops also will prevent depletion of soil minerals. Each plant needs a different combination of minerals; some need a particular mineral in very large amounts. When the same plants are grown in the same spot year after year, they literally can "eat" that mineral out of the soil. This results in poor harvests.

▼ Let plants help each other. Certain plants seem to help other plants by deterring harmful insects or providing nutrients the other plants need. Try planting marigolds and garlic with tomatoes. Plant oregano around the garden to attract bees, which help pollination. Grow peas and beans, except near plants of the onion/garlic family, to make nitrogen available to vegetables planted later in same soil. Set in nasturtiums with cabbage, squash or cucumbers. Use rosemary with beans, carrots or cabbage.

▼ Keep the garden clean. Don't leave dead or diseased leaves, stems, or other plant parts around the garden to provide a haven for pests.

▼ Avoid keeping the garden damp. Water at ground level, not overhead, to discourage the spread of viruses and mildew that thrive on wet leaves. Don't walk in the garden right after a rain. You inadvertently may spread disease, such as mildew, from one plant to another.

▼ Entice birds to your yard. Birds eat enormous amounts of insects every day, so let them help you in the battle against bugs. Plant berry-bearing plants, such as dogwood, viburnum or juniper. Hang bird feeders from nearby trees. Put up birdhouses.

▼ Control aphids organically. Let ladybugs loose in your garden; they're natural enemies of aphids.

▼ Pick beetles off plants by hand. Better to touch a bug than a poison!

▼ Seduce slugs with beer. Sink a shallow pan in the earth until the rim is at ground level and fill it with beer. The slugs, attracted to the beer, will crawl into the pan and drown.

▼ Hunt slugs at night armed with a flashlight and salt shaker. Sprinkle slugs with the salt to dehydrate and kill them.

▼ Use a homemade insect spray. Boil 2 onions, 4 to 5 garlic cloves, and a handful of hot peppers in 2 gallons of water until you have a "soup." Strain the liquid, and add more water to make 2 gallons again. Spray the solution on your vegetables. You can pick and eat the vegetables the same day you spray them, as long as you wash them thoroughly.

▼ Or mix ¼ cup of water with ¼ cup of liquid dishwashing soap. Spray the soap solution on house or garden plants when you find insects on them. The soap spray kills the insects already on the plants, and keeps other insects away.

▼ Buttermilk spray controls spider mites and other mites. Mix together ½ cup of buttermilk, 4 cups of wheat flour, and 5 gallons of water. Use the spray as often as necessary.

▼ Use a natural pest control for cutworms. Make dough balls out of raw flour and water, and put the balls around plants susceptible to cutworms. Soon after eating the dough, the cutworms expand and burst.

V·E·G·E·T·A·B·L·E G·R·O·W·I·N·G G·U·I·D·E

H·A·R·D·Y
(Can be sown in the garden as soon as the ground can be worked in spring; tolerate very cold weather and heavy frosts)

Vegetable	Space Between Plants	Space Between Rows	No. Per/ Size of Container	Weeks to First Harvest*	Notes**
Beets	2 to 3 inches	15 to 18 inches	4 to 5/8 to 10 inches	7 to 9	A
Broccoli	1 to 1½ feet	1½ to 2 feet	1/1 gallon	8 to 11	B, T
Brussels Sprouts	2 feet	2½ to 3 feet	1/3 gallons	13 to 14	T
Cabbage	1 to 1½ feet	1½ to 2½ feet	1/1 gallon	8 to 13	B, T
Carrots	2 to 3 inches	12 to 15 inches	5 to 6/1½ gallons	8 to 12	A
Cauliflower	1½ to 2 feet	2½ to 3 feet	1/1 gallon	7 to 11	T
Celery	6 to 8 inches	10 inches	N.A.	15 to 17	T
Collards	12 to 15 inches	2 to 3 feet	4 to 5/3 gallons	8 to 9	B
Garlic	4 to 6 inches	12 to 15 inches	6 to 8/1½ gallons	4 to 5	B
Kale	1 foot	2½ feet	1 to 2/1½ gallons	8 to 9	B
Kohlrabi	3 to 4 inches	12 to 15 inches	2/3 gallons	7 to 8	B
Leeks	6 inches	2 feet	5 to 6/3 gallons	16 to 18	N.A.
Mustard Greens	8 inches	2 feet	8 to 10/3 gallons	6 to 7	B
Onions (plants)	4 to 6 inches	6 to 12 inches	5 to 6/3 gallons	10 to 11	B,T
Onions (sets)	2 to 3 inches	12 to 15 inches	10 to 12/1½ gallons	9 to 12	B
Parsnips	4 to 6 inches	1 to 1½ feet	6 to 8/1 to 2 gallons	15	N.A.
Peas	2 inches	3 feet	15/15 gallons	7 to 10	A,B
Potatoes, Irish	1 foot	2½ feet	4 to 5/1½ gallons	13 to 15	N.A.
Radishes	1 to 2 inches	12 to 15 inches	10 to 12/8 inches	3 to 4	A,B
Spinach	5 to 6 inches	1½ to 2 feet	6 to 8/3 gallons	6 to 10	B
Turnips	3 to 5 inches	12 to 15 inches	2 to 3/8 to 10 inches	5 to 8	A,B

S·E·M·I - H·A·R·D·Y
(Tolerate light frosts)

Escarole	8 to 10 inches	12 to 15 inches	8 to 10/3 gallons	6 to 7	B
Lettuce, Head	10 to 12 inches	15 inches	1/4 inches	10 to 13	B
Lettuce, Leaf	8 to 10 inches	15 inches	6 to 8/1½ gallons	6 to 8	A,B
Romaine	1 foot	1½ feet	8 to 10/2 to 3 gallons	11 to 12	B
Strawberries	1 foot	1 foot	4/3 gallons	12 to 16	T
Summer Spinach	8 to 10 inches	1½ to 2 feet	4 to 6/3 gallons	10	N.A.
Swiss Chard	4 to 6 inches	1½ to 2 feet	6 to 8/2 to 3 gallons	7 to 8	A

T·E·N·D·E·R
(Cannot tolerate frost; plant in the garden after all danger of frost has passed, and the soil has warmed up)

Vegetable	Space Between Plants	Space Between Rows	No. Per/ Size of Container	Weeks to First Harvest*	Notes**
Artichokes	4 to 6 feet	4 to 6 feet	1/3 gallons	23 to 25	T
Beans, Bush †	4 to 6 inches	15 to 18 inches	5 to 6/3 gallons	6 to 8	A
Beans, Pole	8 to 10 inches	3 feet	N.A.	8 to 9	N.A.
Corn ‡	8 to 12 inches	2½ to 3 feet	6/15 gallons	9 to 13	N.A.
Cucumbers	1 foot	4 to 5 feet	2 to 3/3 gallons	8 to 10	H
Eggplant	16 to 18 inches	2 feet	1/3 gallons	9 to 11	T
Melons	2 feet	4 to 6 feet	1 to 2/5 gallons	11 to 14	H only
Okra	10 to 12 inches	1½ to 2 feet	3/3 gallons	7 to 10	N.A.
Peanuts	8 to 12 inches	3 feet	3 to 4/3 gallons	16 to 17	N.A.
Peppers	10 to 12 inches	1½ to 2 feet	1/3 gallons	9 to 11	T
Potatoes, Sweet	15 to 18 inches	3 to 4 feet	3 to 4/3 gallons	14 to 21	T
Pumpkins	2 to 3 feet	6 to 10 feet	2/3 gallons	12 to 17	H
Squash, Zucchini/Summer	1 to 1½ feet	3 to 4 feet	3 to 4/5 gallons	7 to 8	H
Squash, Winter	3 feet	6 to 8 feet	3 to 4/3 gallons	10 to 12	H
Tomatoes	1½ to 3 feet	2 to 3 feet	1/3 gallons	8 to 11	T

* = from the time seeds or transplants are set out in the garden; we give a broad span to accommodate different varieties.
**A = sow 2 or 3 times at 10-day intervals for longer harvest; sow beets at 3-week intervals throughout season.
B = sow again in midsummer for fall harvest.
T = transplants; start seeds indoors.

N.A. = not applicable.
H = plant in "hills;" groups of 4 to 5 seeds thinned after germination to the strongest 3 or 4 plants; space hills 3 to 4 feet apart for cucumbers and zucchini/summer squash, 5 to 6 feet for melons and winter squash, and 6 to 8 feet for pumpkins.
†Lima beans, whether bush or pole, take 9 to 12 weeks to mature.
‡Plant in blocks of at least 4 rows side by side, not in single long rows.

Canning: Hot Water Bath Method

Follow the directions exactly; do not take shortcuts.
▼ Place the hot water bath canner on the stove. Add water to fill the canner half way, cover the canner, and bring the water to boiling.
▼ Wash the jars in hot, sudsy water. Rinse them well, and leave them in hot water.
▼ Place new domed lids in a bowl, and cover them with boiling water. Keep the lids in water.
▼ Follow the individual recipe directions.
▼ Remove the jars from the hot water, one at a time, and place them on a clean cloth. Pack or ladle food into the jars, leaving headroom specified in the recipe.
▼ Wipe the tops and outside rims of the jars with a clean cloth. Place the domed lids on top. Screw the metal rings on tightly, but do not use force.
▼ Place the jars in the canner rack, and lower them into rapidly boiling water. Add boiling water if the water level is not 2 inches above the jars. Cover the canner, and return the water to a full boil.

▼ Process following the recipe; calculate the processing time from when the water comes to a second boil. If you live above sea level, add 1 minute for each 1,000 feet when the recipe calls for processing for 20 minutes or less. When processing for more than 20 minutes, add 2 minutes for each 1,000 feet.
▼ Remove the jars from the canner with tongs, and place them at least 3 inches apart on a wire rack until they are cool, for about 12 hours.
▼ Test the seal on all the jars by tapping them with a spoon. A clear ringing sound means a good seal. If a jar is not properly sealed, store it in the refrigerator and use the food within a month, or reprocess.
▼ Remove the metal rings. Wipe the jars with a dampened clean cloth. Label, date and store the jars in a cool, dark, dry place.

B·L·O·O·M·I·N·G
B·U·L·B·S

God the first garden made.
—Abraham Cowley

Planting and Forcing Bulbs Indoors

Bring spring into your kitchen a little early this year. Around the second week in January, after the Christmas decorations have been taken down and the house looks empty, brighten the scene with pots of flowering bulbs you have forced into bloom. Forcing tricks the bulbs into thinking it's spring by cooling them with an artificial winter. You need to start early, because most bulbs need about 12 weeks of cold storage before forcing, so plant bulbs in October for brilliant January blossoms.

Containers

You can grow bulbs successfully in just about any type of container—clay, wooden, ceramic, plastic, even a recycled coffee can.

▼ Use a container that is at least twice as deep as the bulbs are long; a 2-inch-long bulb needs a 4-inch-deep pot. The container should have one large or several small drainage holes in the bottom.

▼ Soak new clay pots in water overnight before planting in them. This prevents the pots from drawing moisture out of the soil after the bulbs are planted.

▼ Scrub previously used clay pots.

Soil

Bulbs need a rich, fast-draining soil mix.

▼ Combine 1 part each of packaged soil, milled or ground peat moss, and horticultural or builders' sand. Add 1 cup of vermiculite to each quart of mix.

▼ Before adding the peat moss to the soil mix, soak the peat in a bucket of hot water and squeeze it almost dry.

Planting

▼ Put a handful of bulb fungicidal dust in a bag, drop in a few bulbs at a time, and shake the bag to coat them.

▼ Cover the container drainage hole or holes with rocks, pieces of broken clay pots, or a piece of fiberglass screening.

▼ Fill the container with the soil mix. Set a bulb on the soil surface. The tip of the bulb should be ½ inch below the container rim; add or remove soil mix until the level is correct.

▼ Set all the other bulbs to be planted in the container gently on the soil surface. For spectacular results, plant as many bulbs as possible in the container, placing the bulbs just so they are not touching each other.

▼ For a beautiful effect, plant different varieties of bulbs together, such as early-blooming tulips with hyacinths, or irises with daffodils.

Suddenly Springtime

Colorful tulips, dazzling daffodils, sweet-smelling hyacinths—who wouldn't want one of these glorious blooms brightening their kitchen? The indoor beauties shown in the photo at left are White Dream tulips. You can enjoy beautiful flowers like these from Christmas to Easter by forcing bulbs to bloom months earlier than they would outdoors. *(For more blooming beauties, see pages 174-175.)*

WHY YOU CAN FORCE BULBS

Each bulb contains an incomplete flower, leaves, a stem, and a built-in supply of food to nourish the plant as it matures. All you have to provide is the right environment.

▼ *Cold period.* The bulb needs this time to develop healthy roots. Once the roots are well-established, the stem and leaves appear. At this point, the bulb can be forced to bloom.

▼ *Warming-up period.* When you move the bulb to a slightly warmer area, you fool the bulb into thinking that spring has arrived. The bulb has no way of knowing whether the cold lasted for only 6 weeks or for 3 months, as would have happened if the bulb had been planted outdoors. The bulb will flower beautifully, giving you a preview of springtime while it still is winter outside.

▼ Set tulip bulbs in the container with their flat sides facing the container wall. The flat sides produce the first leaves, which will form a neat border around the rim of the container.

▼ Fill in soil around the bulbs. Don't press the bulbs down; their roots need loose, lightly packed soil in which to grow.

▼ Water the bulbs slowly and gently. Fill soil depressions caused by the water with more soil.

▼ Using waterproof ink, label each container with the types of bulbs planted in it, and the planting date.

Cold Storage

▼ Store the containers in a cold, dark area for up to 12 weeks; the temperature should be between 32° and 45°. Keep the soil barely moist.

▼ If late autumn and winter temperatures stay consistently below 40° where you live, keep the containers in an unheated sunporch, cellar, garage or terrace. To protect bulbs from the damaging below-freezing temperatures, cover the containers with several inches of shredded newspaper, or a sheet of black plastic. Lay the cover loosely over the soil surface so the stems have room to grow.

▼ If you live in an area where late autumn and winter temperatures tend to rise above 45°, or if you live in an apartment, store the containers in the refrigerator (see Forcing Bulbs in the Sunbelt, at right).

▼ You also can store the containers outdoors in the ground. Choose a protected spot close to your house that drains well and does not get full sun. Dig a 10-inch-deep trench, and spread gravel or rocks on the bottom. Set the containers in the trench. Fill in around the containers with sharp builders' sand to just below the container rims. Cover the containers with a 2-inch-thick layer of leaves, wood chips or straw. Top that with 2 to 3 inches of soil or sand. Keep the bulbs watered until the first freeze. Then mulch over the bed again with a 4-inch layer of straw, hay, evergreen boughs, or other organic material.

Forcing Blooms

▼ After 4 weeks of cold storage, begin to check the bulbs periodically. The bulbs are ready to force when the stems are 2 to 3 inches tall, and the root mass is visible. To check the root mass, turn over the container. Rap the rim gently on the edge of a table to loosen the soil ball, and catch the ball as it comes out.

▼ When the bulbs are ready to force, remove the containers from cold storage and place them in a dark, 55° area for 7 to 10 days. During this period, the top growth will develop height and strength.

▼ Then put the containers in or near a north window with bright light but no direct sun.

▼ When the buds have formed and you can see a bit of color, move the containers to a sunny, airy spot.

Care of Flowering Bulbs

These guidelines will keep forced blooms healthy and long-lasting.

▼ *Water* Keep the soil moist, but not too wet. Drain the water from container saucers.

▼ *Heat* Forced blooms deteriorate in temperatures above 65°. To prolong the life of the flower, place the containers at night in a cool room where the temperature does not fall below 32°. Do not put the containers near a radiator.

▼ *Drafts* Keep the bulbs in a draft-free location.

▼ *Light* When the blooms are fully opened, move the plants out of direct sun.

▼ *Fertilizer* After the blooms begin to fade, feed the plants once with 5-10-5 fertilizer, and continue watering as before until the foliage turns brown.

Getting Bulbs to Bloom Again

Except for amaryllis (see page 179), bulbs cannot be forced to bloom indoors a second time. However, bulbs can be planted outdoors after they have been forced, and they will rebloom in a year or two.

▼ After the indoor flowers are spent, cut off the stems at the soil line. Leave the foliage until it turns brown.

▼ When the foliage is completely withered, unpot the bulbs, cut off the foliage and dead roots, and remove the soil from the bulbs.

▼ Place each variety of bulb in a separate paper bag, and label the bags.

▼ Leave the bags open, or perforate them with vent holes and staple them closed at the top.

▼ Store the bags in a dark, dry spot until autumn.

Forcing Bulbs in the Sunbelt

If you live in Florida, southern California or Hawaii, you can force anemones, crocuses, daffodils, freesias, hyacinths, paper-white narcissus, or oxalis species with one of these methods.

▼ *In Fiber* Peat moss, coconut fiber, or "bulb fiber" sold in garden centers can be used to force all the bulbs listed above.

1. Use a shallow container with a drainage hole (a bulb pan may also be used).

2. Soak fiber in hot water, and squeeze it almost dry. Pack down the fiber lightly in the container.

3. Place the bulbs in the container so their tips are just below the container rim. Fill in fiber around the bulbs, leaving the tips exposed.

4. Place the container in a cool, dark spot, such as a closet or refrigerator, for a few weeks. Keep the fiber barely moist.

5. Follow the steps in Forcing Blooms, at left.

▼ *In Water* Hyacinths can be forced in special "hyacinth glasses," which are hourglass-shaped containers filled with water. No cold storage is needed.
1. Scrape the bulb base gently with a knife blade to stimulate root growth.
2. Fill the glass with spring or distilled water. Drop in a few horticultural charcoal chips to keep the water from getting sour.
3. Change the water about once a week.

▼ *On Water-Covered Pebbles* Paperwhite narcissus, daffodils and most other narcissus, as well as crocuses and hyacinths, can be brought into bloom on moist pebbles. The roots grow down into the water, and spread over the pebbles. No cold storage is needed.
1. Set the bulbs on pebbles in a container. Pour in enough water so the tops of the pebbles remain dry. The bulbs should not sit in water.
2. Add horticultural charcoal chips to keep the water from getting sour.

> **If you have two loaves of bread,**
> **sell one**
> **and buy a hyacinth.**
> — Persian saying

COUNTRY WAYS
The Language of Flowers
Throughout the ages, flowers have carried their own secret meanings. Many blooms were given to convey a specific message to the receiver.

▼ *Forever Yours*
  Red chrysanthemum: I love. *Forget-me-not:* true love. *Myrtle, red rose:* love. *White rose:* I am worthy of you. *Mixed white and red roses:* unity. *Red tulip:* declaration of love.
▼ *Sweet Reverie*
  Artemesia: absence. *Pansy:* you occupy my thoughts. *Blue salvia:* I think of you. *Zinnia:* thoughts of absent friends.
▼ *My Beloved*
  Red, pink, or scented leaf geranium: preference. *Heliotrope:* devotion. *Ivy:* marriage, fidelity. *Blue violet:* faithfulness.
▼ *Broken Hearts*
  Japanese anemone: forsaken. *Red carnation:* alas for my poor heart. *Marigold:* jealousy. *Pennyroyal:* flee away. *Full blown rose over two buds:* secrecy. *Yellow tulip:* hopeless love.

COUNTRY WAYS
Birthday Flowers
Each month has a flower, or flowers, known as "birth flowers." Surprise someone this year with an entirely appropriate birthday bouquet.

▼ *January:* Carnation
▼ *February:* Violet
▼ *March:* Jonquil
▼ *April:* Sweet pea
▼ *May:* Daisy
▼ *June:* Rose
▼ *July:* Larkspur
▼ *August:* Gladiolus
▼ *September:* Lavender
▼ *October:* Aster
▼ *November:* Chrysanthemum
▼ *December:* Holly

Pink Perfection and Delft Blue hyacinths

A *Bevy of Blooming Bulbs*

Just a few of the glorious blossoms that can be yours: hyacinths, tulips, irises, narcissus, daffodils. Don't restrict yourself to planting only one type of bulb in a pot. Try mixing bulbs together to create a more natural — and colorful — look.

Tulips and Dutch irises

Daffodils

Tulips

Paperwhite narcissus

Tulips and hyacinths

V·A·R·I·E·T·I·E·S O·F B·U·L·B·S T·O F·O·R·C·E

(Planted indoors, early bulbs bloom before late ones, just as they do outdoors)

H·Y·A·C·I·N·T·H·S

Bulbs	Bloom Time	Color
Amsterdam	Early	Pink
Anna Marie	Early	Light pink
Blue Jacket	Late	Deep blue
Carnegie	Early	White
Delft Blue	Early	Soft lilac blue
Eros	Late	Deep pink
Jan Bos	Early	Carmine red
Marconi	Late	Deep pink
Pink Pearl	Early	Rose pink
Pink Perfection	Early	Pink

T·U·L·I·P·S

Bulbs	Bloom Time	Color
Angelique	Late	Pink
Apricot Beauty	Early	Pink
Atilla	Early	Plum
Bellona	Early	Yellow
Bing Crosby	Early	Red
Christmas Marvel	Early	Pink
Danton	Late	Scarlet
Edith Eddy	Late	Red, edged white
Golden Eddy	Late	Red, edged yellow
Hibernia	Early	White
Madame Spoor	Early	Red, edged yellow
Merry Widow	Early	White and red
Monte Carlo	Early	Yellow
Peerless Pink	Late	Pink
Prominence	Late	Red
Thule	Early	Yellow and red
White Dream	Early	White
Yokohama	Late	Yellow

D·A·F·F·O·D·I·L·S

Bulbs	Color
Barrett Browning	White, apricot corona
Dutch Master	Yellow
February Gold (dwarf)	Yellow
Geranium	Creamy white, apricot corona
Honolulu (double)	White, orange and white corona
Ice Follies	White, yellow blush in corona
Paperwhite	White
Tête-à-Tête (dwarf)	Golden yellow

M·I·N·O·R B·U·L·B·S

Bulbs	Color
Dutch iris	Many hues
Dwarf *Iris danfordiae*	Yellow
Dwarf *Iris reticulata*	Deep blue or purple, orange accents
Giant crocus Flower Record	Deep purple
Grape hyacinth *Muscari*	Blue

COUNTRY WAYS
Insect Weather Forecasters

In farming communities, weather conditions determined how people lived, what they ate, or even if they ate. Favorable weather meant good crops and prosperity. Bad weather that ruined crops brought hardship to a family or an entire community. Weather was so important to the lives of country folks that they devised all sorts of ways to predict it. Insects often turned out to be accurate forecasters.

▼ Some folks relied on bees to predict the weather. When bees stayed close to their hive, rain was on the way, but " a swarm of bees in July, does little more than bring a dry." These observations have been substantiated by beekeepers today.

▼ Some folks said that flies bit more before a rain, which is a fact. Humidity in the air makes it difficult for the insects to fly, so they tend to cling. In addition, moist air causes sweating and the release of body odors, which makes people more appetizing targets.

▼ Believe it or not, crickets can function as thermometers. They chirp faster in warm weather, and slower in cold weather. If you count a cricket's chirps for 14 seconds and add 40, you'll know the temperature wherever the cricket is.

COUNTRY WAYS
Matrimonial Magic

▼ *Something old, something new, something borrowed, something blue.* At a wedding, something old symbolizes the happy married life of an elder. Something new denotes the new experience for the bride and groom. Something borrowed often is made of gold and symbolizes the sun, the source of life. Something blue represents purity.

▼ *Bridal veil.* In Far Eastern weddings, a canopy was carried over the bride during the ceremony to protect her against any ill-omened glances from spectators.

▼ *Bridesmaids and groomsmen.* It was an ancient Roman custom to present these women and men at a wedding in order to outwit jealous demons who might be trying their best to spoil the event.

▼ *Throwing rice.* In Hindu and Chinese religious rites, rice symbolizes prosperity and bestows fertility on the bridal pair. It also provides food for evil spirits, diverting their attention from carrying out envious schemes against the couple.

▼ *The honeymoon.* The rite originated in early Teutonic society, where newly married couples drank mead (wine made of honey) for 30 days, or one complete cycle of the moon. Hence, our name for today's postnuptial vacation.

***May I a small house,
and large garden have!***
—Abraham Cowley

Beautiful and Easy-to-Grow Amaryllis

With its large, lily-like flowers, the Dutch amaryllis is one of the most popular indoor bulbs. It's also one of the easiest to grow. When you get it, the amaryllis bulb is ready to bring into bloom; it doesn't need cold storage or forcing. The bulb will reflower for years if you give it proper care.

▼ Use a container that leaves 2 inches of space between the bulb and the container edge.

▼ Place the bulb in the container, and pack soil firmly around the bulb base. Leave the bulb neck and about a quarter of the bulb exposed.

▼ Set the container in a cool (60° to 65°) room in good light, such as from an east window; direct sunlight isn't necessary.

▼ Keep the soil barely moist.

▼ Move the plant to a warmer (70° to 75°) area once the stalk and strap-like leaves begin to develop.

▼ In about 2 months, a cluster of three to four large flowers will form on top of the stalk. Larger bulbs may produce a second flower stalk when the first flowering stalk begins to die.

▼ When the amaryllis blooms, feed it every 2 weeks while it's in flower with 5-10-5 fertilizer diluted to one quarter strength. Keep the soil evenly moist.

▼ When the flowers die, cut back the stalk or stalks to about 2 inches, and continue regular watering.

▼ After the last spring frost, place the container outdoors in the ground in a partly shady part of the garden. Leave the container and bulb there during the summer months.

▼ In the autumn, before the first frost, bring the container into a cool room with subdued light, snip off all the foliage, and let the bulb rest for a month without water or food.

▼ After one month, begin to water the bulb to spur new growth, keeping the soil barely moist, and maintain the plant as before.

COUNTRY WAYS
The Language of Herbs
Herbs, like flowers, have their own sweet, and sometimes barbed, meanings.

▼ *Peppermint:* warmth of feeling.
▼ *Rosemary:* remembrance.
▼ *Mint:* virtue.
▼ *Sage:* esteem, domestic virtue.
▼ *Basil:* hatred.
▼ *Lavender:* distrust.

WATERING WAYS
There are three ways to water your houseplants: from the top, from the bottom or with a wick.

▼ *From the top.* Pour the water around the inside rim of the pot, not near the center of the plant (this can cause rot). Be careful not to get water on the leaves of plants, such as African violets, which spot. Keep watering until the water seeps out the drainage holes into the saucer. When the plant has drained all excess water, empty the saucer.

▼ *From the bottom.* Fill a large container with one to three inches of water (depending on the pot size). Set the pots, without their saucers, in the water and let them sit until moisture beads up on the soil surface. Thoroughly drain the plants before setting them back in their saucers. This method takes more time, but is particularly effective with plants susceptible to crown rot or leaf spot.

▼ *With a wick.* Before potting a plant, thread a piece of nylon clothesline, acrylic yarn or strips cut from nylon stockings through the drainage hole. Hold the wick upright while you partially fill the pot with soil. Put more soil on top, then the plant. Place the end of the wick extending from the drainage hole into a container of water; keep the container filled. Watering with a wick works best if you pot the plant with vermiculite or a soilless medium. Wash off the old soil from the plant's roots before potting. This method of watering is particularly effective for plants that prefer evenly moist soil.

DO·IT·YOURSELF·DECOR

M·A·K·E A·N
H·E·R·B W·R·E·A·T·H

*I have here only made a nosegay
of culled flowers, and have brought
nothing of my own but the thread
that ties them together.*
— Michel Eyquem de Montaigne

HERB WREATH

Materials: Wire coat hanger; branches of fresh herbs and flowers; floral tape; floral wire; wire cutters.

Directions:

1. Snip off the coat hanger hook just above the hook base. Bend the coat hanger into a heart shape, or other desired shape. If using a heart shape, place the base of the hook at the center top of the heart. Starting at the base of the hook, wrap the hanger with the floral tape.

2. Gather the branches of each variety of herb and flower into bunches, and wire each bunch together. Leave a few individual flowers loose.

3. Working down one side of the coat hanger at a time, wire the herb and flower bunches to the hanger; overlap the bunches so the stem ends are hidden. Mix plant colors and textures, such as grayish lavender with dark green basil, or spikes of salvia blossoms with clusters of heliotrope.

4. From time to time, hold up the wreath and check for skimpy spots. Fill these in with leafy, fluffy branches such as artemesia.

5. Wire on the individual flowers, scattering them around the wreath for accent color. Tuck the stem ends under the tops of the bunched branches.

COUNTRY
C·O·O·K·I·N·G

Cooking is like love. It should be entered into with
abandon or not at all.
—Harriet Van Horne

No book on the Country Kitchen is complete without a chapter devoted to cooking.

On the following pages you'll find our favorite homestyle recipes that capture the essence of country fare: hearty food that's simply prepared, and tastes delicious. There are recipes for warming breakfasts, savory suppers, tasty accompaniments. You can even make your own soups, with our special mix 'n match guide. Try pairing a cup of homemade soup with one of our special sandwiches for a terrific meal.

And of course, we couldn't forget about dessert: there are fragrant pies, berry cobblers, creamy parfaits. And for kids and the young at heart, we even have yummy jumbo cookies, shown at left.

The pleasures of country cooking is what a country kitchen is all about. We hope these recipes help you savor the experience.

S·U·P·P·E·R·T·I·M·E

Sunday Supper Roast Chicken

**Seeing is deceiving.
It's eating that's believing.**
—James Thurber

SUNDAY SUPPER ROAST CHICKEN

Bake at 350° for 1 hour and 30 minutes.
Makes 6 servings, plus leftovers.

Nutrient Value Per Serving: 611 calories, 56 g protein, 39 g fat, 5 g carbohydrate, 250 mg sodium, 199 mg cholesterol.

- 1 roasting chicken (about 6 pounds)
  Apple Nut Stuffing (recipe, at right)
- ¼ cup (½ stick) butter or margarine, melted
- 2 tablespoons lemon juice
- 1 teaspoon aromatic bitters
  Rice Pilaf (recipe follows)
- 1 ripe red Comice pear, cored and cut into sixths

1. Preheat the oven to moderate (350°). Stuff the chicken neck and body cavities lightly with the Apple Nut Stuffing. Skewer the neck to the body, push the tail inside the bird, and secure the body cavity closed. Tie the legs together, draw the string up and under the wings, and knot it.
2. Place the chicken on a rack in a shallow roasting pan. Combine the melted butter or margarine with the lemon juice, and brush the mixture over the chicken.
3. Roast the chicken in the preheated moderate oven (350°) for 1 hour and 15 minutes, basting several times with the butter mixture.
4. Stir the aromatic bitters into the remaining butter mixture. Brush the bitters mixture onto the chicken to coat the chicken evenly. Roast for 15 minutes more, or until the drumstick moves easily at the joint. Remove the string.
5. Line a serving platter with the Rice Pilaf. Place the chicken on the rice and garnish with the pear slices.

Rice Pilaf: Sauté 1 chopped small onion (¼ cup) and 1 small green apple, halved, peeled, cored and chopped, in ¼ cup (½ stick) of butter or margarine in a medium-sized saucepan over medium heat. Add 2 cups of rice, and stir to coat the rice. Pour 4 cups of water and ½ cup of white wine over the rice. Add 1 teaspoon of salt, ¼ teaspoon of cinnamon, a dash of ground nutmeg, and freshly ground pepper to taste. Bring the rice mixture to boiling. Lower the heat, and cover the saucepan. Simmer for 17 to 20 minutes, or until the liquid is absorbed. Fluff the rice with a fork. Toss in ½ cup of halved seedless green grapes and 3 Italian (prune) plums, halved and pitted, just before placing the rice on a warmed serving platter.
Makes 6 cups.

APPLE NUT STUFFING

Makes 6 servings, or enough to stuff a 6-pound bird.

Nutrient Value Per Serving: 221 calories, 5 g protein, 15 g fat, 19 g carbohydrate, 386 mg sodium, 22 mg cholesterol.

- 1 medium-size onion, chopped (½ cup)
- ¼ cup (½ stick) butter or margarine
- 1 cup chopped apple
- 1 envelope or teaspoon instant chicken broth
- ⅓ cup water
- 6 slices white bread, cubed (3 cups)
- ½ cup chopped peanuts

1. Sauté the onion in the butter or margarine in a large skillet until the onion is soft. Stir in the apple, broth and water. Bring the mixture to boiling. Remove the skillet from the heat.
2. Add the bread cubes and the chopped peanuts to the skillet. Toss the stuffing with a fork until it is moist.

COUNTRY WAYS
Leftovers

Country folk have always been frugal; they never let their leftovers go to waste. Here's a casserole recipe that makes the most of your Sunday Supper Roast Chicken leftovers.
Arrange the remaining Rice Pilaf in a 6-cup shallow casserole dish. Carve the remaining Sunday Supper Roast Chicken from the carcass, and place it over the rice. Cover the casserole dish with plastic wrap, and refrigerate the leftovers. Before reheating them, cook 1 bag (1 pound) of frozen mixed vegetables for 2 minutes, following the package directions. Transfer the vegetables with a slotted spoon to the casserole dish. Combine 1 can of condensed cream of mushroom soup with ¾ cup of the vegetable cooking water, and pour the liquid over the casserole. Bake in a preheated hot oven (400°) until the casserole is bubbly and heated through, for 35 minutes.

A hearty feast for a chilly night: Meatloaf Pizzaiola (recipe, page 188) and Oven Roasted Vegetables (recipe, page 189).

MEATLOAF PIZZAIOLA

Bake at 375° for 1 hour.
Makes 6 servings.

Nutrient Value Per Serving: 427 calories, 28 g protein, 29 g fat, 13 g carbohydrate, 968 mg sodium, 149 mg cholesterol.

❧

1   egg
1½ pounds ground beef, pork and/or veal
2   slices bread, crumbled
1   medium-size onion, grated
1   clove garlic, finely chopped
¼   cup chopped fresh parsley
1   small can evaporated milk
2   tablespoons chopped fresh basil OR: 1½ teaspoons
        dried basil, crumbled
1   teaspoon salt
¼   teaspoon freshly ground pepper
1½ cups tomato sauce
1   cup shredded mozzarella cheese (4 ounces)
    Broccoli flowerets, for garnish (optional)
    Cherry tomatoes, for garnish (optional)
    Oven Roasted Vegetables (recipe, page 189)

1. Preheat the oven to moderate (375°).
2. Combine the egg, ground meat, bread crumbs, onion, garlic, parsley, evaporated milk, basil, salt and pepper in a large bowl just until the ingredients are blended; do not overmix.
3. Press the mixture into a 9 x 5 x 3-inch loaf pan, and unmold the meatloaf into a shallow roasting pan. Pour the tomato sauce over the meatloaf.
4. Bake the meatloaf in the preheated moderate oven (375°) for 50 minutes. Sprinkle the meatloaf with the mozzarella cheese. Bake for 10 minutes more, or until the mozzarella cheese melts. If you wish, garnish the meatloaf with broccoli flowerets and cherry tomatoes. Serve the meatloaf with the Oven Roasted Vegetables.

Note: The meatloaf mixture can be made the night before, shaped and unmolded into a shallow roasting pan, covered with plastic wrap, and refrigerated. One hour and 30 minutes before serving, remove the meatloaf from the refrigerator and unwrap it. Let the meatloaf stand at room temperature for 15 minutes, then bake it in a preheated moderate oven (375°) for 1 hour and 15 minutes, or until it is well cooked.

CASSEROLE TOPPINGS

▼ Cut Italian or French bread into very thin slices. Beat 1 egg white in a small bowl until stiff peaks form. Add ¼ cup of shredded Cheddar cheese. Spread the cheese mixture on the bread slices, and arrange the slices on a small baking sheet. Bake the slices in a preheated hot oven (425°) until they are golden, for 5 minutes. Place the slices on top of the prepared casserole.
▼ Toss 2 cups of small cubes of bread with 2 tablespoons of butter or margarine and 1 clove of garlic in a skillet over medium-high until the cubes are crisp and golden. Sprinkle the cubes over the prepared casserole.
▼ Toss 2 cups of popped popcorn with 3 tablespoons of melted butter or margarine, 1 teaspoon of garlic salt, and 3 tablespoons of grated Parmesan cheese. Spread the mixture on a small baking sheet. Bake the topping in a preheated hot oven (425°) until it is very hot, for 5 minutes. Sprinkle the topping over the prepared casserole.

FREEZING CASSEROLES

Line the casserole dish specified in the individual recipe with heavy-duty aluminum foil, allowing enough overlap to cover the food and make a tight seal. In choosing a casserole dish, remember that the shallower the dish, the quicker the frozen food will heat. Fill the foil-lined casserole dish following the individual recipe. Cover the food with the overlap of foil. Seal the foil package tightly, and label, date and freeze it inside the casserole dish. When the food is frozen solid, remove the foil package from the casserole dish; the frozen casserole will hold its shape without the dish. Casseroles can be frozen for up to 3 months.
To Bake a Frozen Casserole: Remove the aluminum foil from the frozen casserole, and return the casserole to the original dish. Bake the casserole following the recipe directions.
To Microwave a Frozen Casserole: Use a microwave-safe casserole dish, and follow the directions above.

OVEN ROASTED VEGETABLES

Bake these hearty vegetables in the pan with the Meatloaf Pizzaiola (recipe, page 188).

Bake at 375° for 1 hour.
Makes 6 servings.

Nutrient Value Per Serving: 215 calories, 5 g protein, 7 g fat, 36 g carbohydrate, 13 mg sodium, 0 mg cholesterol.

❧

1   acorn squash, sliced, peeled, seeded, cubed
     and parboiled
6   medium-size potatoes, peeled, halved
     and parboiled
3   onions, peeled, halved and parboiled
2   large zucchini, trimmed and cut into chunks
3   tablespoons olive oil OR: vegetable oil
     Salt and freshly ground pepper, to taste
     Dried rosemary, crumbled
     Chopped scallions, for garnish

1. Arrange the squash, potatoes, onions and zucchini in the roasting pan around the Meatloaf Pizzaiola. Brush the vegetables with some of the olive or vegetable oil. Sprinkle them with the salt and pepper and the rosemary.
2. Bake the vegetables in the preheated moderate oven (375°), basting them several times with the remaining oil, until the vegetables are golden, for 1 hour. Garnish the vegetables with the scallions.

CASSEROLE DISH
SUBSTITUTION CHART

4-cup casserole dish:	9-inch pie plate *or* 8 x 1½-inch cake pan
6-cup casserole dish:	10-inch pie plate *or* 9 x 1½-inch cake pan
8-cup casserole dish:	8 x 8 x 2-inch square baking pan *or* 9 x 5 x 3-inch loaf pan
10-cup casserole dish:	9 x 9 x 2-inch square baking pan
12-cup casserole dish:	13 x 9 x 2-inch baking pan
16-cup casserole dish:	13 x 9 x 3-inch baking pan

ZUCCHINI LASAGNA

Zucchini replaces the noodles in a deliciously low-calorie, make-ahead casserole.

Bake at 350° for 1 hour.
Makes 8 servings.

Nutrient Value Per Serving: 279 calories, 3 g protein, 6 g fat, 0 g carbohydrate, 195 mg sodium, 39 mg cholesterol.

❧

½   pound sweet Italian sausage, sliced
1   large onion, chopped (1 cup)
1   can (1 pound, 12 ounces) tomatoes in purée
½   pound mushrooms, sliced
1   teaspoon salt
1   teaspoon dried oregano, crumbled
1   teaspoon mixed Italian herbs, crumbled
1   container (16 ounces) lowfat cottage cheese
2   eggs, beaten
½   cup grated Parmesan cheese
6   large zucchini, thinly sliced lengthwise
     (about 6 inches long)
1½ cups grated lowfat mozzarella cheese (6 ounces)

1. Brown the sausage in a large skillet. Push it to one side, and drain off all but 1 tablespoon of fat.
2. Sauté the onion in the skillet until soft. Add the tomatoes with their purée, the mushrooms, salt, oregano and Italian herbs. Cover the skillet and simmer the sausage mixture for 15 minutes.
3. Combine the cottage cheese, eggs and Parmesan cheese in a small bowl, and stir until all the ingredients are well blended.
4. Preheat the oven to moderate (350°).
5. Layer the ingredients in a 13 x 9 x 2-inch baking pan as follows: half of the sausage mixture, one third of the sliced zucchini, all the cottage cheese mixture, another third of the zucchini, the remaining sausage mixture, and the remaining zucchini. Cover the pan with aluminum foil.
6. Bake the lasagna in the preheated moderate oven (350°) for 45 minutes. Remove the aluminum foil, and sprinkle the lasagna with mozzarella cheese. Bake the lasagna for 15 minutes more, or until the mozzarella cheese is melted.

YANKEE BOILED DINNER

Serve this hearty, one-pot winter dinner on a weekend. Then use the leftovers to prepare the Iowa Bean Bake (recipe, at right).

Makes 24 servings.

Nutrient Value Per Serving: 258 calories, 20 g protein, 11 g fat, 19 g carbohydrate, 1,387 mg sodium, 60 mg cholesterol.

1	shank end ham (about 8 pounds)
	Handful celery leaves
1	large onion, chopped (1 cup)
1	tablespoon mixed pickling spices
8	boiling potatoes, peeled
1	head cauliflower, separated into flowerets
2	acorn squash, quartered
4	large carrots, peeled and quartered
	Prepared mustard (optional)

1. Place the ham in a large kettle, and add water to the kettle to a depth of 2 inches. Add the celery leaves, onion and pickling spices.
2. Bring the water to boiling, lower the heat and cover the kettle. Simmer the ham for 1½ hours, or until the ham is tender when pierced with a 2-tined fork. Remove the ham to a warmed serving platter, and keep the ham warm.
3. Strain the cooking liquid into a large kettle, and skim off the fat. Add the potatoes, cauliflower, squash and carrots. Bring the liquid to boiling, lower the heat and cover the kettle. Simmer the vegetables for 30 minutes, or until the vegetables are tender when pierced with a 2-tined fork.
4. Arrange the vegetables on the serving platter with the ham. Cut the ham into thin slices. If you wish, serve the ham with prepared mustard.
5. Remove all the leftover ham from the bone, and dice it. Reserve the bone and 2 cups of the ham to use for making Iowa Bean Bake *(recipe, at right)*.

IOWA BEAN BAKE

*Bake at 375° for 1 hour and 45 minutes.
Or microwave at defrost for 30 minutes, then at half power for 30 minutes.*

Makes 8 servings.

Nutrient Value Per Serving: 324 calories, 26 g protein, 5 g fat, 44 g carbohydrate, 633 mg sodium, 40 mg cholesterol.

1	bag (1 pound) dried white beans
	Bone and 2 cups diced ham left over from Yankee Boiled Dinner (recipe, at left)
1	large onion, chopped (1 cup)
2	large carrots, grated
1	cup chopped celery
2	teaspoons salt
1	teaspoon dried thyme, crumbled
¼	teaspoon freshly ground pepper
2	leeks, split and sliced
2	large carrots, peeled and diced
1	cup sliced celery

1. Rinse the white beans in a strainer under cold running water. Place them in a large kettle, and add water to cover the beans by 2 inches.
2. Bring to boiling, lower the heat, and simmer for 2 minutes. Remove the kettle from the heat, and let the white beans stand in the cooking water for 1 hour. Add the bone, onion, grated carrots, chopped celery, salt, thyme and pepper.
3. Bring the bean mixture to boiling, lower the heat to simmer, and cover the kettle. Simmer for 2 hours, or until the white beans are tender. Add the leeks, diced carrots and sliced celery. Simmer for 15 minutes. Cool the bean mixture. Stir in the diced ham.
4. To freeze, line a 10-cup casserole dish with aluminum foil following the directions in Freezing Casseroles *(see Tip box, page 188)*. Fill the casserole dish with the bean mixture. Continue with the Tip directions for freezing the casserole.
5. To bake the frozen casserole, remove the aluminum foil package two hours before serving, and return the casserole to the original dish. Preheat the oven to moderate (375°). Bake the casserole in the preheated moderate oven (375°) until it is bubbly hot, for 1 hour and 45 minutes.
6. To microwave the casserole, remove the aluminum foil and return the casserole to the original dish. Cover the casserole dish with wax paper. Microwave at defrost for 30 minutes. Rotate the dish one half turn. Microwave at half power for 30 minutes.

PRIDE OF GLOUCESTER BAKED FISH

Bake at 350° for 30 minutes
Makes 6 to 8 servings.

Nutrient Value Per Serving: 441 calories, 29 g protein, 28 g fat, 18 g carbohydrate, 726 mg sodium, 151 mg cholesterol.

❦

2   pounds whiting OR: other fish fillets
¾   cup bread crumbs
¼   cup Romano cheese, grated
1   large clove garlic, finely chopped
¼   teaspoon freshly ground pepper
1   teaspoon salt
2   tablespoons parsley, chopped
2   eggs
¾   cup hot vegetable oil
2   cups sliced onions
2   cups sliced sweet green peppers
2   cups stewed tomatoes
    Salt and freshly ground pepper, to taste
1   pound spaghetti (optional)
    Parmesan cheese (optional)

1. Cut the fish fillets into 3 pieces each.
2. Combine the bread crumbs, Romano cheese, garlic, the ¼ teaspoon of pepper, the teaspoon of salt and the parsley in a small bowl. Beat the eggs in a separate bowl. Dip the fish pieces into the beaten eggs, then roll them in the bread crumb mixture.
3. Fry the fish pieces in the hot oil.
4. Drain the oil that is left from frying the fish into a saucepan. Sauté the onions and the green peppers in the oil. Add the tomatoes and the salt and pepper. Cook the sauce until the vegetables are tender.
5. Preheat the oven to moderate (350°).
6. Arrange the fish in a casserole dish, and pour the sauce over the fish. Bake the fish, covered, in the preheated moderate oven (350°) for 30 minutes. If you wish, cook 1 pound of spaghetti following the package directions, place the spaghetti on a warmed serving platter, and arrange the fish and sauce over it. Sprinkle with Parmesan cheese, if you wish.

HEARTY RIBS AND BEAN BAKE

This casserole is a stick-to-your-ribs delight!

Bake at 350° for 1¾ to 2 hours.
Makes 6 servings.

Nutrient Value Per Serving: 657 calories, 35 g protein, 30 g fat, 62 g carbohydrate, 1,015 mg sodium, 84 mg cholesterol.

❦

3   to 3½ pounds country-style pork ribs
¼   cup water
1   can (15 ounces) tomato sauce
1   envelope onion soup mix
⅓   cup brown sugar
2   tablespoons prepared mustard
⅛   teaspoon hot pepper sauce
3   cups cooked and drained great northern beans
3   cups cooked and drained red kidney beans
1½ cups thinly sliced celery
1   sweet red or green pepper, cut into thin strips

1. Preheat the oven to moderate (350°).
2. Place the ribs in a 12 x 9-inch baking dish, and add the water. Cover the dish tightly, and bake the ribs in the preheated moderate oven (350°) for 1¼ hours. Remove the ribs to paper toweling. Pour off the cooking liquid, and reserve it. Leave the oven on.
3. Combine the tomato sauce, onion soup mix, brown sugar, prepared mustard and hot pepper sauce in a small saucepan, and cook the tomato mixture slowly for 10 minutes. Remove the excess fat from the ribs' cooking liquid, and add enough water to the remaining liquid to make 1 cup. Stir the liquid into the tomato mixture.
4. Combine the great northern and red kidney beans with the celery, red or green pepper strips and all but ½ cup of the tomato mixture. Place the bean mixture in the baking dish. Arrange the ribs on top of the bean mixture, and brush the ribs with the remaining tomato mixture. Cover the dish tightly, and bake the ribs and beans in the preheated moderate oven (350°) for 30 to 45 minutes. Arrange the ribs and beans on a warmed serving platter, and serve.

*A new version of the classic
French country casserole, this
Cassoulet (recipe page 194) is
served with Savory Baked
Vegetables (recipe, page 195).*

CASSOULET

A perfect choice for your next dinner party, this classic casserole is made with lamb chops. This dish also can be made ahead; see the Note at the end of the recipe.

Bake at 350° for 1 hour and 15 minutes.
Makes 12 servings.

Nutrient Value Per Serving: 690 calories, 31 g protein, 53 g fat, 21 g carbohydrate, 971 mg sodium, 126 mg cholesterol.

❦

2   *ham hocks (about 1 pound each)*
8   *cups water*
4   *carrots, peeled and chopped*
2   *large onions, chopped (2 cups)*
1   *tablespoon salt*
2   *cloves garlic, halved*
2   *bay leaves*
2   *teaspoons dried thyme, crumbled*
3   *sprigs parsley*
1   *package (2 pounds) dried large lima beans*
6   *thick lamb chops (about 4 pounds)*
    Salt and freshly ground pepper, to taste
    Sliced green onion
    Zucchini sticks, for garnish (optional)
    Cherry tomatoes, for garnish (optional)
    Fresh mint, for garnish (optional)
    Savory Baked Vegetables (recipe, page 195)

A man seldom thinks with more earnestness of anything than he does of his dinner.
— Samuel Johnson

1. Place the ham hocks in a large kettle with the water, carrots, onions and the 1 tablespoon of salt.

2. Tie the garlic, bay leaves, thyme and parsley in a piece of cheesecloth. Push the bundle under the liquid in the kettle.

3. Bring the liquid slowly to boiling. Reduce the heat, and cover the kettle. Simmer for 1 hour, or until the ham hocks are tender.

4. While the ham hocks simmer, pick over the lima beans and rinse them under running water. Place the lima beans in a large saucepan, and add water to cover the beans by 2 inches. Bring to boiling, and simmer for 2 minutes. Remove the saucepan from the heat and let the lima beans stand in the cooking water at room temperature for 1 hour.

5. Drain the lima beans, and combine them with the ham hocks and ham broth in the kettle. Simmer the combined mixture for 2 hours, or until the lima beans are tender. Remove the ham hocks, and trim the fat and bones from the meat. Cut the ham into small pieces, and return it to the kettle.

6. While the lima beans simmer, sprinkle some salt on the bottom of a large skillet. Heat the skillet, add the lamb chops and brown them well on both sides. Season the chops with the salt and pepper, and drain the chops on paper toweling.

7. Spoon the lima bean-ham mixture into a 16-cup shallow casserole dish or baking pan; arrange the chops on top.

8. Preheat the oven to moderate (350°).

9. Bake the cassoulet in the preheated moderate oven (350°) until it is bubbly hot, for 1 hour and 15 minutes. Sprinkle the cassoulet with the sliced green onion. If you wish, garnish the cassoulet with zucchini sticks, cherry tomatoes and fresh mint. To serve, cut each lamb chop in half. Place the chops on a warmed serving platter along with the lima bean-ham mixture and the Savory Baked Vegetables.

Note: *To make the cassoulet ahead, prepare it through Step 7. Let it cool to room temperature, cover the casserole dish with aluminum foil, and refrigerate it. When ready to heat the cassoulet, let the casserole dish stand at room temperature for 15 minutes. Loosen the foil around the dish before placing it in the oven.*

SAVORY BAKED VEGETABLES

A vegetable dish that bakes along with your main dish is doubly efficient. It uses the same oven heat that the casserole uses, and takes away pot-watching chores from the cook.

Bake at 350° for 1 hour and 15 minutes.
Makes 12 servings.

Nutrient Value Per Serving: 81 calories, 2 g protein, 4 g fat, 10 g carbohydrate, 94 mg sodium, 11 mg cholesterol.

❧

1   bag (1 pound) carrots
1   pound green beans
¾   cup boiling water
     Salt and freshly ground pepper, to taste
1   teaspoon dried basil, crumbled
4   tablespoons (½ stick) butter or margarine
4   slices white bread, crumbled
2   tablespoons chopped parsley

1. Peel the carrots and cut them into 3-inch sticks. Trim the green beans and cut them into halves. Pile the vegetables in a 6-cup casserole dish. (The recipe can be made ahead up to this point. Cover the casserole dish, and refrigerate the vegetables.)
2. Preheat the oven to moderate (350°).
3. Pour the boiling water over the vegetables. Season with the salt and pepper and the basil. Dot the vegetables with 2 tablespoons of the butter or margarine, and cover the casserole dish.
4. Bake in the preheated moderate oven (350°) until the vegetables are crisply tender, for 1 hour and 15 minutes.
5. Melt the remaining 2 tablespoons of butter in a small skillet, and add the bread crumbs. Sauté, stirring constantly, until the bread crumbs are golden. Add the chopped parsley. Spoon the parsley mixture over the baked vegetables just before serving.

Note: *The vegetables can bake along with other casseroles at different temperatures. Bake at 325° for 1 hour and 30 minutes, at 375° for 1 hour, or at 400° for 50 minutes.*

CREAMY SCALLOPED PARSNIPS

Bake at 325° for 50 minutes.
Makes 8 servings.

Nutrient Value Per Serving: 275 calories, 5 g protein, 15 g fat, 32 g carbohydrate, 655 mg sodium, 45 mg cholesterol.

❧

2   pounds parsnips, pared and cut into
        ¼-inch-thick slices
2   cups half-and-half
3   tablespoons all-purpose flour
3   tablespoons chopped parsley
1½ teaspoons salt
¼   teaspoon freshly ground pepper
1   large onion, coarsely chopped (1 cup)
3   tablespoons butter OR: margarine

1. Preheat the oven to slow (325°). Lightly butter an 8-inch square or other 2-quart baking dish.
2. Bring 1 inch of water to boiling in a medium-size saucepan over medium heat. Add the parsnips and return the water to boiling. Cover the saucepan and cook the parsnips until they are barely tender, for 5 minutes. Drain the parsnips.
3. Meanwhile, stir together the half-and-half and flour in a small saucepan until they are well blended. Cook the cream mixture over low heat until it is thickened, for 3 or 4 minutes. Add the parsley, salt and pepper.
4. Layer half of the parsnips and half of the onion in the prepared dish. Pour half of the cream mixture over the vegetables. Dot the vegetables with half of the butter or margarine. Repeat the layering. Pour the remaining cream mixture over the vegetables and dot the top of the casserole with the remaining butter. Cover the dish.
5. Bake the casserole in the preheated slow oven (325°) for 40 minutes. Remove the cover and bake until the parsnips are tender and the top is lightly golden, for 10 minutes more.

S·O·U·P·S &
S·A·N·D·W·I·C·H·E·S

GAZPACHO

Try serving this Spanish soup with a sandwich to make a tasty light meal.

Makes 2 servings.

Nutrient Value Per Serving: 52 calories, 4 g protein, 1 g fat, 10 g carbohydrate, 457 mg sodium, 0 mg cholesterol.

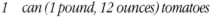

  2   large ripe tomatoes, peeled
 ½   sweet red pepper, seeded
 ½   yellow onion
 ½   cucumber, peeled and seeded
 ¼   cup red wine vinegar
  1   clove garlic
  1   cup tomato juice
       Pinch ground hot red pepper
       Pinch dried dill

1. Coarsely chop the tomatoes, sweet red pepper, onion and cucumber.
2. Mix together the vinegar, garlic and tomato juice in a small bowl. Place the vinegar and vegetable mixtures together in the container of an electric blender. Cover the blender and whirl until the mixture is puréed. Transfer the purée to a serving bowl.
3. Stir in the ground hot red pepper and the dill. Chill the soup for at least 2 hours before serving it.

VEGETABLE FISH CHOWDER

Filled with the rich goodness of the sea, this meal-in-a-bowl is ready in less than 30 minutes.

Makes 4 servings.

Nutrient Value Per Serving: 255 calories, 29 g protein, 3 g fat, 32 g carbohydrate, 1,166 mg sodium, 54 mg cholesterol.

  1   can (1 pound, 12 ounces) tomatoes
  1   bottle (8 ounces) clam broth
  1   teaspoon salt
  1   teaspoon dried thyme, crumbled
 ¼   teaspoon freshly ground pepper
  2   ears of corn, cut into 2-inch pieces
  1   cup frozen lima beans (from a 1-pound bag)
  2   carrots, cut into 2-inch pieces
  1   cup sliced celery
  1   cup sliced green beans
  1   package (1 pound) frozen fillet of flounder
       OR: cod, cut into 1-inch pieces

1. Combine the tomatoes with the broth in a large saucepan. Stir in the salt, thyme and pepper. Bring the mixture to boiling.
2. Add the corn, lima beans, carrots, celery and green beans, and return to boiling. Lower the heat and simmer for 10 minutes, or until the vegetables are crisply tender.
3. Add the frozen fish cubes and simmer for 10 minutes more, or until the fish flakes easily.

COUNTRY WAYS
"Real" Clam Chowder

COUNTRY WAYS
"Real" Clam Chowder

Just as every farmer had his own secrets for raising successful crops and livestock, every cook had her own secret recipes which surfaced once a year at the county or state fair. It was recognized that everyone had his or her own way of doing things, but each person was confident that his or her own way was the "right" way. Take, for example, one New Englander's reaction to a brew called Manhattan Clam Chowder:

"There is a terrible pink mixture (with tomatoes in it, and herbs) called Manhattan Clam Chowder, that is only vegetable soup, and not to be confused with New England Clam Chowder, nor spoken of in the same breath. Tomatoes and clams have no more affinity than ice cream and horseradish. It is sacrilege to wed bivalves with bay leaves, and only a degraded cook would do such a thing."

After reading this indictment, we couldn't help but include *only* a New England Clam Chowder recipe in this chapter!

So munch on, crunch on, take your nuncheon,
Breakfast, supper, dinner, luncheon!
— Robert Browning

NEW ENGLAND CLAM CHOWDER

Makes 4 servings.

Nutrient Value Per Serving: 364 calories, 14 g protein, 17 g fat, 39 g carbohydrate, 608 mg sodium, 52 mg cholesterol.

❦

3   *slices lean bacon, cut into ½-inch dice (2½ ounces)*
1   *medium-size onion, chopped (½ cup)*
2   *tablespoons all-purpose flour*
¼   *teaspoon dried thyme, crumbled*
¼   *teaspoon freshly ground pepper*
3   *cups milk*
1   *can (6½ ounces) clams finely chopped, drained and liquid reserved*
1   *bottle (8 ounces) clam broth*
3   *large red-skinned potatoes (about 1¼ pounds), peeled and cut into ½-inch cubes*
3   *to 4 drops liquid red pepper seasoning (optional)*

1. Cook the bacon in a medium-size saucepan over medium heat for 3 minutes, or until the bacon is golden brown. Add the onion, and sauté until the onion has softened, for 2 to 3 minutes. Stir in the flour, thyme and pepper. Stir in the milk.

2. Add the reserve canned clam liquid, the clam broth and potatoes to the saucepan. Bring to boiling over medium heat, stirring constantly. Lower the heat, partially cover the saucepan, and simmer until the potatoes are tender, for 8 to 10 minutes.

3. Add the clams. Simmer just until the chowder is heated through, for about 2 minutes. If you wish, stir in 3 to 4 drops of liquid red pepper seasoning.

Note: *The chowder can be prepared a day ahead through Step 2.*

M·I·X & M·A·T·C·H
M·A·I·N-D·I·S·H S·O·U·P·S

Some wonderful ways to use up leftovers.

Pour 4 cups of one of the STOCKS, below, into a large saucepan.
Add 1 cup each of STARCH and VEGETABLES. Simmer for 15 to 30 minutes. In the last 10 minutes of cooking time, add the
PROTEIN. Sprinkle with basil, oregano, or parsley. Just before serving, top with croutons or grated Parmesan cheese.

STOCK	STARCH	VEGETABLES	PROTEIN
VEGETABLE STOCK	Cooked brown rice Red kidney beans Cooked macaroni Diced raw potato	Cut green beans Diced yellow turnip Frozen snow peas Canned sliced carrots	Drained flaked tuna Canned minced clams Canned salmon Canned oysters
HEARTY BEEF STOCK	Frozen lima beans Bulgur wheat Sliced raw potatoes Cooked ziti	Sliced yellow squash Frozen chopped broccoli Italian green beans Diced white turnip	Shredded Swiss cheese Cooked sausage Crumbled bacon White kidney beans
RICH TURKEY STOCK	Canned corn Diced raw yams Cooked white rice Raw egg noodles	Sliced acorn squash Canned peas Sliced celery Canned white onions	Diced cooked lamb Diced baked ham Flaked cooked fish Sliced hot dogs

COUNTRY WAYS
Touched by Cupid

▼ Dimples long have been a sign of beauty and
passion. It was said that babies with dimples
were touched by Cupid's finger.
▼ Men with dimples in their chins were
thought to be passionate and lovable.
Women with dimples in their chins were said
to be flirtatious.
▼ It seems that a dimple in the chin was
preferable to dimples in the cheeks, as
evidenced by this old rhyme:
  A dimple in your cheek,
  Many hearts you will seek.
  A dimple in your chin,
  Many hearts you will win.

COUNTRY WAYS
Glorious Garnishes

Dress up soups, salads and main courses with
easy and colorful garnishes. Turn green onions,
leeks, carrots or sweet red and yellow peppers
into corkscrew shapes by cutting very thin
threads from the vegetables with a paring knife,
and placing the threads in ice water for an hour
or two before a meal. Or create free-form wavy
shapes from a carrot by cutting paper-thin strips
with a swivel-bladed vegetable peeler and
putting the strips in ice water. An hour or so
later, the strips will be wavy.

VEGETABLE STOCK

Sautéing the vegetables in oil before simmering adds a deep, hearty flavor to vegetable broth. Use this stock to make gravy, too.

Makes 12 cups.

Nutrient Value Per Serving: 89 calories, 0 g protein, 9 g fat, 2 mg carbohydrate, 560 mg sodium, 0 mg cholesterol.

❦

2   large onions, chopped (2 cups)
2   cloves garlic, finely chopped
6   large carrots, peeled and chopped
4   stalks celery with tops, chopped
2   leeks, chopped and washed (optional)
½   pound mushrooms, sliced (optional)
2   small white turnips, peeled and diced
½   cup vegetable oil
10   cups water
2   bay leaves
1   tablespoon salt
6   whole peppercorns
4   whole cloves

1. Sauté the onions, garlic, carrots, celery, the leeks and mushrooms if you wish, and the turnips in the oil in a kettle or Dutch oven, stirring often, until the vegetables are golden, for about 30 minutes.
2. Add the water, bay leaves, salt, peppercorns and cloves, and stir the ingredients to blend. Bring the stock to boiling. Skim the surface of the stock, lower the heat, and cover the kettle.
3. Simmer the stock until it is rich and flavorful, for about 2 hours. Cool the stock at room temperature. Strain the stock through cheesecloth into a large bowl.
4. Refrigerate the stock for up to 4 days. To freeze the stock, pour it into plastic freezer containers to within ½ inch of the top. Seal, label, date and freeze the stock. Use the frozen stock within 3 months in soups, sauces, gravies or casseroles.

HEARTY BEEF STOCK

Get out the old soup kettle, and start saving all the meat bones and vegetable trims to turn them into appetizing soups.

Roast bones and vegetables at 450° for 30 minutes. Makes 12 cups.

Nutrient Value Per Cup: 23 calories, 1 g protein, 1 g fat, 4 g carbohydrate, 557 mg sodium, 0 mg cholesterol.

❦

3   pounds beef meat bones OR: bones from a roast
3   large carrots, peeled and chopped
2   large onions, halved
1   leek, trimmed (optional)
2   celery stalks with leaves, chopped
10   cups water
     Handful parsley
2   cloves garlic, peeled
1   tablespoon salt
6   whole peppercorns
1   bay leaf

1. Preheat the oven to hot (450°). Put the meat bones, carrots, onions, leek if you wish, and the celery in a roasting pan.
2. Roast the bones and vegetables in the preheated hot oven (450°) until the bones are brown, for 30 minutes.
3. Place the bones and vegetables in a large kettle or Dutch oven. Add the water, parsley, garlic, salt, peppercorns and bay leaf. Cover the kettle.
4. Bring the stock to boiling, and skim its surface. Lower the heat and simmer the stock for 2 hours, or until it is rich and flavorful. Cool the stock to room temperature. Strain the stock through cheesecloth into a large bowl.
5. Refrigerate the stock for up to 4 days, leaving the fat layer on the surface. When you are ready to use the stock, lift off the fat and discard it. To freeze the stock, pour it into plastic freezer containers to within ½ inch of the top. Seal, label, date and freeze the stock. Use the frozen stock within 3 months for soups or sauces.

RICH TURKEY STOCK

Don't let the carcass of your holiday turkey go to waste. Simmer it in a stockpot and enjoy the rich, tasty broth.

Makes 12 cups.

Nutrient Value Per Serving: 45 calories, 1 g protein, 2 g fat, 6 g carbohydrate, 555 mg sodium, 0 mg cholesterol.

1   turkey carcass
2   large onions, quartered
4   carrots, peeled and diced
6   stalks celery, chopped
2   white turnips, peeled and diced
10 cups water
1   clove garlic, halved
2   sprigs parsley
1   tablespoon salt
1   teaspoon dried thyme, crumbled
6   whole peppercorns

1. Combine the turkey carcass, onions, carrots, celery, turnips, water, garlic, parsley, salt, thyme and peppercorns in a large kettle or stock pot. Cover the kettle or pot.
2. Bring the stock to boiling. Skim its surface, lower the heat and simmer for 2 hours, or until the stock is rich and flavorful. Cool the stock.
3. Remove the turkey meat from the bones, and reserve it to use in a casserole. Strain the stock through cheesecloth into a large bowl.
4. Refrigerate the stock for up to 2 days, leaving the fat layer on the surface. When you are ready to use the stock, lift off the fat and discard it. To freeze the stock, pour it into plastic freezer containers to within ½ inch of the top. Seal, label, date and freeze the stock. Use the stock within 2 months.

Note: *This recipe also is a great way to use chicken necks, gizzards and trims. Freeze the assorted parts from different chickens in plastic containers with tight covers until you have about 4 cups. Use the chicken parts in place of the turkey carcass.*

BLACK BEAN SOUP WITH ROASTED PEPPERS

Makes 6 generous servings (about 2½ quarts).

Nutrient Value Per Serving: 386 calories, 18 g protein, 10 g fat, 58 g carbohydrate, 741 mg sodium, 0 mg cholesterol.

1   pound dried black beans, soaked
2   quarts plus 1 cup water
1   medium-size onion, coarsely chopped
2   large cloves garlic, smashed but left whole
3   large onions, chopped (3 cups)
4   large cloves garlic, finely chopped
1   sweet green pepper, halved, cored, seeded and chopped
¼   cup olive oil OR: vegetable oil
2   teaspoons salt
¾   teaspoon freshly ground pepper
½   teaspoon dried oregano, crumbled
2   sweet red peppers
2   tablespoons red wine vinegar
    Dairy sour cream OR: plain yogurt (optional)

1. Drain the black beans, and place them in a large saucepan. Add 2 quarts of the water, the coarsely chopped onion and smashed garlic cloves. Bring the mixture to boiling over medium heat. Lower the heat, cover the saucepan, and simmer until the black beans are almost tender, for 1½ hours.
2. Meanwhile, sauté the 3 cups of chopped onion with the chopped garlic and green pepper in the olive or vegetable oil in a large skillet, stirring often, until the vegetables are soft, for about 10 minutes.
3. Stir the sautéed vegetables into the black beans along with the salt, pepper and oregano. Cover the saucepan and simmer for 1 hour more, or until the black beans are very tender.
4. Char the red peppers on all sides over a gas flame or under the broiler. Place the charred peppers in a paper bag for 5 minutes to loosen the skin. Peel and seed the charred peppers. Reserve about half a red pepper for garnish, and coarsely chop the remainder.
5. Add the chopped red peppers to the soup along with the vinegar and as much of the remaining 1 cup of water as necessary to make a good soup consistency. Simmer the soup for 15 minutes more. Taste and adjust the seasoning.
6. Garnish the soup with the reserved red pepper and, if you wish, dollops of sour cream or plain yogurt.

WALNUT BREAD WITH FIVE TOPPINGS

Bake at 400° for 15 minutes, then at 350° for 15 to 20 minutes.
Makes 1 round loaf (16 slices).

Nutrient Value Per Slice: 204 calories, 6 g protein, 8 g fat, 28 g carbohydrate, 311 mg sodium, 8 mg cholesterol.

❦

- 1   *envelope active dry yeast*
- 1   *teaspoon sugar*
- ¼   *cup warm water (105° to 110°) **
- 1¼   *cups milk*
- 3   *tablespoons butter*
- 2   *teaspoons salt*
- 4   *to 4½ cups unbleached flour*
- ⅓   *cup ground walnuts*
- ½   *cup coarsely chopped walnuts*
- 1   *egg white, slightly beaten*
    Toppings: poppy seeds, sesame seeds, caraway seeds, grated Parmesan cheese, coarse salt

1. Dissolve the yeast and ¼ teaspoon of the sugar in the warm water. Let the yeast mixture stand until it is bubbly, for 5 minutes. Heat the remaining ¾ teaspoon of sugar with the milk, butter and salt in a saucepan until the butter has melted. Cool the butter mixture in a large bowl until it is warm (105° to 110°). Add the yeast mixture. Stir in 2½ cups of the flour and the ground walnuts. Beat until smooth. Add enough of the remaining flour to make a soft, sticky dough.

2. Knead the dough on a floured surface until it is smooth and elastic, for 10 minutes, adding more of the remaining flour as needed. Place the dough in a greased large bowl, and turn the greased side up. Cover the bowl and let the dough rise in a warm place, away from drafts, until it is doubled in size, for 1 to 1½ hours. Poke the dough with your finger; the indentation should remain. If the dough pushes out, let it rise for a few minutes more.

3. Punch down the dough. Pinch off one third of the dough. Pat the remainder into an 8-inch circle. Sprinkle the circle with the chopped walnuts, and press them in gently. Fold over the edges of the circle to meet in the center, shape the dough into a ball, and pinch the center together. Turn the smooth side up. Push your fingertips into the center of the dough, gently pulling the dough apart to form a 2-inch hole. Pinch the center edges together. Place the loaf on a greased baking sheet.

4. Divide the remaining dough into 5 equal pieces.

Roll each piece into a thin 12-inch-long rope. Fold each rope in half, and twist its ends together. Arrange the ropes on the loaf top, spacing them evenly. Tuck the rope ends under the loaf. Cover the loaf with a towel, and let the loaf rise until it is doubled in size, for 1 hour.

5. Preheat the oven to hot (400°).

6. Brush the loaf with the egg white. Sprinkle each section of the loaf with a different topping.

7. Bake the loaf in the preheated hot oven (400°) for 15 minutes. Lower the oven to moderate (350°). Bake the loaf until it is golden brown and sounds hollow when lightly tapped with your fingertips, for 15 to 20 minutes more.

*Note: *Warm water should feel tepid when dropped on your wrist.*

Walnut Bread Sandwich: Slice the Walnut Bread loaf in half horizontally. Spread the inside of the bread with hot-and-sweet mustard. Layer arugula, radicchio, sliced cooked chicken breast, sliced red onion, Black Forest ham, crumbled blue cheese and sliced Red Bartlett pears on one of the loaf halves. For a more attractive filling, fold the slices of chicken and ham. Top with the other loaf half, and slice the sandwich into wedges with a serrated knife.
Makes 6 to 8 servings.

KEEPING YOUR COOL IF THE FREEZER FAILS

▼ Keep the freezer door closed tightly. If the freezer is fully stocked, the contents will stay frozen for at least two days; if the freezer is half-full, the food will stay frozen for about one day.

▼ For extended periods without power, buy dry ice (25 pounds for each cubic foot of freezer space), and place large chunks on top of the food. Always wear gloves when handling dry ice. If the freezer is fully stocked, the dry ice will keep the food frozen for three to four days; in a half-filled freezer, for two to three days.

▼ If foods have partially thawed, but still have ice crystals in their packages, they can be refrozen safely. To make sure food is only partially thawed when you can't see ice crystals, slip a thermometer between the food and its wrapping. If the temperature is 40° or lower, the food can be refrozen safely.

▼ If uncooked foods have thawed, cook them, and refreeze them. Frozen cooked foods that have thawed should be heated and eaten.

ROAST BEEF AND ONION TRIPLE-DECKER SANDWICH

Adjust the amount of horseradish in this recipe to suit your taste.

Makes 4 servings.

Nutrient Value Per Serving: 457 calories, 32 g protein, 24 g fat, 30 g carbohydrate, 435 mg sodium, 112 mg cholesterol.

❦

8   slices caraway rye bread
4   ounces soft cream cheese
6   to 12 teaspoons bottled horseradish
12 ounces thinly sliced roast beef
¼   teaspoon freshly ground pepper
4   outer leaves iceberg lettuce
½   cup thinly sliced onion
4   thin slices tomato

1. Layer the following ingredients on one slice of the bread to make one sandwich: 1½ tablespoons of the cream cheese, 1 to 2 teaspoons of the horseradish, 3 ounces of the roast beef, a dash of freshly ground pepper, 1 lettuce leaf, 1 bread slice, 1½ tablespoons of the cream cheese, 1 to 2 teaspoons of the horseradish, ¼ cup of the onion, 2 tomato slices, 1 bread slice, 1½ of the tablespoons of the cream cheese, 1 to 2 teaspoons of the horseradish, 3 ounces of the roast beef, a dash of freshly ground pepper, 1 lettuce leaf, and 1 bread slice.
2. Repeat with the remaining ingredients to make a second sandwich.
3. Cut each sandwich in half, and serve.

SAVORY BROCCOLI TOASTS

A great accompaniment to a soup or salad.

Broil for 2 minutes.
Makes 4 servings.

Nutrient Value Per Serving: 227 calories, 8 g protein, 5 g fat, 37 g carbohydrate, 445 mg sodium, 9 mg cholesterol.

❦

8   ounces broccoli
8   diagonal slices (about ¾ inch thick) Italian bread
¼   cup Creamy Salad Dressing (recipe, below)
¼   cup shredded mozzarella cheese

1. Cut off the woody ends of the broccoli stalks. Peel the stalks, if necessary. Separate the broccoli tops into flowerets, and cut the stalks into pieces. Blanch the broccoli in boiling water for 1 minute. Drain the broccoli, rinse it with cold water, drain again, and let the broccoli dry.
2. Place the bread slices on a baking sheet, and toast one side only of the slices under the broiler or in a toaster oven.
3. Reserve a few small broccoli flowerets for garnish. Chop the remaining flowerets and the stalks, and place them in a bowl. Stir in the Creamy Salad Dressing. Spread the broccoli mixture on the toasted sides of the bread slices. Sprinkle the mozzarella cheese over the broccoli mixture.
4. Broil the toasts for about 2 minutes, or until the mozzarella cheese melts. Garnish the toasts with the reserved broccoli flowerets.

Creamy Salad Dressing: Whisk together ½ cup creamy salad dressing, ¼ cup plain nonfat yogurt, 1 teaspoon catsup, ½ teaspoon lemon juice and ¼ teaspoon freshly ground pepper in a small bowl until the dressing is smooth. Cover the bowl, and refrigerate the dressing until serving time.
Makes about ¾ cup.

DILLED SALMON BURGERS

Makes 4 servings.

Nutrient Value Per Serving: 392 calories, 26 g protein, 18 g fat, 30 g carbohydrate, 1,221 mg sodium, 118 mg cholesterol.

❧

    1   egg
    1   can (16 ounces) salmon, drained and flaked
   ½   cup finely chopped celery
   ¼   cup finely chopped onion
    1   cup fresh bread crumbs (2 slices bread)
    2   tablespoons chopped fresh dill
 1½   tablespoons lemon juice
   ¾   teaspoon grated lemon zest
          (yellow part of rind only)
   ½   teaspoon salt
   ⅛   teaspoon freshly ground pepper
    2   tablespoons vegetable oil
    4   hamburger buns
          Dill Spread (recipe follows)
          Lettuce leaves
          Sliced tomato

1. Combine the egg, salmon, celery, onion, bread crumbs, dill, lemon juice, lemon zest, salt and pepper in a large bowl. Shape the salmon mixture into 4 patties. Cook the patties in the oil in a large skillet for 5 minutes. Carefully turn over the patties, and cook them for 5 minutes more.
2. Spread the buns with the Dill Spread. Top with the burgers, then with the lettuce and the sliced tomato.

Dill Spread: Combine 2 tablespoons of reduced-calorie mayonnaise with 1 tablespoon of Dijon-style mustard and 2 tablespoons of chopped fresh dill.

BLUE CHEESE AND ROASTED PEPPER SANDWICH

A flavorful sandwich for blue cheese lovers.

Makes 4 servings.

Nutrient Value Per Serving: 471 calories, 15 g protein, 32 g fat, 34 g carbohydrate, 1,184 mg sodium, 32 mg cholesterol.

❧

    1   jar (8 ounces) marinated mushrooms
    6   ounces blue cheese, crumbled (about 1 cup)
    1   oval loaf (8 x 4 inches) pumpernickel bread,
          unsliced OR: 6 slices pumpernickel bread
    1   jar (7 ounces) roasted red peppers, drained
    4   large leaves romaine lettuce

1. Drain the mushrooms, reserving the marinade. Finely chop the mushrooms.
2. Mix the mushrooms with the blue cheese and 1 tablespoon of the reserved mushroom marinade in a small bowl.
3. If using the pumpernickel loaf, cut it with a serrated knife into 3 equal-size horizontal slices. Brush a third of the reserved marinade over the bottom slice. Layer the remaining ingredients in the following order: half the blue cheese-mushroom mixture, half the roasted red peppers, 2 of the romaine lettuce leaves, the middle slice of bread, another third of the reserved marinade, the remaining blue cheese-mushroom mixture, the remaining roasted red peppers, and the remaining 2 romaine lettuce leaves. Brush the remaining marinade on the cut side of the top slice of bread, and place the slice on top of the sandwich. If using the sliced pumpernickel bread, make two sandwiches with the same layering.
4. Slice the sandwich or sandwiches into 4 equal portions, and serve.

Cheese — milk's leap toward
immortality.
— Clifton Fadiman

B·R·E·A·K·F·A·S·T
F·A·R·E

*Life, within doors, has few
pleasanter prospects than a neatly
arranged and well-provisioned
breakfast-table.*
— Nathaniel Hawthorne

BLUEBERRY BRAN MUFFINS

Bake at 425° for 23 minutes.
Makes 12 muffins.

Nutrient Value Per Muffin: 164 calories, 3 g protein, 6 g fat, 25 g carbohydrate, 195 mg sodium, 33 mg cholesterol.

❧

- ⅓ cup unsalted butter, softened
- ½ cup sugar
- 1 egg
- ¾ cup milk
- ¼ teaspoon vanilla
- 1⅔ cups plus 1 tablespoon sifted all-purpose flour
- 2½ teaspoons baking powder
- ½ teaspoon salt
- ¼ cup unprocessed bran
- 1 generous cup fresh blueberries OR: unsweetened frozen blueberries, slightly thawed

1. Preheat the oven to hot (425°). Grease the bottoms only of twelve 2½-inch muffin-pan cups.
2. Beat the butter with the sugar in a large mixing bowl until the mixture is light colored and fluffy. Beat in the egg, then the milk and the vanilla. Mix the ingredients well; the mixture may look separated.
3. Sift together 1⅔ cups of the flour, the baking powder and salt into a medium-size bowl. Stir in the bran. Add the flour mixture to the butter mixture. Stir the combined mixture briskly with a fork just until the dry ingredients are moistened. Do not overmix; the batter will not be smooth.
4. Toss the blueberries with the remaining 1 tablespoon of flour in a small bowl. Fold the blueberries into the batter.
5. Using a large spoon and a rubber spatula, fill each prepared muffin-pan cup two thirds full of batter.
6. Bake in the preheated hot oven (425°) until the muffins are golden brown, for 23 minutes. Remove the muffin-pan to a wire rack. Loosen the muffins with a spatula, and remove them from the pan at once to prevent steaming. Serve the muffins piping hot.

APPLESAUCE MUFFINS

Bake at 400° for 25 minutes.
Makes 12 muffins.

Nutrient Value Per Muffin: 211 calories, 4 g protein, 12 g fat, 24 g carbohydrate, 211 mg sodium, 56 mg cholesterol.

❧

- ½ cup (1 stick) unsalted butter, softened
- ⅓ cup sugar
- 2 eggs
- 1 cup applesauce
- 1¾ cups sifted all-purpose flour
- 3 teaspoons baking powder
- ½ teaspoon salt
- ½ cup chopped walnuts

1. Preheat the oven to hot (400°). Grease the bottoms only of twelve 2½-inch muffin-pan cups.
2. Beat the butter with the sugar in a large bowl until the mixture is light colored and fluffy. Beat in the eggs, one at a time. Beat in the applesauce; the mixture may look separated.
3. Sift together the flour, baking powder and salt over the butter mixture. Add the chopped walnuts. Stir the mixture briskly with a fork just until all the dry ingredients are moistened. Do not overmix; the batter will look lumpy.
4. Using a large spoon and a rubber spatula, fill each prepared muffin-pan cup two thirds full of batter.
5. Bake in the preheated hot oven (400°) until the muffins are golden brown, for 25 minutes. Remove the muffin-pan to a wire rack. Loosen the muffins with a spatula and remove them from the pan at once to prevent steaming. Serve the muffins piping hot.

COUNTRY WAYS
Busy Morning Breakfasts

Weekday mornings may be chaotic with everyone running around trying to get ready for school or work, so plan ahead for breakfast. On Sunday night, make muffins or biscuits. Split them in half and fill them with scrambled eggs and ham, sausage or bacon. Place these breakfast sandwiches in self-sealing plastic bags, and freeze them. In the morning, just pop them in the microwave for a minute or two to heat them. The whole family — and you! — will be ready to face the day with a hot meal inside.

PUMPKIN MUFFINS

Bake at 400° for 20 to 25 minutes.
Makes 10 muffins, or 12 small savarins (ring molds).

Nutrient Value Per Serving: 168 calories, 4 g protein, 6 g fat, 25 g carbohydrate, 212 mg sodium, 36 mg cholesterol.

———————— ❧ ————————

1¾ cups unsifted all-purpose flour
¼   cup sugar
2   teaspoons baking powder
½   teaspoon ground cinnamon
½   teaspoon ground nutmeg
½   teaspoon salt
1   egg, slightly beaten
1   cup solid-pack pumpkin purée
        (not pumpkin pie filling)
¾   cup milk
¼   cup (½ stick) unsalted butter, melted

1. Preheat the oven to hot (400°). Butter ten 2½-inch muffin-pan cups or twelve ½-cup savarin molds.
2. Stir together the flour, sugar, baking powder, cinnamon, nutmeg and salt in a medium-size bowl.
3. Whisk together the egg, pumpkin purée, milk and melted butter in a medium-size bowl until they are well blended.
4. Add the dry ingredients all at once to the pumpkin mixture. Stir just until the dry ingredients are moistened; do not overmix.
5. Scoop a scant ¼ cup of batter into each prepared muffin-pan cup or savarin mold. Gently press down the batter with your fingertips.
6. Bake in the preheated hot oven (400°) until a wooden pick inserted in the centers of the muffins comes out clean, for 20 to 25 minutes. Run a knife around the muffins to loosen them. Turn out the muffins onto a wire rack, and cool them slightly before serving them.

GINGER APRICOT MUFFINS

Delicious for breakfast, these muffins also are good with lunch or afternoon tea.

Bake at 400° for 25 minutes.
Makes 12 muffins.

Nutrient Value Per Muffin: 154 calories, 3 g protein, 6 g fat, 22 g carbohydrate, 195 mg sodium, 33 mg cholesterol.

———————— ❧ ————————

1¾ cups sifted all-purpose flour
3   tablespoons sugar
2½ teaspoons baking powder
1½ teaspoons ground ginger
½   teaspoon salt
1   egg
¾   cup milk
⅓   cup unsalted butter, melted
¾   cup finely chopped dried apricots
1½ teaspoons grated lemon zest
        (yellow part of rind only)
        Additional finely chopped dried apricots,
        for garnish (optional)

1. Preheat the oven to hot (400°). Grease the bottoms only of twelve 2½-inch muffin-pan cups.
2. Sift together the flour, sugar, baking powder, ginger and salt into a large bowl.
3. Lightly beat the egg in a small bowl. Beat in the milk and the melted butter. Stir in the apricots and the lemon zest. Pour the egg mixture all at once into the flour mixture. Stir the combined mixture briskly with a fork just until the dry ingredients are moistened. Do not overmix; the batter will look lumpy.
4. Using a large spoon and a rubber spatula, fill each prepared muffin-pan cup two thirds full of batter.
5. Bake in the preheated hot oven (400°) until the muffins are golden brown, for 25 minutes. Remove the muffin-pan to a wire rack. Loosen the muffins with a spatula, and remove them from the pan at once to prevent steaming. Garnish with additional finely chopped dried apricots, if you wish. Serve the muffins piping hot.

MORNING SPICE MUFFINS

Lightly spiced and plump with raisins, these muffins are perfect breakfast fare.

Bake at 400° for 20 minutes.
Makes 12 muffins.

Nutrient Value Per Muffin: 161 calories, 3 g protein, 6 g fat, 25 g carbohydrate, 191 mg sodium, 32 mg cholesterol.

———————— ❧ ————————

1	cup sifted all-purpose flour
½	teaspoon salt
1	teaspoon baking powder
½	teaspoon baking soda
½	teaspoon ground cinnamon
½	teaspoon ground ginger
¼	teaspoon ground nutmeg
¾	cup stirred whole wheat flour
⅓	cup firmly packed light brown sugar
1	egg
1	cup buttermilk
⅓	cup unsalted butter, melted
½	cup raisins, plumped *

1. Preheat the oven to hot (400°). Grease the bottoms only of twelve 2½-inch muffin-pan cups.
2. Sift together the all-purpose flour, salt, baking powder, baking soda, cinnamon, ginger and nutmeg into a large bowl. Stir in the whole wheat flour and the brown sugar.
3. Lightly beat the egg in a small bowl. Beat in the buttermilk and the melted butter. Stir in the raisins. Pour the egg mixture all at once into the flour mixture. Stir the combined mixture briskly with a fork just until the dry ingredients are moistened. Do not overmix; the batter will look lumpy.
4. Using a large spoon and rubber spatula, fill each prepared muffin-pan cup two thirds full of batter.
5. Bake in the preheated hot oven (400°) until the muffins are golden brown, for 20 minutes. Remove the muffin-pan to a wire rack. Loosen the muffins with a spatula, and remove them from the pan at once to prevent steaming. Serve the muffins piping hot.

***Note:** To plump the raisins, cover them with hot water in a small bowl and let them stand for 5 minutes. Drain the raisins well.*

OATMEAL MUFFINS

These muffins are studded with dried apricots and pecans. They can be made ahead of time, frozen, and thawed in the refrigerator overnight.

Bake at 375° for 20 to 25 minutes.
Makes 12 medium-size muffins, or 36 mini-muffins.

Nutrient Value Per Medium-Size Muffin (or 3 Mini-Muffins): 189 calories, 4 g protein, 8 g fat, 26 g carbohydrate, 145 mg sodium, 24 mg cholesterol.

———————— ❧ ————————

1	cup quick-cooking oatmeal (not instant)
1	cup buttermilk
1	cup all-purpose flour
1	teaspoon baking powder
½	teaspoon baking soda
¼	teaspoon salt
⅓	cup vegetable oil
½	cup firmly packed light brown sugar
1	egg
⅓	cup chopped dried apricots
2	tablespoons chopped pecans
1½	tablespoons granulated sugar

1. Combine the oatmeal with the buttermilk in a small bowl, and stir to mix them well. Cover the bowl, and let the oatmeal mixture stand for 30 minutes.
2. Preheat the oven to moderate (375°). Line 12 medium-size muffin-pan cups (measuring 2½ inches in diameter), or 36 mini-muffin-pan cups (measuring 1¾ inches in diameter), with paper liners.
3. Stir together the flour, baking powder, baking soda and salt in a medium-size bowl until they are well mixed. Set aside the flour mixture.
4. Combine the oil, brown sugar and egg in a small bowl until they are well mixed. Stir the egg mixture into the oatmeal mixture. Pour the oatmeal-egg mixture into the flour mixture. Stir just to moisten the dry ingredients. Gently stir in the apricots and the chopped pecans. Divide the batter evenly among the prepared muffin-pan cups, filling each three quarters full. Sprinkle the tops evenly with the granulated sugar.
5. Bake either size muffins in the preheated moderate oven (375°) for 20 to 25 minutes. Remove the muffins from the muffin-pan cups. Serve the muffins warm or at room temperature.

TOASTED DOUBLE HAM AND CHEESE SANDWICHES

A savory "knife-and-fork" sandwich that's ideal for Sunday brunch.

Makes 6 servings.

Nutrient Value Per Serving: 391 calories, 24 g protein, 21 g fat, 25 g carbohydrate, 1,179 mg sodium, 118 mg cholesterol.

❧

1   unsliced 9-inch round loaf white bread
¼   pound thinly sliced baked ham
¼   pound thinly sliced Swiss cheese
¼   pound thinly sliced prosciutto OR: capocollo
¼   pound thinly sliced hot pepper cheese
½   cup milk
1   egg
2   tablespoons butter

1. With a serrated knife, cut two ½-inch-thick horizontal slices from the center of the loaf. Reserve the top and bottom of the loaf for the Egg, Bacon and Cheese Monster Muffin *(recipe, at right).*
2. Layer the ham, Swiss cheese, prosciutto or capocollo and the hot pepper cheese between the bread slices. Cut the sandwich into 6 equal wedges.
3. Mix the milk with the egg in a pie plate. Dip both sides of each sandwich wedge in the egg mixture. Set aside the wedges.
4. Heat the butter in a large skillet. Sauté the sandwich wedges over medium heat, turning once, until they are golden brown on both sides. Serve the sandwich wedges immediately.

Being kissed by a man who didn't wax his moustache was — like eating an egg without salt.
— Rudyard Kipling

EGG, BACON AND CHEESE MONSTER MUFFIN

This breakfast favorite gets extra zip from Dijon mustard and Provolone cheese.

Heat bread at 350° for 10 minutes.
Makes 4 servings.

Nutrient Value Per Serving: 402 calories, 20 g protein, 24 g fat, 25 g carbohydrate, 900 mg sodium, 320 mg cholesterol.

❧

    Top and bottom slices (about ½ inch thick) of
      9-inch round loaf white bread, left over from
      Toasted Double Ham and Cheese Sandwiches
      (recipe, at left)
1   tablespoon mayonnaise
2   teaspoons Dijon-style mustard
4   slices Canadian bacon (2 ounces)
2   tablespoons butter or margarine
4   eggs
4   slices smoked or plain Provolone (4 ounces)

1. Preheat the oven to moderate (350°). Wrap the bread slices in aluminum foil, and heat them in the preheated moderate oven (350°) for about 10 minutes.
2. Meanwhile, mix the mayonnaise with the mustard in a small cup, and set the mayonnaise mixture aside.
3. Sauté the bacon on both sides in the butter or margarine in a large skillet until the bacon is heated through. Set aside the bacon, and keep it warm.
4. Break each egg into the skillet. Cook the eggs over low heat until the yolks begin to set. Place a slice of the Provolone cheese over each egg. Cover the skillet with a tight-fitting lid, and cook for 1 minute more, or until the Provolone cheese has melted. Remove the skillet from the heat.
5. Remove the bread slices from the oven. Spread the cut sides with the mayonnaise mixture. Place the eggs on the bottom slice of bread. Top with the bacon, and cover with the top slice of bread.
6. Cut the muffin sandwich into 4 equal wedges, and serve them immediately.

APPLE CHEESE OMELET

Bake at 400° for 5 minutes.
Makes 2 servings.

Nutrient Value Per Serving: 328 calories, 17 g protein, 19 g fat, 24 g carbohydrate, 394 mg sodium, 305 mg cholesterol.

❦

- 1   large Golden Delicious apple (8 ounces)
- ½   cup thinly sliced leeks, white part only
- 2   eggs
- ½   cup skim or nonfat milk
       Pinch salt
       Pinch freshly ground pepper
- 2   teaspoons margarine
- 1   cup sliced mushrooms
- ½   cup (2 ounces) shredded Cheddar cheese
- 2   teaspoons chopped flat-leaf Italian parsley,
          for garnish

1. Preheat the oven to hot (400°). Wrap the handle of a nonstick skillet with aluminum foil; if the skillet has a metal handle or the handle is removable, the aluminum foil is not necessary.
2. Peel, core and thinly slice the apple. Rinse the leeks in a strainer or colander under running water to remove all the sand.
3. Beat together the eggs, milk, salt and pepper in a small bowl until they are combined.
4. Heat the margarine in the prepared skillet over medium heat. Add the apple, leeks and mushrooms, and sauté until the apple and vegetables are crisply tender, for 3 to 5 minutes. Evenly distribute the apple mixture in the pan. Sprinkle the Cheddar cheese over the apple mixture.
5. Reduce the heat to medium-low. Stir the egg mixture and pour it into the skillet, tilting the skillet and lifting the edges of the omelet with a spatula to let the egg run underneath. Cook the omelet until it is almost set and its bottom is lightly browned, for 3 to 4 minutes.
6. Place the skillet with the omelet in the preheated hot oven (400°) and bake until the top of the omelet is set, for 5 minutes. Invert the omelet onto a serving platter. Cut the omelet in half, garnish it with the parsley, and serve it immediately.

RARAKOR
(Swedish Potato Pancakes)

Serve these tasty potato pancakes instead of hash browns. Traditionally, this recipe includes snipped chives; add 1 or 2 tablespoons, if you wish.

Makes 4 to 6 servings.

Nutrient Value Per Serving: 382 calories, 3 g protein, 31 g fat, 25 g carbohydrate, 983 mg sodium, 25 mg cholesterol.

❦

- 4   large baking potatoes
- 1   tablespoon lemon juice
- 2   teaspoons salt
       Freshly ground black pepper, to taste
- ¼   cup (½ stick) butter or margarine
- ½   cup vegetable oil
       Cooked sausage links
       Sautéed apple wedges OR: warmed applesauce
          (optional)

1. Peel the potatoes and coarsely grate them. Transfer the grated potatoes to a large bowl, and cover them with cold water mixed with the lemon juice.
2. At serving time, drain the grated potatoes on paper toweling. Stir in the salt and the black pepper.
3. Melt half the butter or margarine with half the oil in a large skillet over high heat until the foam subsides.
4. Drop three or four 2-tablespoon mounds of the potato mixture into the hot skillet. Flatten the mounds with a spatula to make 3-inch circles. Fry the pancakes over medium-high heat for 2 or 3 minutes, or until the pancakes are crisp and golden. Turn the pancakes and fry the second sides until they are crisp and golden. Remove the pancakes to a serving platter lined with paper toweling, and keep the pancakes warm. Continue with the remaining potato mixture, adding more of the remaining butter and oil, if necessary.
5. Serve the potato pancakes with the sausages and, if you wish, with the apple wedges or applesauce.

ORANGE BREAD PUDDING

Bake at 350° for 45 minutes.
Makes 6 servings.

Nutrient Value Per Serving: 436 calories, 12 g protein, 17 g fat, 60 g carbohydrate, 452 mg sodium, 220 mg cholesterol.

10 to 12 slices (about ¾ inch thick) French bread,
        with crust
¼ cup (½ stick) butter or margarine, softened
4 eggs
½ cup sugar
2 teaspoons grated orange zest
        (orange part of rind only)
⅔ cup orange juice (2 oranges)
2¾ cups milk
        Boiling water
¼ cup orange marmalade, melted
        Light cream OR: whipped cream (optional)

1. Spread one side of each bread slice generously with the butter or margarine. Arrange the bread slices, buttered side up and overlapping, in a lightly buttered 2-quart shallow baking dish.
2. Beat together the eggs, sugar and orange zest in a bowl just until they are blended. Gradually stir in the orange juice and the milk. Pour the egg mixture evenly over the bread slices, and let stand for 15 minutes.
3. Preheat the oven to moderate (350°).
4. Set the baking dish in a large baking pan, and place the baking pan on the oven rack. Pour boiling water into the baking pan until the water level is halfway up the sides of the baking dish.
5. Bake in the preheated moderate oven (350°) until a knife inserted in the center of the pudding comes out clean, for 45 minutes. The center will be almost set but still soft.
6. Remove the pudding from the water bath. Cool the pudding for at least 30 minutes.
7. Brush the melted marmalade over the top of the pudding. Serve the pudding warm or chilled. If you wish, serve the pudding with light cream to pour over each serving, or with whipped cream on the side.

BLINI ROLL-UPS
(Russian Buckwheat Pancakes)

Buckwheat flour usually is available at health food stores. If it is unavailable, substitute 2 cups of all-purpose flour and 1 cup of whole wheat flour.

Makes 4 to 6 servings.

Nutrient Value Per Serving: 969 calories, 30 g protein, 74 g fat, 49 g carbohydrate, 2,328 mg sodium, 357 mg cholesterol.

1½ cups buckwheat flour
½ cup all-purpose flour
1 package active dry yeast
¼ cup warm water (105° to 115°)*
2¾ cups milk
4 eggs
1 tablespoon sugar
1 teaspoon salt
3 tablespoons butter or margarine, melted
4 egg whites
1 container (16 ounces) dairy sour cream
⅓ cup chopped fresh dill
1 cup (2 sticks) butter or margarine, melted
½ pound thinly sliced smoked salmon
        OR: thinly sliced smoked turkey
        Fresh dill sprigs, for garnish
        Salmon Rose (recipe follows), for garnish

1. Mix together the buckwheat and all-purpose flours on a piece of wax paper. Remove ¾ cup of the flour mixture to a large bowl.
2. Sprinkle the yeast over the warm water in a small bowl, and stir. Let the yeast mixture stand for 5 minutes. Heat ¾ cup of the milk to lukewarm in a small saucepan over medium heat. Whisk the heated milk into the yeast mixture.
3. Gradually stir the yeast mixture into the flour mixture in the bowl until smooth. Cover the bowl, and let the yeast rise in a warm place, away from drafts, for 2 hours.
4. Beat the whole eggs in a small bowl until they are well blended. Gradually beat in the sugar, salt and the 3 tablespoons of melted butter or margarine. Add the egg mixture to the yeast mixture.

5. Heat the remaining 2 cups of milk to lukewarm in a small saucepan over medium heat. Stir the milk into the yeast mixture, then stir in the remaining flour mixture until it is well blended.

6. Beat the egg whites until they are stiff but not dry in a medium-size bowl with an electric mixer at high speed. Fold the egg whites into the yeast mixture with a wire whisk or spatula.

7. Lightly grease an electric griddle or frying pan set at 360°. Or place a heavy griddle or skillet over medium heat, then lightly grease the bottom.

8. Ladle the batter with a ¼-cup measure onto the griddle, cooking 3 or 4 pancakes at a time. When bubbles appear on the surface, turn over the pancakes and cook until the second sides are golden. Remove the pancakes to a heated serving platter. Let the pancakes stand only until they are cool enough to handle. Roll up the pancakes, place them seam side down on the serving platter, and keep them warm. Cook and roll up the remaining pancakes.

9. Combine the sour cream with the chopped dill in a small bowl until they are well blended. Unroll the pancakes, one at a time, and drizzle them with part of the 1 cup of melted butter or margarine. Spoon about 2 tablespoons of the sour cream mixture onto each pancake, top with a piece of the smoked salmon or turkey, and roll up each pancake again. Garnish the serving platter with the fresh dill sprigs and the Salmon Rose.

Note: *Warm water should feel tepid when dropped on your wrist.*

Salmon Rose: Cut a ¾ x 3-inch strip of salmon, and roll it up tightly. Place the salmon roll on a plate, flat side down. Open up the roll to form "petals." If you wish, decorate with green pepper leaves.

BLUEBERRY PANCAKES

You may want to combine the dry ingredients and keep the "mix" on hand.

Makes 12 pancakes.

Nutrient Value Per Pancake: 105 calories, 3 g protein, 6 g fat, 11 g carbohydrate, 174 mg sodium, 58 mg cholesterol.

- ½ cup whole wheat flour
- ⅓ cup unsifted all-purpose flour
- 2 tablespoons cornmeal
- 1 tablespoon light brown sugar
- 1½ teaspoons baking powder
- ¼ teaspoon baking soda
- ¼ teaspoon salt
- 2 tablespoons unsalted butter, melted
- 2 eggs, separated
- 1 cup buttermilk
- 1 cup blueberries
- 2 to 3 tablespoons softened butter

1. Combine the whole wheat flour and all-purpose flours with the cornmeal, brown sugar, baking powder, baking soda and salt in a medium-size bowl. Stir to mix the ingredients well.

2. Combine the melted butter, egg yolks and buttermilk in a bowl. Stir to mix the ingredients.

3. Beat the egg whites in a small bowl until stiff peaks form. Stir the buttermilk mixture into the flour mixture until they are combined. Fold in the egg whites. Gently fold in the blueberries.

4. Heat a heavy griddle or large skillet until it is hot. Brush the griddle with some of the softened butter. Using a ¼-cup measure, ladle the batter onto the griddle, allowing spreading room between the pancakes. Cook the pancakes until their edges look dry and bubbles form on the surface. Turn the pancakes over, and cook until the second sides are browned. Repeat until all the batter is used.

5. Stack the pancakes on top of each other to keep them warm. Or place the pancakes in a warm oven on a baking sheet until all are cooked.

*Fragrant and warm from the oven:
Caraway Rye Bread and Corn Sticks
(recipes, page 214), Whole Wheat Bread
(recipe, page 215), and Oatmeal Bread
and Rolls (recipe, page 116).*

CARAWAY RYE BREAD

Molasses and caraway seeds give special character to this fragrant loaf.

Bake at 400° for 35 minutes.
Makes 2 loaves (16 slices per loaf).

Nutrient Value Per Slice: 129 calories, 3 g protein, 1 g fat, 26 g carbohydrate, 139 mg sodium, 0 mg cholesterol.

❦

2	envelopes active dry yeast
2½	cups very warm water (120° to 125°) *
¼	cup light molasses
2	teaspoons salt
2	tablespoons vegetable shortening
2½	cups rye flour
1	tablespoon caraway seeds, crushed
6	cups all-purpose flour
	Cornmeal

1. Sprinkle the yeast into ½ cup of the very warm water in a 1-cup measure. Stir in 1 teaspoon of the molasses, and continue stirring until the yeast dissolves. Let the yeast mixture stand until it is bubbly, for 10 minutes.

2. Combine the remaining 2 cups of very warm water and the remaining molasses with the salt and the vegetable shortening in a large bowl. Stir in the yeast mixture, rye flour and caraway seeds. Add enough of the all-purpose flour to make a soft dough.

3. Turn out the dough onto a lightly floured pastry cloth or board. Knead the dough for 10 minutes, or until it is smooth and elastic, using enough of the remaining all-purpose flour to keep the dough from sticking.

4. Place the dough in a large greased bowl, and turn the greased side up. Cover the bowl with plastic wrap, and let the dough rise in a warm place, away from drafts, until it is doubled in size, for 1½ hours.

5. Grease a large baking sheet, and sprinkle it with the cornmeal.

6. Punch down the dough, and turn it out onto the lightly floured pastry cloth or board. Knead the dough a few times, invert the bowl over it, and let the dough rest for 10 minutes. Divide the dough in half, and knead each half a few times. Shape each half into a loaf. Place the loaves at least 4 inches apart on the prepared baking sheet. Cover the loaves with plastic wrap, and let them rise in a warm place, away from drafts, until they are doubled in size, for 45 minutes.

7. Preheat the oven to hot (400°).

8. Brush the tops of the loaves with water, and bake the loaves in the preheated hot oven (400°) until they are brown and sound hollow when tapped with your fingertips, for 35 minutes. Remove the loaves from the baking sheet to a wire rack, and cool them completely before slicing them.

Note: *Very warm water should feel comfortably warm when dropped on your wrist.*

CORN STICKS

These golden goodies are fabulous served with butter and orange marmalade.

Bake at 400° for 12 minutes.
Makes 16 corn sticks.

Nutrient Value Per Serving: 148 calories, 4 g protein, 4 g fat, 23 g carbohydrate, 198 mg sodium, 27 mg cholesterol.

❦

⅔	cup raisins (optional)
2	cups cornmeal
1	cup all-purpose flour
¼	cup sugar
2	teaspoons baking powder
½	teaspoon salt
2	eggs
1	cup buttermilk
1	teaspoon baking soda
¼	cup vegetable shortening, melted

1. Preheat the oven to hot (400°). Grease 16 corn stick pans generously.

2. If you are using the raisins, rinse them and place them on paper toweling to drain.

3. Place the cornmeal in a large bowl. Sift together the flour, sugar, baking powder and salt over the cornmeal. Stir with a wooden spoon to blend all the ingredients.

4. Beat the eggs with a wire whisk in a small bowl. Add the buttermilk and baking soda, and stir until they are well blended.

5. Pour the egg mixture over the cornmeal mixture, and mix just until the ingredients are blended. Stir in the melted shortening and, if using, the raisins.

6. Fill each prepared corn stick pan to the top with the batter.

7. Bake in the preheated hot oven (400°) until the corn sticks are golden, for 12 minutes. Serve the corn sticks hot.

WHOLE WHEAT BREAD

Just what whole grain lovers are looking for—a loaf made with 100% whole wheat flour.

Bake loaves at 375° for 1 hour; bake rolls at 375° for 25 minutes.

Makes 3 large loaves, or 3 dozen rolls.

Nutrient Value Per Slice: 148 calories, 5 g protein, 3 g fat, 28 g carbohydrate, 253 mg sodium, 2 mg cholesterol.

❧

2   cups milk
1/3   cup honey OR: molasses
4   teaspoons salt
2   envelopes active dry yeast
2   cups very warm water (120° to 125°) *
10   cups whole wheat flour
1/3   cup vegetable shortening, melted

1. Combine the milk with the honey or molasses and the salt in a small saucepan. Heat the milk mixture until it is very hot. Remove the saucepan from the heat, and cool the milk mixture to lukewarm.

2. Sprinkle the yeast over ½ cup of the very warm water in a large bowl, and stir until the yeast dissolves. Let the yeast stand for 10 minutes, or until it is bubbly.

3. Stir in the remaining 1½ cups of very warm water and the cooled milk mixture. Add 5 cups of the flour, and beat until smooth. Add the melted vegetable shortening and enough of the remaining 5 cups of flour to make a stiff dough.

4. Cover the bowl with plastic wrap, and let the dough rise in a warm place, away from drafts, until it is doubled in size, for 1 hour.

5. Turn out the dough onto a lightly floured pastry cloth or board, and knead the dough until it is smooth, adding as little of the remaining flour as possible to keep the dough from sticking.

6. Place the dough in a greased bowl, and turn the greased side up. Cover the dough with plastic wrap, and let it rise, away from drafts, until it is doubled in size, for 40 minutes. Punch down the dough, and divide it into thirds.

7. To make loaves, shape each third of the dough into a 12 x 9-inch rectangle. Roll up the rectangle, jelly-roll style and place it, seam side down, in a greased 9 x 5 x 3-inch loaf pan.

8. To make the rolls, shape each third of the dough into 12 pieces. To make Round Rolls: Shape each piece of dough into a ball. Place the balls, 1 inch apart, on a large baking sheet. To make Muffin-Pan Rolls: Place the balls in greased muffin-pan cups. To make Bow Knot Rolls: Roll each piece of dough into an 8-inch-long rope. Make a loop in the center of the rope and pull one end through. Place the bow knots, 1 inch apart, on large baking sheets.

9. Cover the loaves or rolls with plastic wrap, and let them rise in a warm place, away from drafts, for 30 minutes.

10. Preheat the oven to moderate (375°).

11. Bake the loaves in the preheated moderate oven (375°) for 1 hour, or until the loaves sound hollow when tapped with your fingertips. Bake the rolls in the preheated moderate oven (375°) for 25 minutes.

12. Invert the loaves onto wire racks, and cool them completely. Remove the rolls with a spatula from the baking sheet or muffin-pan, and cool them completely on wire racks. Wrap the loaves or rolls in plastic bags to store them.

Note: *Very warm water should feel comfortably warm when dropped on your wrist.*

"No business before breakfast, Glum!" says the King. "Breakfast first, business next."
—William Makepeace Thackeray

OATMEAL BREAD AND ROLLS

Bake loaves at 450° for 15 minutes, then at 350° for 30 minutes; bake rolls at 450° for 15 minutes, then at 350° for 7 minutes.
Makes 2 loaves, 1 loaf and 18 rolls, or 3 dozen rolls.

Nutrient Value Per Slice (12 slices per loaf): 144 calories, 4 g protein, 1 g fat, 29 g carbohydrate, 139 mg sodium, 0 mg cholesterol.
Nutrient Value Per Roll: 96 calories, 3 g protein, 3 g fat, 19 g carbohydrate, 93 mg sodium, 0 mg cholesterol.

2 cups quick-cooking rolled oats
    (not instant oatmeal)
1½ cups boiling water
2 envelopes active dry yeast
½ cup very warm water (120° to 125°) *
½ cup molasses
1½ teaspoons salt
1 tablespoon vegetable shortening
5 cups all-purpose flour
    Melted vegetable shortening

1. Place the rolled oats in a large bowl. Pour the boiling water over the oats, and stir with a wooden spoon to blend them. Allow the oats to stand for 30 minutes.
2. Sprinkle the yeast into the very warm water in a 1-cup measure, and stir until the yeast dissolves. Let the yeast stand for 10 minutes, or until it is bubbly.
3. Stir the dissolved yeast into the oats along with the molasses, salt and vegetable shortening until the ingredients are well blended.
4. Stir the flour into the oat mixture, part at a time, to make a soft dough. Turn out the dough onto a lightly floured pastry cloth or board. Knead the dough until it is smooth, for 5 minutes.
5. Place the dough in a large greased bowl and turn the greased side up. Cover the bowl with plastic wrap and let the dough rise in a warm place, away from drafts, until it is doubled in size, for 1½ hours.
6. Punch down the dough and turn it out onto the lightly floured pastry cloth or board. Knead the dough a few times.
7. Divide the dough in half. Shape each half of the dough into a 12 x 9-inch rectangle, roll it up jelly-roll style, and place it, seam side down, in a greased 9 x 5 x 3-inch loaf pan. Or shape each half into 18 even-size pieces for rolls. Or shape half of the dough into a loaf and half into rolls.

8. To make Round Rolls: Shape each piece of dough into a ball. Place the balls, 1 inch apart, on a large baking sheet. To make Muffin-Pan Rolls: Place the balls in greased muffin-pan cups. To make Bow Knot Rolls: Roll each piece of dough into an 8-inch-long rope. Make a loop in center of the rope and pull one end through. Place the bow knots, 1 inch apart, on large baking sheets. Brush a little melted shortening over the surfaces of the loaves and rolls, and cover them with plastic wrap. Let the loaves and rolls rise in a warm place, away from drafts, for 1 hour.
9. Preheat the oven to very hot (450°).
10. Bake the loaves and rolls in the preheated very hot oven (450°) for 15 minutes. Lower the oven temperature to moderate (350°). Bake the loaves until they sound hollow when tapped with your fingertips, for 30 minutes more. Bake the rolls for 7 minutes more.
11. Invert the loaves onto wire racks, and cool them completely before slicing them. Remove the rolls with a spatula from the baking sheet or muffin-pan, and cool them on wire racks.

Note: *Very warm water should feel comfortably warm when dropped on your wrist.*

Better is bread with a happy heart
Than wealth with vexation.

—Amenemope

T·H·E
D·E·S·S·E·R·T C·A·R·T·

RHUBARB 'N CREAM

Makes 6 servings.

Nutrient Value Per Serving: 367 calories, 2 g protein, 15 g fat, 59 g carbohydrate, 27 mg sodium, 54 mg cholesterol.

❦

2   pounds fresh rhubarb OR: thawed frozen
      rhubarb, cut into 1½-inch pieces
¾   cup granulated sugar
¾   cup firmly packed light brown sugar
2   tablespoons chopped, peeled fresh gingerroot
1   cup whipping cream
½   teaspoon vanilla

1. Combine the rhubarb, granulated and brown sugars and ginger in a heavy saucepan. Cook the mixture, uncovered, over very low heat, stirring occasionally, until the rhubarb is very tender, for 35 minutes.
2. Drain the mixture in a sieve (the liquid can be reserved and used for ice cream topping). Purée the rhubarb and ginger in a food processor, force them through a food mill, or mash them very well with a potato masher. Transfer the purée to a large bowl. Cover the bowl with plastic wrap and refrigerate the purée for several hours, or until it is very cold.
3. Beat the cream with the vanilla in a medium-size bowl until it forms soft peaks. Gently fold the whipped cream into the chilled rhubarb purée, leaving streaks of red and white. Spoon the rhubarb and cream mixture into individual dessert glasses.

YOGURT-TOPPED FRUIT

Makes 4 servings.

Nutrient Value Per Serving: 93 calories, 3 g protein, 1 g fat, 20 g carbohydrate, 38 mg sodium, 2 mg cholesterol.

❦

2   cups blueberries, washed
⅓   canteloupe, peeled, seeded and diced
⅔   cup plain nonfat yogurt
1   tablespoon light brown sugar
¼   teaspoon vanilla

Combine the blueberries with the cantaloupe. Spoon the fruit into 4 individual dessert glasses. Gently stir together the yogurt, brown sugar and vanilla in a small bowl. Spoon the yogurt mixture over the fruit, and serve immediately.

APPLESAUCE PARFAITS

Makes 4 servings.

Nutrient Value Per Serving: 113 calories, 3 g protein, 113 g fat, 24 g carbohydrate, 42 mg sodium, 3 mg cholesterol.

❦

2   cups chilled unsweetened applesauce
1   cup plain nonfat yogurt
2   tablespoons sugar
⅛   teaspoon ground cinnamon
¼   teaspoon vanilla

Spoon the applesauce equally into 4 individual dessert glasses. Gently stir together the yogurt, sugar, cinnamon and vanilla just until they are blended. Spoon the yogurt mixture over the applesauce. Chill until serving time.

*Delectable desserts to tempt any palate:
Country Berry Trifle (recipe, page 220),
Orange Cranberry Roll (recipe, page
221), Autumn Fruits Cobbler and Apple
Berry Cobbler (recipes, page 222), and
Rhubarb 'N Cream (recipe, page 217).*

COUNTRY BERRY TRIFLE

A perfect choice for entertaining, this creamy trifle can be assembled several hours before serving.

Bake sponge cake at 350° for 30 minutes.
Makes 8 servings.

Nutrient Value Per Serving: 438 calories, 9 g protein, 20 g fat, 55 g carbohydrate, 113 mg sodium, 358 mg cholesterol.

———————— ❦ ————————

Sponge Cake:
- ½   cup sifted cake flour
- ¼   teaspoon baking powder
      Dash salt
- 3   eggs, separated
- 6   tablespoons sugar
- 1   teaspoon almond extract
- ⅛   teaspoon cream of tartar

Custard:
- 2½ cups milk
- 6   egg yolks
- ¾   cup sugar
- 3   tablespoons all-purpose flour
- 1   teaspoon vanilla

- ⅓   cup strawberry jam, heated and forced through a sieve
- ¼   cup sherry
- 2   cups fresh raspberries OR: frozen dry-pack raspberries, thawed and drained
- 1   cup whipping cream
- 2   tablespoons sugar

1. Preheat the oven to moderate (350°).
2. Prepare the Sponge Cake: Sift together the flour, baking powder and salt onto wax paper. Set aside the flour mixture.
3. Beat the egg yolks with 3 tablespoons of the sugar in a large bowl with an electric mixer at high speed until the mixture is thick and lemon colored, for about 5 minutes. Stir in the almond extract.
4. Beat the egg whites with clean beaters in a large bowl until they are foamy-white. Add the cream of tartar and continue beating until soft peaks form. Gradually beat in the remaining 3 tablespoons of sugar. Continue beating until stiff, glossy peaks form.

5. Fold the flour mixture into the yolk mixture; the combined mixture will be very stiff. Stir one quarter of the beaten whites into the flour-yolk mixture to lighten it. Fold in the remaining whites until no streaks of white remain. Pour the batter into an ungreased 8-inch springform pan.
6. Bake in the preheated moderate oven (350°) until the cake begins to pull away from the sides of the pan and a wooden pick inserted in the center comes out clean, for 30 minutes. Cool the cake in the pan for 5 minutes. Carefully run a thin metal spatula around the edge of the cake, and remove the side of the pan. Carefully run the spatula under the bottom of the cake, and remove the pan bottom. Invert the cake onto a wire rack to cool completely.
7. Prepare the Custard: Warm the milk in a medium-size, heavy saucepan over medium heat until bubbles appear around the edge. Beat together the egg yolks, sugar and flour in a medium-size bowl. Beat one third of the hot milk into the yolk mixture. Stir the milk-yolk mixture back into the remaining hot milk. Cook, stirring constantly, until the custard is thickened, for 10 to 15 minutes; do not let it boil.
8. Quick-chill the custard by setting the saucepan in a large bowl of ice water. Stir the custard as it chills to prevent a skin from forming. Stir in the vanilla. Press plastic wrap directly onto the surface of the custard, and refrigerate the custard until ready to use it.
9. Cut the cake in half horizontally. Brush one side of each half with the strawberry jam, then sprinkle with the sherry. Cut each cake half into thin wedges. Reserve 3 wedges for the top of the trifle. Line the bottom and sides of a 2-quart glass bowl with the remaining wedges, jam-covered sides facing inward; if necessary, trim the cake to fit neatly. Spoon half the custard into the bowl. Cover the custard with 1 cup of the raspberries; reserve the remaining raspberries for garnish. Spoon the remaining custard into the bowl.
10. Beat the whipping cream with the sugar in a small bowl until stiff peaks form. Spread or pipe the whipped cream over the top of the trifle. Arrange the reserved cake wedges on top of the whipped cream. Cover the bowl with plastic wrap, and refrigerate the trifle for several hours. Garnish with the remaining raspberries just before serving.

ORANGE CRANBERRY ROLL

Bake at 400° for 25 to 30 minutes.
Makes 10 servings.

Nutrient Value Per Serving: 352 calories, 4 g protein, 14 g fat, 55 g carbohydrate, 321 mg sodium, 27 mg cholesterol.

❧

Cranberry Sauce:
 3 cups fresh cranberries OR: frozen cranberries
1½ cups sugar
 ⅓ cup coarsely chopped navel orange,
       rind included
 ½ teaspoon cinnamon

Dough:
 2 cups sifted all-purpose flour
 2 tablespoons sugar
2½ teaspoons baking powder
 ½ teaspoon salt
 6 tablespoons (¾ stick) margarine
 1 teaspoon grated orange zest
       (orange part of rind only)
 ½ cup milk

Filling:
 2 tablespoons melted margarine
 1 tablespoon light brown sugar
 ½ cup finely chopped pecans

Garnish:
 ¼ cup fresh cranberries OR: frozen cranberries
 3 tablespoons light corn syrup
    Orange slices
    Fresh mint leaves (optional)
    Softly whipped cream (optional)

1. Preheat the oven to hot (400°). Grease and flour a baking sheet.
2. Prepare the Cranberry Sauce: Combine the cranberries, sugar, orange and cinnamon in a saucepan. Bring the mixture to boiling. Lower the heat and simmer, uncovered, stirring occasionally, until the cranberries have popped and the sauce is very thick, for 10 to 15 minutes. Cool the sauce completely.
3. Meanwhile, prepare the Dough: Sift together the flour, sugar, baking powder and salt in a large bowl. Cut in the margarine with a pastry blender until the mixture is crumbly. Stir in the orange zest. Gradually stir in the milk with a fork to form a soft dough.
4. Turn out the dough onto a lightly floured surface, and roll it out to a 14 x 11-inch rectangle. Transfer the dough to the prepared baking sheet.

5. To fill the roll, brush the dough with the melted margarine. Sprinkle with the brown sugar and the chopped pecans. Spread the dough with the cooled cranberry sauce, leaving a 2-inch border all around. With a long side of the dough facing you, fold the left and right short sides inward so that the ends touch the edges of the cranberry sauce. Beginning with the long side, roll up the dough jelly-roll style. Gently seal the edges with your fingers. Turn the roll seam side down.
6. Bake in the preheated hot oven (400°) until the roll is golden brown, for 25 to 30 minutes. Carefully transfer the roll to a wire rack to cool.
7. Prepare the Garnish: Combine the cranberries with the corn syrup in a small saucepan. Cook over low heat, stirring, just until the cranberries begin to pop, for 2 to 3 minutes. Cool the cranberry syrup.
8. Transfer the roll to a serving plate and garnish it with the cranberry syrup, orange slices and, if you wish, mint leaves. Serve with dollops of whipped cream, if you wish.

AUTUMN FRUITS COBBLER

Bake at 375° for 40 minutes.
Makes 8 servings.

Nutrient Value Per Serving: 279 calories, 3 g protein, 4 g fat, 62 g carbohydrate, 191 mg sodium, 8 mg cholesterol.

❧

2	pounds firm, ripe Bosc pears, peeled, cored and cut into 1½-inch pieces (6 cups)
¾	cup golden raisins
¼	cup brown sugar
¼	cup unsweetened apple juice
2	tablespoons water
¾	teaspoon vanilla

Pastry:

¾	cup sifted all-purpose flour
¼	cup whole wheat flour
1	tablespoon granulated sugar
1	teaspoon baking powder
¼	teaspoon baking soda
¼	teaspoon salt
2	tablespoons butter
⅓	cup buttermilk

Glaze:

⅓	cup peach jam, melted and forced through a sieve

1. Preheat the oven to moderate (375°).
2. Combine the pears, golden raisins, brown sugar, apple juice and water in a saucepan. Bring the mixture slowly to boiling and boil, stirring, for 1 minute. Remove the saucepan from the heat. Stir in the vanilla. Cool the mixture to room temperature.
3. Meanwhile, prepare the Pastry: Combine the all-purpose and whole wheat flours with the granulated sugar, baking powder, baking soda and salt in a large bowl. Cut in the butter with a pastry blender until the mixture is crumbly. Gradually mix in the buttermilk with a fork just until the dough forms a ball.
4. Roll out the dough on a lightly floured surface to an 8-inch circle.
5. Spoon the pear mixture into an ungreased 9-inch pie plate. Ease the pastry onto the center of the pear mixture, allowing some of the pears to show around the edges. Decoratively crimp the edges of the pastry, and cut several steam vents on top.
6. Bake in the preheated moderate oven (375°) until the pastry is golden brown and the pear mixture is bubbly, for 40 minutes. Brush the top with the peach glaze. Serve the cobbler warm or at room temperature.

APPLE BERRY COBBLER

Bake at 375° for 40 minutes.
Makes 8 servings.

Nutrient Value Per Serving: 322 calories, 5 g protein, 16 g fat, 42 g carbohydrate, 256 mg sodium, 66 mg cholesterol.

❧

1	cup sifted all-purpose flour
1	teaspoon baking powder
¼	teaspoon salt
¼	cup (½ stick) butter or margarine
½	cup brown sugar
1	egg
2	teaspoons grated lemon zest (yellow part of rind only)
2	tablespoons lemon juice
⅓	cup coarsely ground walnuts
¼	cup milk
1¼	cups sliced fresh raspberries OR: frozen dry-pack raspberries, thawed and drained
1¼	cups apples, peeled, cored and cut into chunks (Rome Beauty or Cortland)

Streusel Topping:

½	cup sifted all-purpose flour
¼	cup firmly packed light brown sugar
¼	cup (½ stick) butter or margarine

1. Preheat the oven to moderate (375°). Grease an 8 x 8 x 2-inch square baking pan.
2. Sift the 1 cup of flour with the baking powder and the salt onto wax paper.
3. Beat together the ¼ cup of butter or margarine and the brown sugar in a large bowl with an electric mixer at high speed until the mixture is light and fluffy, for about 4 minutes. Beat in the egg, lemon zest and lemon juice. Stir in the walnuts, then the milk. Stir in the flour mixture, then the raspberries and apples. Spread the batter in the pan.
4. Prepare the Streusel Topping: Mix together the flour and the brown sugar in a small bowl. Cut in the butter or margarine with a pastry blender until the mixture is crumbly. Sprinkle the streusel in an even layer over the batter.
5. Bake in the preheated moderate oven (375°) until a wooden pick inserted in the center of the cobbler comes out clean and the cake begins to pull away from the sides of the pan, for 40 minutes. Cool the cobbler on a wire rack.
6. Cut the cobbler into large squares, and serve.

SPICY PUMPKIN PIE

Bake at 375° for 10 minutes, then at 325° for 70 to 75 minutes.
Makes 12 servings.

Nutrient Value Per Serving: 182 calories, 4 g protein, 8 g fat, 23 g carbohydrate, 183 mg sodium, 59 mg cholesterol.

———————— ❦ ————————

3   eggs
1½ cups firmly packed mashed, cooked pumpkin
        OR: 1 can (16 ounces) solid-pack pumpkin
        purée (not pumpkin pie filling)
½   teaspoon ground cinnamon
¼   teaspoon ground nutmeg
2   cups milk
¾   cup sugar
¼   teaspoon salt
        10-inch unbaked pie shell
        Whipped Cream (optional)

1. Preheat the oven to moderate (375°).
2. Beat together the eggs, mashed pumpkin or pumpkin purée, cinnamon, nutmeg, milk, sugar and salt in a medium-size bowl until the mixture is smooth. Pour the mixture into the pie shell.
3. Bake the pie in the preheated moderate oven (375°) for 10 minutes. Lower the oven temperature to slow (325°). Bake until the center of the pie is just set and a wooden pick inserted midway between the rim and the center comes out speckled, for 70 to 75 minutes more.
4. Cool the pie on a wire rack to room temperature. Cut the pie into 12 slim wedges. Top with dollops of whipped cream, if you wish.

PERFECT PIE CRUST

▼ The easiest way to roll a pie crust is on wax paper or a pastry sheet. To keep the wax paper from curling or sliding around, wipe your countertop with a damp cloth or sponge before placing the paper on it. The moisture will keep the paper flat and prevent it from sliding around.
▼ To protect the edges of your pie crust from browning too quickly, make your own reusable crust shield. Take a lightweight, disposable aluminum pie pan and punch a hole in its center. Make five straight cuts up to the rim, then cut out the center so only the outer rim remains. Place the shield on the pie before baking.

GINGERED LEMON CURD

Serve this tart creamy delight with fresh fruit, in pre-cooked tart shells or as a filling for cake.

Makes 2½ cups.

Nutrient Value Per Tablespoon: 59 calories, 1 g protein, 4 g fat, 5 g carbohydrate, 40 mg sodium, 68 mg cholesterol.

———————— ❦ ————————

9   egg yolks
1   cup sugar
2   tablespoons grated lemon zest
        (yellow part of rind only)
¾   cup lemon juice (6 lemons)
½   cup (1 stick) butter, cut into 8 pieces
1½ teaspoons grated fresh gingerroot

1. Combine the egg yolks and the sugar in the top of a double boiler set over simmering water. Whisk the mixture until it is smooth. Add the lemon zest and lemon juice, the butter and ginger. Cook the mixture, stirring constantly with a rubber spatula, until the curd is thickened, for about 15 to 20 minutes. Do not let the curd boil.
2. Pour the curd into sterilized screw-top jars. Cover the tops of the jars with wax paper and place them in the refrigerator. Chill the curd thoroughly. Place the screw-top caps on the jars once the curd is chilled. The curd can be refrigerated for up to 3 weeks.

Little Miss Muffet
Sat on a tuffet,
Eating some curds and whey.
Along came a spider,
And sat down beside her,
And frightened Miss Muffet away.
—Anonymous

PERFECT PECAN PIE

Bake at 350° for 40 to 45 minutes.
Makes 16 servings.

Nutrient Value Per Serving: 266 calories, 2 g protein, 14 g fat, 35 g carbohydrate, 143 mg sodium, 51 mg cholesterol.

❦

1   cup pecan halves
     9-inch unbaked pie shell with high fluted edge
3   eggs
1   cup firmly packed light brown sugar
        OR: ½ cup each firmly packed light brown and
        dark brown sugars
1   cup light corn syrup
1   teaspoon lemon juice
1½   teaspoons vanilla
6   tablespoons melted butter or margarine
     Whipped Cream (optional)

1. Preheat the oven to moderate (350°). Scatter the pecans over the bottom of the pie shell. Set the pie shell aside.

2. Beat together the eggs, brown sugar, corn syrup, lemon juice and vanilla in a small bowl just until they are combined. Beat in the melted butter or margarine, a tablespoon at a time. Pour the egg mixture over the pecans in the pie shell.

3. Bake in the preheated moderate oven (350°) until the filling is puffed and quivers slightly when you nudge the pie pan, for 40 to 45 minutes. Cool the pie on a wire rack to room temperature; the filling should fall. Cut the pie into 16 slim wedges. Top with dollops of the whipped cream, if you wish.

PERFECT PECANS

When cracking pecans, gently tap on the round side of each shell — not the seam — with a small hammer. You'll get perfect halves every time!

STRAWBERRY RHUBARB PIE

Bake at 400° for 50 to 60 minutes.
Makes 8 servings.

Nutrient Value Per Serving: 402 calories, 3 g protein, 18 g fat, 56 g carbohydrate, 304 mg sodium, 10 mg cholesterol.

❦

1   package (11 ounces) pie crust mix
1   cup sugar
⅓   cup all-purpose flour
     Grated zest of 1 orange
        (orange part of rind only)
2½   cups fresh strawberries
2½   cups cut fresh rhubarb
        OR: thawed frozen rhubarb
¼   cup orange juice
1   tablespoon butter

1. Prepare the pie crust mix following the package directions. Shape the dough into a ball, wrap it in wax paper, and refrigerate it for 30 minutes.

2. Preheat the oven to hot (400°).

3. Divide the dough in half. Roll out one half on a lightly floured surface to a 12-inch circle. Fit the circle into a 9-inch pie plate.

4. Combine the sugar, flour and orange zest in a large bowl. Toss the flour mixture with the strawberries, rhubarb and orange juice. Scrape the filling into the bottom crust, and dot the filling with the butter.

5. Roll out the remaining dough into an 11-inch circle, and place it over the filling. Seal, trim and flute the edges. Cut slits in the top for vents.

6. Bake in the preheated hot oven (400°) until the top of the pie is nicely browned, for 50 to 60 minutes. If the edges brown too quickly, cover them with aluminum foil. Cool the pie on a wire rack. Serve the pie at room temperature.

FRENCH VANILLA ICE CREAM

Makes 12 half-cup servings.

Nutrient Value Per ½ Cup: 265 calories, 4 g protein, 19 g fat, 20 g carbohydrate, 130 mg sodium, 196 mg cholesterol.

❧

6   egg yolks, slightly beaten
1   cup sugar
½   teaspoon salt
2   cups milk
2   cups heavy cream
2   tablespoons vanilla

1. Combine the egg yolks, sugar, salt and milk in a heavy 2-quart saucepan. Cook the custard over medium heat, stirring constantly, until it thickens enough to lightly coat a spoon; do not let the custard boil, or it will curdle. Strain the custard through a sieve into a large bowl, and let the custard cool.
2. Stir the cream and the vanilla into the custard. Cover the bowl, and chill the custard.
3. Place the custard in the container of an ice cream maker. Freeze the mixture following to the manufacturer's directions.

Chocolate Ice Cream: Grate 9 ounces of bittersweet chocolate, and add it to the hot custard in Step 1 above. Stir until the chocolate is completely incorporated.

PLUM PEACH BUTTERMILK SHERBET

Makes 10 servings.

Nutrient Value Per Serving: 133 calories, 3 g protein, 1 g fat, 30 g carbohydrate, 83 mg sodium, 3 mg cholesterol.

❧

¾   pound ripe plums, pitted and coarsely chopped
½   pound ripe peaches, peeled, pitted and chopped
1   tablespoon lemon juice
3   cups lowfat buttermilk
1   cup sugar
1   egg white

1. Combine the plums, peaches, lemon juice and ½ cup of the buttermilk in the container of a food processor or electric blender. Whirl until the fruits are puréed. Stir in the remaining 2½ cups of buttermilk, the sugar and egg white. Refrigerate the fruit mixture, covered, until it is cold.
2. Prepare the sherbet in an ice cream maker following the manufacturer's directions. Pack the sherbet into freezer containers, and freeze it.

STRAWBERRY WINE ICE

Makes about 2 pints.

Nutrient Value Per ½ Cup: 107 calories, 0 g protein, 0 g fat, 23 g carbohydrate, 2 mg sodium, 0 mg cholesterol.

❧

¾   cup water
⅔   cup sugar
2   pints ripe strawberries, halved
¾   cup fruity white wine, such as California Riesling
1   tablespoon lemon juice

1. Place the water and the sugar in a small saucepan, and bring the mixture to boiling, stirring until the sugar dissolves. Simmer the mixture, uncovered, for 3 minutes. Cool the syrup completely.
2. Purée the strawberries in the container of a food processor. Combine the syrup with the strawberry purée in a bowl, and let the strawberry mixture stand for 30 minutes.
3. Add the wine and the lemon juice to the strawberry mixture. Pour the combined mixture into an 8-inch square metal pan. Freeze until the ice is almost frozen, for 2 to 4 hours, stirring several times so the ice freezes evenly.
4. Transfer the ice to the container of the food processor or to a large chilled bowl. Quickly process or beat the ice until it is smooth and fluffy. Return the ice to the pan, and freeze it for 30 minutes. Process or beat the ice again.
5. Freeze the ice, tightly covered, until it is almost firm, for 1 to 2 hours. If the ice freezes solid, soften it in the refrigerator for 30 minutes.

My advice to you is not to inquire why or whither, but just enjoy your ice cream while it's on your plate.
— Thornton Wilder

MINCEMEAT SQUARES

Bake at 375° for 25 minutes.
Makes 24 squares.

Nutrient Value Per Square: 194 calories, 2 g protein, 7 g fat, 31 g carbohydrate, 209 mg sodium, 16 mg cholesterol.

2½   cups all-purpose flour
1½   teaspoons baking soda
 ½   teaspoon salt
1½   cups quick-cooking rolled oats
        (not instant oatmeal)
 1   cup firmly packed dark brown sugar
 ¾   cup (1½ sticks) butter or margarine
 1   jar (16 ounces) prepared mincemeat

1. Preheat the oven to moderate (375°). Grease an 11 x 7 x 1-inch baking pan.
2. Sift together the flour, baking soda and salt into a large bowl. Stir in the oats and the brown sugar until they are blended.
3. Cut in the butter or margarine with a pastry blender until the oat mixture is crumbly. Pat half the oat mixture into the prepared pan. Spread the mincemeat on top. Sprinkle the remaining oat mixture over the mincemeat and press it into the mincemeat.
4. Bake in the preheated moderate oven (375°) until the topping is golden, for 25 minutes. Cool the squares in the pan on a wire rack for 15 minutes.
5. With a sharp knife, cut 3 times lengthwise and 5 times crosswise to make 24 squares.
6. Remove the squares from the pan with a spatula. Store the squares, layered between sheets of wax paper, in a metal tin with a tight-fitting lid.

OATMEAL CRUNCHIES

Bake at 375° for 10 minutes.
Makes 4 dozen cookies.

Nutrient Value Per Cookie: 121 calories, 1 g protein, 6 g fat, 16 g carbohydrate, 36 mg sodium, 5 mg cholesterol.

1½   cups all-purpose flour
 ½   teaspoon baking soda
 ½   teaspoon salt
 ¼   teaspoon ground mace
 1   cup butter-flavored vegetable shortening
1¾   cups firmly packed brown sugar
 1   egg
 ¼   cup milk
1¾   cups quick-cooking rolled oats
        (not instant oatmeal)
 1   cup chopped walnuts
 1   cup raisins

1. Preheat the oven to moderate (375°). Grease several baking sheets.
2. Sift together the flour, baking soda, salt and mace onto wax paper.
3. Beat the vegetable shortening with the brown sugar in a large bowl with an electric mixer at high speed until the mixture is light and fluffy. Lower the mixer speed. Beat in the egg and the milk until they are well blended. Sift in the flour mixture, and blend well with a wooden spoon to make a thick batter. Fold in the oats, chopped walnuts and raisins.
4. Drop the dough by teaspoonfuls 2 inches apart on the prepared baking sheets.
5. Bake in the preheated moderate oven (375°) until the cookies are lightly golden, for 10 minutes. Remove the cookies from the oven, and let them stand for 1 minute on the baking sheets. Remove the cookies with a wide spatula to a wire rack to cool completely. Store the cookies in a cookie jar with a tight-fitting lid.

Oatmeal Raisin Jumbos

Served with a big glass of milk, these extra-large cookies are a perfect after-school treat.

Bake at 375° for 15 minutes.
Makes 15 very large cookies.

Nutrient Value Per Cookie: 347 calories, 5 g protein, 18 g fat, 43 g carbohydrate, 103 mg sodium, 28 mg cholesterol.

1½	cups all-purpose flour
½	teaspoon baking powder
½	teaspoon salt
¼	teaspoon ground cinnamon
1	cup butter-flavored vegetable shortening
1¼	cups firmly packed brown sugar
2	eggs
1¾	cups old-fashioned rolled oats (not instant oatmeal)
1	cup raisins
1	cup sliced natural almonds

1. Preheat the oven to moderate (375°).
2. Sift together the flour, baking powder, salt and cinnamon onto wax paper.
3. Beat the vegetable shortening with the brown sugar in a large bowl with an electric mixer at high speed until the mixture is light colored and fluffy. Beat in the eggs, one at a time, until the mixture is smooth and creamy.
4. Turn the mixer speed to low. Add the flour mixture, and mix until the ingredients are well blended. Stir in the oats, raisins and ¾ cup of the sliced almonds with a wooden spoon until they are well blended.
5. Drop the batter, ¼ cupful at a time, 4 inches apart on ungreased baking sheets. Spread the batter to make 3-inch rounds. Sprinkle the rounds with the remaining ¼ cup of sliced almonds.
6. Bake in a moderate oven (375°) until the cookies are golden, for 15 minutes. Cool the cookies on baking sheets on wire racks for 5 minutes. Loosen the cookies with a spatula, and remove the cookies to the wire racks to cool. Store the cookies in a metal tin with a tight-fitting lid.

Date Pecan Chews

Bake at 350° for 25 minutes.
Makes 4 dozen bars.

Nutrient Value Per Bar: 56 calories, 1 g protein, 2 g fat, 10 g carbohydrate, 20 mg sodium, 13 mg cholesterol.

¾	cup all-purpose flour
½	teaspoon baking powder
½	teaspoon ground cinnamon
¼	teaspoon salt
3	eggs
1	cup sugar
2	tablespoons orange juice
1	package (8 ounces) pitted dates, chopped
1	cup pecans, chopped
2	tablespoons grated orange zest (orange part of rind only)

1. Preheat the oven to moderate (350°). Grease a 13 x 9 x 2-inch baking pan.
2. Sift together the flour, baking powder, cinnamon and salt onto wax paper.
3. Beat the eggs until they are light colored and foamy in a large bowl with an electric mixer at high speed. Slowly add the sugar, beating continually, until the mixture is thick and fluffy. Stir in the orange juice.
4. Fold in the flour mixture, chopped dates, chopped pecans and orange zest. Pour the batter into the prepared pan, and spread it evenly with a spatula.
5. Bake in the preheated moderate oven (350°) until the top of the chews springs back when pressed with your fingertip, for 25 minutes. Cool the chews in the pan on a wire rack for 15 minutes.
6. Cut the chews lengthwise into 6 strips, and crosswise into 8 strips to make 48 bars. Remove the chews from the pan with a spatula, and store them in a metal tin with a tight-fitting lid.

Prune Walnut Chews: Substitute 1½ cups of chopped pitted prunes for the dates, and 1 cup of chopped walnuts for the pecans.

BEST EVER BROWNIES

Bake at 350° for 30 minutes.
Makes 16 brownies.

Nutrient Value Per Brownie: 173 calories, 2 g protein, 12 g fat, 17 g carbohydrate, 101 mg sodium, 42 mg cholesterol.

2   squares (1 ounce each) unsweetened chocolate
½   cup (1 stick) butter or margarine
2   eggs
1   cup sugar
1   teaspoon vanilla
½   cup all-purpose flour
¼   teaspoon salt
¾   cup chopped walnuts

1. Melt the chocolate with the butter or margarine in a small saucepan over low heat. Cool the chocolate mixture to lukewarm.
2. Preheat the oven to moderate (350°). Grease an 8 x 8 x 2-inch baking pan.
3. Beat the eggs in a small bowl with an electric mixer at high speed. Gradually beat in the sugar until the mixture is fluffy and thick. Stir in the chocolate mixture and the vanilla.
4. Fold in the flour and the salt until they are well blended. Stir in the chopped walnuts. Spread the batter in the prepared pan.
5. Bake in the preheated moderate oven (350°) until the brownies are shiny and firm on top, for 30 minutes. Cool the brownies in the pan on a wire rack. Cut the brownies into 16 squares.

GIANT CHOCOLATE CHIPPERS

Bake at 350° for 15 minutes.
Makes 20 very large cookies.

Nutrient Value Per Cookie: 266 calories, 3 g protein, 16 g fat, 30 g carbohydrate, 179 mg sodium, 46 mg cholesterol.

2¾   cups all-purpose flour
1   teaspoon baking powder
½   teaspoon salt
1   cup (2 sticks) butter or margarine
⅔   cup granulated sugar
⅔   cup firmly packed brown sugar
2   eggs
1   teaspoon vanilla
1   package (12 ounces) semisweet chocolate pieces
1   cup chopped walnuts (optional)

1. Preheat the oven to moderate (350°). Grease several baking sheets.
2. Sift together the flour, baking powder and salt onto a piece of wax paper.
3. Beat the butter or margarine with the granulated and brown sugars in a large bowl with an electric mixer at high speed until the mixture is light colored and fluffy. Beat in the eggs, one at a time, until they are well blended. Beat in the vanilla.
4. Turn the mixer speed to low. Add the flour mixture, and mix until all the ingredients are well blended. Using a wooden spoon, stir in the semisweet chocolate pieces and, if you wish, chopped walnuts until they are incorporated into the dough.
5. Drop the batter, ¼ cupful at a time, 4 inches apart onto the prepared baking sheets. Spread the batter to make 3-inch rounds.
6. Bake in the preheated moderate oven (350°) until the cookies are golden, for 15 minutes. Cool the cookies on the baking sheets on wire racks for 5 minutes. Remove the cookies with a spatula to the wire racks to cool. Store the cookies in a metal tin with a tight-fitting lid.

CHOCOLATE NUT ROUNDS

Bake at 350° for 12 minutes.
Makes 5 dozen cookies.

Nutrient Value Per Cookie: 53 calories, 1 g protein, 3 g fat, 6 g carbohydrate, 55 mg sodium, 10 mg cholesterol.

❧

2   cups all-purpose flour
1   teaspoon baking powder
1/2 teaspoon salt
1/4 teaspoon baking soda
3/4 cup (1 1/2 sticks) butter or margarine
3/4 cup firmly packed brown sugar
2   squares (1 ounce each) unsweetened
        chocolate, melted
1   egg
1   teaspoon vanilla
1/4 teaspoon aromatic bitters
1/4 cup milk
     Granulated sugar
     Walnut halves

1. Sift together the flour, baking powder, salt and baking soda onto a piece of wax paper.
2. Beat the butter or margarine and the brown sugar in a large bowl with an electric mixer at high speed until the mixture is fluffy. Beat in the melted chocolate, egg, vanilla, aromatic bitters and milk. Continue beating until the chocolate mixture is smooth.
3. Turn the mixer speed to low. Sift in the flour mixture, a third at a time, blending well after each addition, to make a soft dough. Refrigerate the dough for several hours, or until it is firm enough to handle.
4. Preheat the oven to moderate (350°).
5. Roll the dough, one teaspoonful at a time, between the palms of your hands, into round balls. Roll the balls in the granulated sugar. Place the balls 3 inches apart on ungreased baking sheets, and flatten the balls with the tines of a fork. Top each flattened ball with a walnut half.
6. Bake in the preheated moderate oven (350°) until the cookies are firm, for 12 minutes. Carefully remove the cookies from the baking sheets with a spatula to wire racks to cool. Store the cookies in a cookie jar.

CHOCO-PEANUT BARS

Bake at 350° for 35 minutes.
Makes 3 dozen bars.

Nutrient Value Per Bar: 150 calories, 3 g protein, 8 g fat, 17 g carbohydrate, 109 mg sodium, 27 mg cholesterol.

❧

1   cup crunchy peanut butter
2/3 cup butter or margarine, softened
1   teaspoon vanilla
2   cups firmly packed light brown sugar
3   eggs
1   cup all-purpose flour
1/2 teaspoon salt
1/2 teaspoon ground nutmeg
1/2 cup semisweet chocolate morsels
1   teaspoon vegetable shortening

1. Preheat the oven to moderate (350°). Grease a 13 x 9 x 2-inch baking pan.
2. Combine the peanut butter with the butter or margarine and the vanilla in a large bowl, and beat with an electric mixer at medium speed until the ingredients are blended. Beat in the brown sugar until the mixture is light colored and fluffy. Beat in the eggs, one at a time, until they are well blended.
3. Stir in the flour, salt and nutmeg just until they are well blended. Spread the batter in the prepared pan.
4. Bake in the preheated moderate oven (350°) until the center of the cake springs back when lightly touched with your fingertip, for 35 minutes. Remove the pan from the oven to a wire rack to cool slightly.
5. Melt the chocolate with the vegetable shortening in a metal cup over simmering water. Drizzle the melted chocolate over the top of the cake to cover it thinly. When the chocolate is cool, use a sharp knife to cut the cake into 36 bars. Carefully lift the bars out of the pan with a wide spatula, and store them in a metal tin with a tight-fitting lid.

C·R·A·F·T·S B·A·S·I·C·S &
A·B·B·R·E·V·I·A·T·I·O·N·S

HOW TO KNIT

THE BASIC STITCHES

Get out your needles and yarn, and slowly read your way through this special section. Practice the basic stitches illustrated here as you go along. Once you know them, you're ready to start knitting.

CASTING ON: This puts the first row of stitches on the needle. Measure off about two yards of yarn (or about an inch for each stitch you are going to cast on). Make a slip knot at this point by making a medium-size loop of yarn; then pull another small loop through it. Place the slip knot on one needle and pull one end gently to tighten (FIG. 1).

FIG. 1

• Hold the needle in your right hand. Hold both strands of yarn in the palm of your left hand securely but not rigidly. Slide your left thumb and forefinger between the two strands and spread these two fingers out so that you have formed a triangle of yarn.
• Your left thumb should hold the free end of yarn, your forefinger the yarn from the ball. The needle in your right hand holds the first stitch (FIG. 2).

FIG. 2

You are now in position to cast on.
• Bring the needle in your right hand toward you; slip the tip of the needle under the front strand of the loop on your left thumb (FIG. 3).

FIG. 3

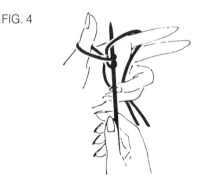

• Now, with the needle, catch the strand of yarn that is on your left forefinger (FIG. 4).

FIG. 4

• Draw it through the thumb loop to form a stitch on the needle (FIG. 5).

FIG. 5

KNITTING ABBREVIATIONS AND SYMBOLS

Knitting directions are always written in standard abbreviations. Although they may look confusing, with practice you'll soon know them:

beg—beginning; **bet**—between; **bl**—block; **ch**—chain; **CC**—contrasting color; **dec(s)**—decrease(s); **dp**—double-pointed; ″ or **in(s)**—inch(es); **incl**—inclusive; **inc(s)**—increase(s); **k**—knit; **lp(s)**—loop(s); **MC**—main color; **oz(s)**—ounces(s); **psso**—pass slipped stitch over last stitch worked; **pat(s)**—pattern(s); **p**—purl; **rem**—remaining; **rpt**—repeat; **rnd(s)**—round(s); **sk**—skip; **sl**—slip; **sl st**—slip stitch; **sp(s)**—space(s); **st(s)**—stitch(es); **st st**—stockinette stitch; **tog**—together; **yo**—yarn over; **pc**—popcorn stitch.

* (asterisk)—directions immediately following * are to be repeated the specified number of times indicated in addition to the first time—i.e. "repeat from * 3 times more" means 4 times in all.

( ) (parentheses)—directions should be worked as often as specified—i.e., "(k 1, k 2 tog, k 3) 5 times" means to work what is in ( ) 5 times in all.

• Holding the stitch on the needle with your right index finger, slip the loop off your left thumb (FIG. 6). Tighten up the stitch on the needle by pulling the freed strand back with your left thumb, bringing the yarn back into position for casting on more stitches (FIG. 2).

FIG. 6

• *Do not cast on too tightly.* Stitches should slide easily on the needle. Repeat from * until you have cast on the number of stitches specified in your instructions.

KNIT STITCH (k): Hold the needle with the cast-on stitches in your left hand (FIG. 7).

FIG. 7

• Pick up the other needle in your right hand. With yarn from the ball in *back* of the work, insert the tip of the right-hand needle from *left to right* through the front loop of the first stitch on the left-hand needle (FIG. 8).

FIG. 8

• Holding both needles in this position with your left hand, wrap the yarn over your little finger, under your two middle fingers and over the forefinger of your right hand. Hold the yarn firmly, but loosely enough so that it will slide through your fingers as you knit. Return the right-hand needle to your right hand.
• With your right forefinger, pass the yarn under (from right to left) and then over (from left to right) the tip of the right-hand needle, forming a loop on the needle (FIG. 9).

FIG. 9

• Now draw this loop through the stitch on the left-hand needle (FIG. 10).

FIG. 10

• Slip the original stitch off the left-hand needle, leaving the new stitch on right-hand needle (FIG. 11).

FIG. 11

Note: *Keep the stitches loose enough to slide along the needles, but tight enough to maintain their position on the needles until you want them to slide.* Continue until you have knitted all the stitches from the left-hand needle onto the right-hand needle.

• To start the next row, pass the needle with stitches on it to your left hand, reversing it, so that it is now the left-hand needle.

PURL STITCH (p): Purling is the reverse of knitting. Again, keep the stitches loose enough to slide, but firm enough to work with. To purl, hold the needle with the stitches in your left hand, with the yarn in **front** of your work. Insert the tip of the right-hand needle from **right to left** through the front loop of the first stitch on the left-hand needle (FIG. 12).

FIG. 12

• With your right hand holding the yarn as you would to knit, but in **front** of the needles, pass the yarn over the tip of the right-hand needle, then under it, forming a loop on the needle (FIG. 13).

FIG. 13

• Holding the yarn firmly so that it won't slip off, draw this loop through the stitch on the left-hand needle (FIG. 14).

FIG. 14

• Slip the original stitch off of the left-hand needle, leaving the new stitch on the right-hand needle (FIG. 15).

FIG. 15

SLIPSTITCH (sl st): Insert the tip of the right-hand needle into the next stitch on the left-hand needle, as if to purl, unless otherwise directed. Slip this stitch off the left-hand needle onto the right, but **do not** work the stitch (FIG. 16).

FIG. 16

BINDING OFF: This makes a finished edge and locks the stitches securely in place. Knit (or purl) two stitches. Then, with the tip of the left-hand needle, lift the first of these two stitches over the second stitch and drop it off the tip of the right-hand needle (FIG. 17).

FIG. 17

One stitch remains on the right-hand needle, and one stitch has been bound off.
• Knit (or purl) the next stitch; lift the first stitch over the last stitch and off the tip of the needle. Again, one stitch remains on the right-hand needle, and another stitch has been bound off. Repeat from * until the required number of stitches have been bound off.
• Remember that you work two stitches to bind off one stitch. If, for example, the directions read, "k 6, bind off the next 4 sts, k 6 . . ." you must knit six stitches, then knit **two more** stitches before starting to bind off. Bind off four times. After the four stitches have been bound off, count the last stitch remaining on the right-hand needle as the first stitch of the next six stitches. When binding off, always knit the knitted stitches and purl the purled stitches.
• Be careful not to bind off too tightly or too loosely. The tension should be the same as the rest of the knitting.
• To end off the last stitch on the bound-off edge, if you are ending this piece of work here, cut the yarn leaving a 6-inch end; pass the cut end through the remaining loop on the right-hand needle and pull snugly (FIG. 18).

FIG. 18

SHAPING TECHNIQUES

Now that you are familiar with the basic stitches, you are ready to learn the techniques for shaping your knitting projects.

INCREASING (inc): This means adding stitches in a given area to shape your work. There are several ways to increase.

1. *To increase by knitting twice into the same stitch:* Knit the stitch in the usual way through the front loop (FIG. 19), but **before** dropping the stitch from the left-hand needle, knit **another** stitch on the same loop by placing the needle into the back of the stitch (FIG. 20). Slip the original stitch off your left-hand needle. You now have made two stitches from one stitch.

FIG. 19

FIG. 20

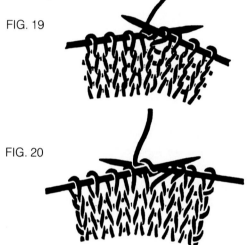

2. *To increase by knitting between stitches:* Insert the tip of the right-hand needle under the strand of yarn **between** the stitch you've just worked and the following stitch; slip it onto the tip of the left-hand needle (FIG. 21).

FIG. 21

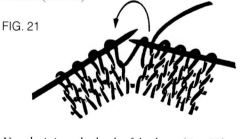

Now knit into the back of the loop (FIG. 22).

FIG. 22

3. *To increase by "yarn-over" (yo):* Pass the yarn ***over*** the right-hand needle after finishing one stitch and before starting the next stitch, making an extra stitch (see the arrow in FIG. 23). If you are knitting, bring the yarn ***under*** the needle to the back. If you are purling, wind the yarn ***around*** the needle once. On the next row, work all yarn-overs as stitches.

FIG. 23

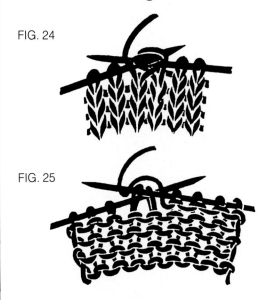

DECREASING (dec): This means reducing the number of stitches in a given area to shape your work. Two methods for decreasing are:

1. *To decrease by knitting* (FIG. 24) ***or purling*** (FIG. 25) ***two stitches together:***

FIG. 24

FIG. 25

Insert the right-hand needle through the loops of two stitches on the left-hand needle at the same time. Complete the stitch. This is written as "k 2 tog" or "p 2 tog."

• If you work through the ***front*** loops of the stitches, your decreasing stitch will slant to the right. If you work through the ***back*** loops of the stitches, your decreasing stitch will slant to the left.

2. *Slip 1 stitch, knit 1 and psso:* Insert the right-hand needle through the stitch on the left-hand needle, but instead of working it, just slip it off onto the right-hand needle (see FIG. 16). Work the next stitch in the usual way. With the tip of the left-hand

needle, lift the slipped stitch over the last stitch worked and off the tip of the right-hand needle (FIG. 26). Your decreasing stitch will slant to the left. This is written as "sl 1, k 1, psso."

FIG. 26

Pass Slipped Stitch Over (psso): Slip one stitch from the left-hand needle to the right-hand needle and, being careful to keep it in position, work the next stitch. Then, with the tip of the left-hand needle, lift the slipped stitch over the last stitch and off the tip of the right-hand needle (FIG. 26).

ATTACHING YARN

When you finish one ball of yarn, or if you wish to change colors, attach the new ball of yarn at the start of a row. Tie the new yarn to an end of the previous yarn, making a secure knot to join the two yarns. Continue to work (FIG. 27).

FIG. 27

HOW TO CROCHET

THE BASIC STITCHES

Most crochet stitches are started from a base of chain stitches. However, our stitches are started from a row of single crochet stitches which gives body to the sample swatches and makes practice work easier to handle. When making a specific item, follow the stitch directions as given.

• Holding the crochet hook properly (FIG. 1), start by practicing the slip knot (FIG. 2 through FIG. 2C) and base chain (FIG. 3 through FIG. 3B).

FIG. 1   HOLDING THE HOOK

FIG. 2   THE SLIP KNOT
(BASIS FOR CHAIN STITCH)

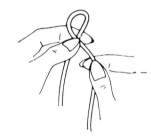

FIG. 2a

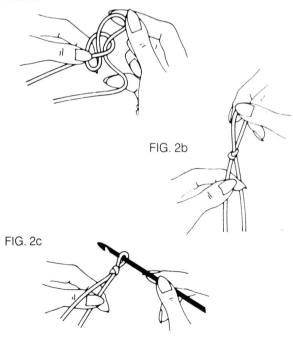

FIG. 2b

FIG. 2c

FIG. 3   CHAIN STITCH (CH)

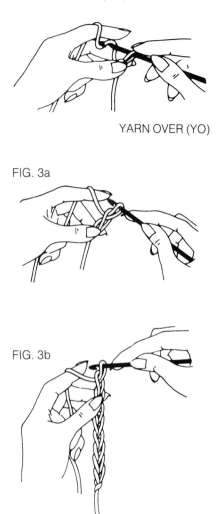

YARN OVER (YO)

FIG. 3a

FIG. 3b

CHAIN STITCH (ch): Follow the steps in FIG. 3 through FIG. 3B. As you make the chain stitch loops, the yarn should slide easily between your index and middle fingers. Make about 15 loops. If they are all the same size, you have maintained even tension. If the stitches are uneven, rip them out by pulling on the long end of the yarn. Practice the chain stitch until you can crochet a perfect chain.

From here on, we won't be showing hands—just the hook and the stitches. **Note:** *Left-handed crocheters can use the illustrations for right-handed crocheting by turning the book upside down in front of a free-standing mirror. The reflected illustrations will provide left-handed instructions.*

CROCHET ABBREVIATIONS AND SYMBOLS

The following is a list of standard crochet abbreviations with definitions of the terms given. To help you become accustomed to the abbreviations used, we have repeated them throughout our instructions.

beg—begin, beginning; **ch**—chain;
dc—double crochet; **dec**—decrease;
dtr—double treble crochet;
hdc—half double crochet; **in(s)** or **″**—inch(es);
inc—increase; **oz(s)**—ounce(s); **pat**—pattern;
pc—picot; **rem**—remaining; **rnd**—round;
rpt—repeat; **sc**—single crochet;
skn(s)—skein(s); **sk**—skip;
sl st—slip stitch; **sp**—space; **st(s)**—stitch(es);
tog—together; **tr**—triple crochet; **work even**—continue without further increase or decrease;
yo—yarn over.
* (asterisk)—directions immediately following * are to be repeated the specified number of times indicated in addition to the first time.
( ) (parentheses)—directions should be worked as often as specified.

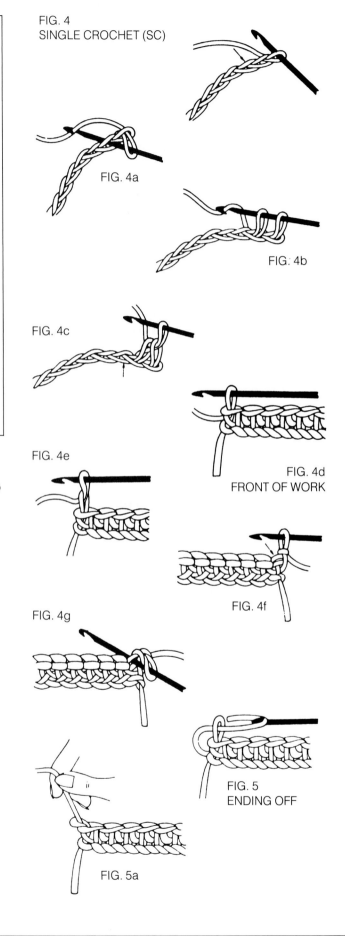

FIG. 4
SINGLE CROCHET (SC)

FIG. 4a

FIG: 4b

FIG. 4c

FIG. 4e

FIG. 4d
FRONT OF WORK

FIG. 4f

FIG. 4g

FIG. 5
ENDING OFF

FIG. 5a

SINGLE CROCHET (sc): Follow the steps in FIG. 4. To practice, make a 20-loop chain (this means 20 loops in addition to the slip knot). Turn the chain, as shown, and insert the hook in the second chain from the hook (see arrow) to make the first sc stitch. Yarn over (yo); for the second stitch, see the next arrow. Repeat to the end of the chain. Because you started in the second chain from the hook, you end up with only 19 sc. To add the 20th stitch, ch 1 (called a turning chain) and pull the yarn through. Now turn your work around (the "back" is now facing you) and start the second row of sc in the first stitch of the previous row (at the arrow). Make sure your hook goes under both of the strands at the top of the stitch. Don't forget to make a ch 1 turning chain at the end before turning your work. Keep practicing until your rows are perfect.

ENDING OFF: Follow the steps in FIG. 5. To finish off your crochet, cut off all but 6-inches of yarn and end off as shown. (To "break off and fasten," follow the same procedure.)

DOUBLE CROCHET (dc): Follow the steps in Fig. 6. To practice, ch 20, then make a row of 20 sc. Now, instead of a ch 1, you will make a ch 3. Turn your work, yo and insert the hook in the second stitch of the previous row (at the arrow), going under both strands at the top of the stitch. Pull the yarn through. You now have three loops on the hook. Yo and pull through the first two, then yo and pull through the remaining two—one double crochet (dc) made. Continue across the row, making a dc in each stitch (st) across. Dc in the top of the turning chain (see arrow in Fig. 7). Ch 3. Turn work. Dc in second stitch on the previous row and continue as before.

FIG. 7

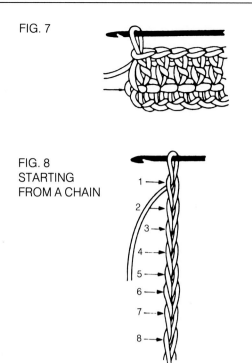

FIG. 8
STARTING
FROM A CHAIN

FIG. 6
DOUBLE CROCHET
(DC)

FIG. 6a

FIG. 6b

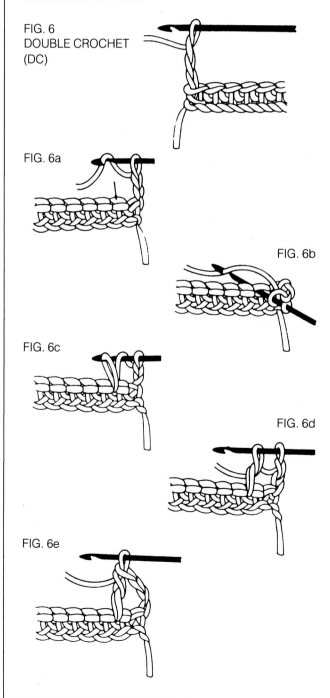

Note: *You may also start a row of dc on a base chain (omitting the sc row). In this case, insert the hook in the fourth chain from the hook, instead of the second (Fig. 8).*

FIG. 6c

FIG. 6d

SLIP STITCH (sl st): Follow the steps in Fig. 9. This is the stitch you will use for joining, shaping and ending off. After you chain and turn, **do not** yo. Just insert the hook into the **first** stitch of the previous row (see Fig. 9A), and pull the yarn through the stitch, then through the loop on the hook—the sl st is made.

FIG. 9
SLIP STITCH
(SL ST)

FIG. 6e

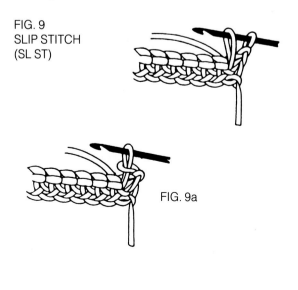

FIG. 9a

HALF DOUBLE CROCHET (hdc): Follow the steps in FIGS. 10 and 10A.

To practice, make a chain and a row of sc. Ch 2 and turn; yo. Insert the hook in the second stitch, as shown; yo and pull through to make three loops on the hook. Yo and pull the yarn through *all* three loops at the same time—hdc made. This stitch primarily is used as a transitional stitch from an sc to a dc. Try it and see—starting with sc's, then an hdc and then dc's.

FIG. 10
HALF DOUBLE CROCHET

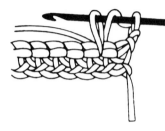

FIG. 10a

SHAPING TECHNIQUES FOR CROCHETING

Now that you have practiced and made sample squares of all the basic stitches, you are ready to learn the adding and subtracting stitches that will shape your project by changing the length of a row as per the instructions. This is done by increasing (inc) and decreasing (dec).

To increase (inc): Just make two stitches in the same stitch in the previous row (see arrow in FIG. 11). The technique is the same for any kind of stitch.

FIG. 11   INCREASING (INC)
FOR SINGLE CROCHET

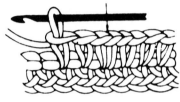

To decrease (dec) for single-crochet (sc): Yo and pull the yarn through two stitches to make three loops on the hook (see steps in FIG. 12). Pull the yarn through all the loops at once—dec made. Continue in the stitches called for in the instructions.

FIG. 12   DECREASING (DEC)

FOR SINGLE CROCHET   FIG. 12

To decrease for double crochet (dc): In a dc row, make the next stitch and stop when you have two loops on the hook. Now yo and make a dc in the next stitch. At the point where you have three loops on the hook, pull yarn through all loops at the same time. Finish the row with regular dc.

HOW TO BLOCK LIKE A PRO

These step-by-step instructions for blocking will insure that your needlework has a professional finished look.

MATERIALS:

• **A Blocking Board** An absolute *must* for professional-looking blocking. You can usually buy a blocking board at craft and sewing centers.
• **Rustproof T-pins and Staples** Used to hold the needlework pieces in place.
• **Undyed Cotton Cloth** A dampened cloth covers the needlework while it is being pressed.
• **Iron** With a dry setting.
• **Yellow Soap** Dels Naptha or Kirkman. For blocking needlepoint. Restores natural sizing to canvas and helps prevent infestations of insects.

KNITTED OR CROCHETED WORK:

The purpose of blocking is to align the stitches, loft the yarn and straighten the knitted or crocheted pieces.
• Pin the work or the pieces, right side down, to the blocking board with the T-pins. Place the pins close together to avoid ripples in the work.
• Dampen a cotton cloth with water and wring it out; the cloth should be moist, not dripping wet. Place the cloth over the work on the board.
• Set the iron on "dry" and select a temperature setting suited to the fibers in the work.
• Gently iron over the cloth in the direction of the stitches. **Do not** apply pressure to the iron or iron against the grain. You may need to remoisten the cloth and iron the work several times, until it is moist and warm to the touch.
• Carefully remove the cloth. If the cloth clings, leaving the work damp and rippled, don't panic. This occurs when a synthetic fiber is pressed with steam that is too hot. No permanent damage can be done unless pressure is used and the stitches are flattened. To restore the work to the desired shape, pat the pieces gently with your hands.
• Allow the work to dry on the board in a flat position for at least 24 hours.
• When the work is completely dry, remove the pins; the pieces are ready to be assembled.

Note: You can ease or stretch pieces a bit to achieve the desired size, but you can't turn a size 10 sweater into a size 16, or shrink a size 40 vest into a size 34.

NEEDLEPOINT PROJECTS:

Blocking needlepoint realigns the threads of the canvas, lofts the yarn and naturally sets each stitch.
*Note: Check for yarn color fastness before you begin to needlepoint. If you've completed a work, and are unsure of the color fastness, **do not block.** Press the work on the wrong side with a warm iron. This won't yield the same results, but avoids color streaking.*
• Place a bar of yellow soap *(see Materials)* in a bowl of warm water and let it stand until the water becomes slick to the touch.
• Place the needlepoint, right side down, on the blocking board.
• Dip a cotton cloth into the soapy water and wring it out. Place the damp cloth over the needlepoint.
• Set an iron on "dry" and select a temperature suited to the fibers in the work. Lightly pass the iron over the cloth; **do not** apply pressure.
• Repeat dampening the cloth and pressing until the canvas is very soft and flexible; moist, but not wet.
• Turn the needlepoint right side up on the board.
• Keeping the threads of the canvas parallel to the grid on the blocking board, staple the canvas to the board leaving 1 inch between the staples and the edge of the needlepoint. (Remove tape or selvages before stapling.) The staples should be fairly close together (staples are preferable to pins because they maintain a straight line and even tension across the work).
• Staple along the bottom edge of the canvas, again, maintaining an even tension across the work. Gently pull one side of the canvas to align the fabric grain with the grid lines on the board, and staple along this edge. Repeat on the other side of the canvas. (**Do not** stretch the canvas; just pull it gently into its original size.) As you are stretching the third and fourth sides, wrinkles may appear in the center of the work; as the fourth side is eased into alignment, these should disappear. If the canvas is pulled off the grain while being blocked, remove the staples and realign the sides. When the grain of the work is perfectly square, the stitching should be aligned; remember, you are not straightening the stitching, you are squaring the threads of the canvas.
• Allow the needlepoint to dry on the board for at least 24 hours.
• When the needlepoint is completely dry, gently pull it up from the board; the staples will pull out easily. Your needlepoint is now ready to be finished.

Note: If the design becomes distorted, reblock the piece. This can be avoided if you use enough soapy steam on the canvas and staple it carefully into a perfect square.

E·M·B·R·O·I·D·E·R·Y
S·T·I·T·C·H G·U·I·D·E

CROSS STITCH

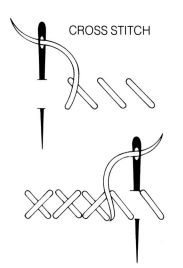

CHAIN STITCH

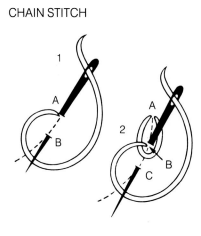

STEM STITCH

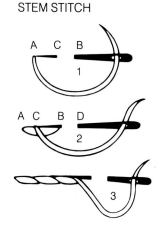

FRENCH KNOT

 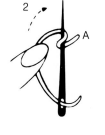 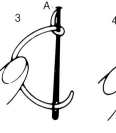 

BACKSTITCH

WHIPPED STEM STITCH

LAZY DAISY STITCH

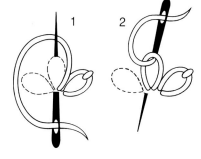

LONG AND SHORT STITCH

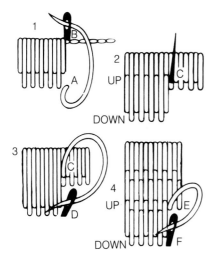

HOW TO ENLARGE PATTERNS AND DESIGNS

If the pattern or design is not already marked off in squares, make a tracing of it. Mark the tracing off in squares: For a small design, make the squares ¼-inch; for larger designs, use ½- or 2-inch squares, or use the size indicated in the directions. Check the instructions for desired size of the finished project. On a second piece of tracing paper, mark off an enlarged grid with the same number of squares as appears on the original pattern. For example, if you wish the finished project to be 6 times larger than the original pattern, each new square must be 6 times larger than on the original. Copy the design outline from the original pattern or tracing onto the second, enlarged grid, square by square. Using a dressmaker's carbon and a tracing wheel, transfer the enlarged design onto the material you are using for your project.

SLIP STITCH

SPLIT STITCH

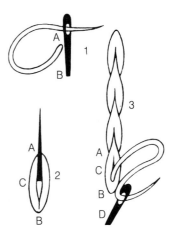

CRETAN STITCH

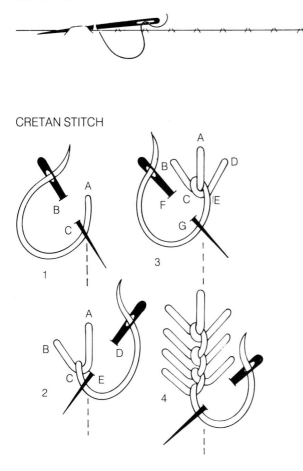

SATIN STITCH

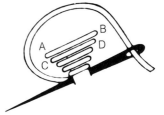

LOVELY AS LACE TABLECLOTH
(directions, page 136)

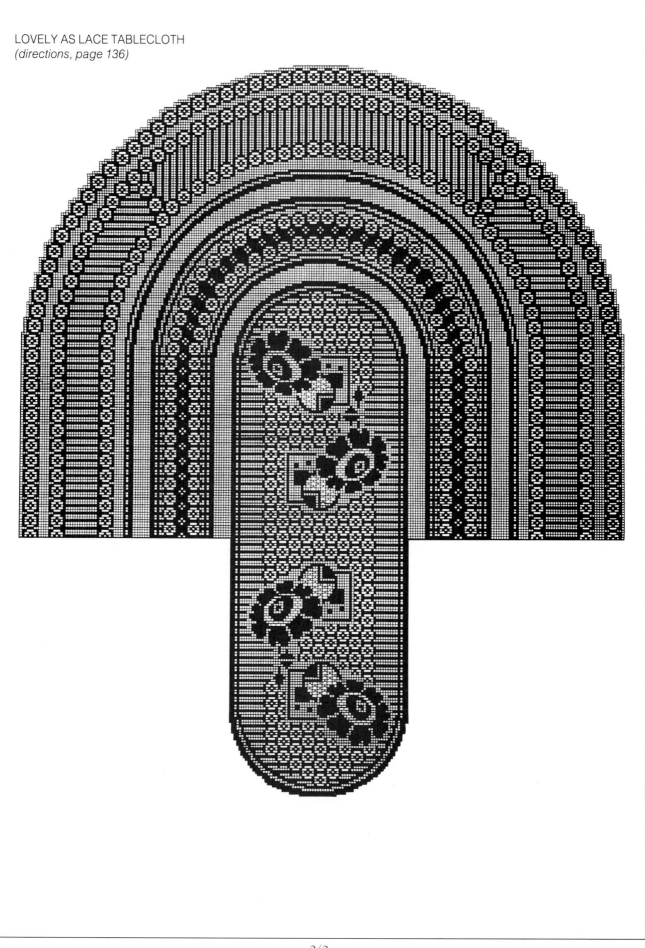

I·N·D·E·X

Italicized Page Numbers Refer To Photographs

PHOTOGRAPHY CREDITS

Jean Mitchell Allsopp: Pages 106-107. **Jon Aron:** Pages 144-145. **Bill Arsenault:** Pages 91, 158-159.
Roslyn Banish & Laurie Black: Page 27. **Laurie Black:** Page 51.
Ralph Bogertman: Pages 40, 78, 84, 92, 112, 123, 132, 150, 153, 154, 155, 160.
Jon Bonjour: Pages 49, 73. **Fran Brennan:** Page 23.
Chuck Crandall: Pages 170, 174, 175, 178. **Lisl Dennis:** Pages 66-67.
David Frazier: Page 100. **Tim Fuller:** Pages 56-57. **David Glomb:** Page 29.
Anne Gummerson: Page 36. **Kari Haavisto:** Page 96.
Ronald G. Harris: Pages 184, 186-187, 192-193.
Michael Jensen: Page 20. **Pamela Bar Kentin:** Pages 88, 102.
Leombruno-Bodi: Page 120. **Elyse Lewin:** Page 2.
Maris/Semel: Cover Photo and pages 4, 34, 38-39, 42-43, 45, 46, 54, 95.
McGinn/Velez: Pages 114, 117, 126, 137, 148.
Jeff McNamara: Page 19. **Keith Scott Morton:** Page 87.
Leonard Nones: Page 138. **Bradley Olman:** Pages 16-17, 82. **Dean Powell:** Page 119.
Carin & David Riley: Pages 68, 74, 129, 142. **Jeremy Samuelson:** Page 85.
Ron Schwerin: Pages 204, 218-219. **Semarco Company Inc.:** Page 8. **Michael Skott:** Page 156.
Gordon E. Smith: Pages 182, 212-213. **William P. Steele:** Pages 58-59, 62, 80, 108, 180, 181.
William Stites: Pages 6,11, 13, 24, 30, 60-61, 83, 99, 101, 104-105. **Bob Stoller:** Pages 71, 76, 125.